THE THAI BUREAUCRACY:
Institutional Change and Development

The THAI BUREAUCRACY
INSTITUTIONAL CHANGE AND DEVELOPMENT

by William J. Siffin

EAST-WEST CENTER PRESS – HONOLULU

for ALFRED D. FOX *in memory*

and for PRINYA CHAVALITTAMRONG *with affection*

FOREWORD

ONE WHO contemplates a bureaucracy may be inclined to para-
phrase the Apostle Paul: "How mysterious are its ways; how incom-
prehensible are its judgments!" And then to add: "How many are
the perspectives from which to view it."

This book attempts to portray the institutional characteristics of
the Thai bureaucracy and their evolution, using a rather simple
social-system perspective. In another volume, *Thailand: The Modernization of a Bureaucratic Polity,* my colleague, Professor Fred W.
Riggs, examines the politics of Thailand and finds it rooted in the
bureaucracy.

These two books are the products of separate efforts from different
perspectives. Professor Riggs and I have made no efforts at systematic
co-ordination, although we discussed our ongoing work, and have
hoped that the outcomes would be complementary rather than confusing or duplicative. A brief observation about our respective approaches is in order.

In developing nations, bureaucracies are usually much more than
administrative instrumentalities, and Thailand is no exception. Given
the character of Thai society it is not inappropriate to talk of
"bureaucratic politics," or of "a bureaucratic polity."

To ignore or disavow the political significance of the Thai bureaucracy would be unfortunate. The sheer existence, persistence, and
normative content of that bureaucracy are matters of elemental
political consequence. But the involvement of the Thai bureaucracy
in the shaping of political policy is quite a complicated matter. On
one hand, Thai bureaucratic institutions are not much oriented
toward policy making. Yet, on the other hand, policies are made in
the Thai government, and the policy makers have usually emerged
out of bureaucratic seedbeds. There is no other place in the society
from which they might come. Hence the expression, "a bureaucratic
polity."

In justification for my own efforts, which take small account of bureaucratic policy making, I would argue only that there are in Thailand significant differences between bureaucrats and politicians, and that there is much utility in looking at Thai bureaucratic institutions from a perspective which focuses upon broadly conceived structural characteristics.

Modest as this effort is, debts have been incurred in its making. Only a few are acknowledged here. To the graduate students of the Institute of Public Administration at Thammasat University I am indebted beyond repayment. Whether they have taught me well and wisely you may judge; they tried. Some of my obligations to them are noted in my footnotes; a series of M.A. theses prepared under my supervision in Bangkok have served me as valuable sources of data.

My colleague, Dr. Choop Karnjanaprakorn, also sought to balance my innocence with his wisdom, and found it necessary to add much patience in the bargain. I am grateful—and wish only I had made more use of his talents.

My friend and associate, Professor Woodwarth G. Thrombley, for three years chief adviser to the Institute of Public Administration in Bangkok has also helped me a great deal, with both data and perceptive judgments I have shamelessly made my own.

Finally, I must acknowledge a lasting debt to Dr. Malai Huvanandana, Dean of the Institute of Public Administration. I have learned much from him, and at times the lessons were almost lost in the pleasure of our association.

From Indiana University's Advisory Committee on International Studies I received a modest grant that helped make this study possible. The final draft was prepared during a stay at the Institute of Advanced Projects, East-West Center, University of Hawaii. Mrs. Sonja Gay at Bloomington, Indiana, and Mrs. Carol Uno Kunishige in Honolulu met my typing needs with more skill and aplomb than I deserved, and Mrs. Hazel Tatsuno of the Institute of Advanced Projects facilitated my work in myriad ways.

For my wife this book has meant a real sacrifice. May there be at least a bit of compensating pleasure in its completion.

WM. J. SIFFIN

Honolulu, June 21, 1965

CONTENTS

THE THAI BUREAUCRACY:
Institutional Change and Development

Chapter 1

THE NATURE OF THE CASE

THE SUBJECT of "bureaucracy" has acquired a new lustre, a result of current concerns with the emergence of a host of new nations. The reason for this refreshing interest in the administrative apparatus of government is elemental: no government of any size or significance can exist, assert meaningful goals, and seek to implement them without some sort of administrative machinery. Public administrative organizations are necessary—if not always sufficient—instruments of governmental action, prime means of converting aim and edict into achievement, in all save the most diffuse, primitive socio-political systems.

This banal premise has served as a point of departure for some lively journeys in the realms of both practice and theory. The need for effective administrative systems has led to myriad efforts at their establishment, efforts often marked by anguish and sometimes marred by disaster. And these have added to our understanding.

One of the things we have learned and learned again is that bureaucracies are more than mere implementive mechanisms of the state. They are important parts of the system of society. They may help hold it together, reflect its cultural foundations, nurture and suppress various forces within it, define and assert and enforce important social goals, and greatly affect the ability of a given social system to survive and change.

Of course, we have known this for a long time. Yet practitioners and technical consultants in recent years have often been encouraged to ignore this sort of knowledge, in short-run attempts to improve or extend the administrative machinery of particular governments. Some of these efforts have been desperate; others—from some perspectives at least—have seemed droll.

In the United States we are wiser than we were at the beginning of our commitment to help in the development of "modern" govern-

1

ments across the face of the world. Part of our wisdom is reflected in the expanding array of concepts we have applied in portraying and evaluating the mechanisms of government and administration. In a short time we have soared beyond rather pristine ideas of "efficiency" and "economy," a simple Weberian typology, and an obsession with specific techniques in our conceptualization of bureaucracies. Now we have more powerful abstractions, many of them sociological in their source, which enable us to think and talk in terms of such functions as integration, goal gratification, and cultural maintenance and transmission, and to grope with some assurance toward an ordered perception of the relationships between bureaucratic systems and their contexts. For our concepts are expanded into typologies; we can classify patterns to the extent that they can be perceived; and out of this comes enhanced understanding of the complexities of the administrative institutions with which we are concerned.

Concepts—and typologies—can be, and certainly have been, further expanded into theories, explanations of interdependence and causation—some of them vast, wonderful, provocative, but difficult of application; others mere fragments, useful but limited in scope.

In fact, efforts to study such phenomena as public administrative systems in developing nations have been both blessed and vexed by the sheer riches of available concepts, categories, and theories. The choice of a perspective itself becomes a challenge to the researcher. The assertion of it may prove to be an equally difficult problem, for the distance between empirical observation and abstract concept may be chasmal, if not cosmic. Then, too, there is always the temptation to modify or supplement the existing array of schemes—to play Linnaeus in the course of cultivating one small garden. And while this may not be totally unmeritorious, it does add to the confusion.

What follows is no grand effort at the construction of theory, and it involves only the smallest modifications of a rather well-established conceptual scheme. This is simply a case study in an area some scholars call "administrative development." It is a description and analysis of an effort at administrative modernization that in its own small way was both heroic and unique, which led to outcomes that could not possibly have been anticipated by those engaged in the attempt. It is, in short, a study of the "modernization" of the Thai bureaucracy.

The examination was undertaken in response to two simple questions: "What is the Thai bureaucracy *really* like?" and "What has caused the Thai administrative system to be what it is?"—questions which have been asked many times, in many ways, often with intense emotion and in colorful language.

Thailand, formerly Siam, has intrigued many people over the years, as well it may, for it is an extraordinary place. The only territory of Southeast Asia which did not come under Western imperial control, Thailand has a long and lively history. One part of the nation's fairly recent past involved the construction, in the latter nineteenth century, of an impressively effective bureaucracy, an administrative apparatus which persists today only slightly changed in many salient respects, but significantly different in others. What caused— and enabled—its construction? What led to certain modifications in the central values of the Thai bureaucracy after it had been established? What is it like today; what evident shifts are occurring in it, and why? These are the questions of our concern.

They have been stimulated by personal involvement with the Thai bureaucracy, by the penetrating portrait of "Thai Administrative Behavior" drawn a few years ago by Professor James Mosel,[1] by Walter Vella's discerning survey of *The Impact of the West on Government in Thailand*,[2] by David Wilson's recent study on *Politics in Thailand*,[3] and by some of the work of my own colleague, Professor Fred W. Riggs.

This effort to trace and assess a particular instance of administrative development has also been motivated by the fact that the Thai case, having run its course, offers a historical perspective that is available in only a few instances, for most of the concerted efforts at modernization have occurred in only the past two decades.

In its particulars the Thai case is unique; it really *proves* nothing. The substantial conditions of its occurrence can never be duplicated. But there still may be merit in studying it. Even a particular case affords a basis for a probing of the generalizations which have been made about administrative development and political modernization. A case, too, can test and perhaps demonstrate the utility of concepts which have flourished in the study of modern and modernizing government and politics. Finally, the Thai case has the intrinsic merit of its own charm—a charm tinged with quaintness when viewed from the sometimes grim and murky circumstances of these tumultuous times.

Administrative modernization in Thailand began in the latter part of the nineteenth century, but by then the Thai case already had a long and interesting history. The foundations of the administrative system were laid in the fifteenth century by an almost legendary king with a genius for organization. The system survived and in some ways evolved over the centuries, and its characteristics were to have a profound influence upon the course of events in Thailand during and after the efforts at modernization known as the "Chakkri Reformation."

I have sought to sketch the major characteristics of the traditional society and its governmental apparatus—not to produce a definitive and critical restatement of Thai cultural and political history, but to set the scene for the events of the nineteenth and twentieth centuries, and to identify patterns and forces which affected the Thai response to those events.

Standard sources have been used for data, but not always for interpretations. I have tried to avoid involvement in occasional issues which may be important to some Thai scholars, but which may not make much difference here. For my purposes, the exact date of King Trailok's statute governing the bureaucratic hierarchy does not matter greatly. Much use has been made of H. G. Quaritch Wales's unique study of ancient Siamese government, an invaluable source of information, but I would not always care to be identified with his interpretations—of the absoluteness of the Khmerized Thai kings, for example, or of the causes of bureaucratic decay in the decades before the Chakkri Reformation.

The attempt to modernize the Thai bureaucracy was a response to exogenous forces, or, in simple terms, to the impact of the West in the nineteenth century. This has been ably described and assessed by Walter Vella, and I am indebted to him for a systematic study from which I have drawn extensively.

The Thai response to the impact of the West included the construction of a new administrative system, whose central characteristics I have sought to describe, relying largely upon the record of the Ministry of Interior, which in many ways was the leading sector in Thai bureaucratic reconstruction.

Perhaps unfortunately, the Thai case does not simply end on a note of triumph in 1910 or thereabouts. The Chakkri Reformation ran its course, and was followed by changes in the environment of the bureaucracy, which in turn were reflected within the administrative apparatus. It is a thesis of this work that the contemporary civil bureaucracy of Thailand is a product of its past, including the ancient tradition, the Chakkri Reformation, and the aftermath of that Reformation.

It is also a tentative premise of the study that new forces of change are once more at work in Thailand, and that the "contemporary bureaucracy" is undergoing modifications that may affect the characteristics described in the latter chapters of this book. It is too soon to say. In any case, such changes must proceed from base lines which are the central characteristics of the more or less contemporary bureaucracy; and such changes will have to deal with the potent stabilizing forces which are among those contemporaneous characteristics.

In short, the Thai bureaucracy of 1965 is not the bureaucracy of the latter 1950s in all respects. But one cannot yet assess the magnitude and the depth of the changes that are taking place. However, the point of departure for significant change can be, and is, identified. And interesting and pertinent questions can be raised about the nature of the requisites for producing such change.

Chapter 2

TRADITIONAL SOCIETY AND TRADITIONAL GOVERNMENT

Thailand to the Mid-Nineteenth Century

WELL INTO the nineteenth century, Thailand was a traditional Oriental kingdom. The place had an aura of timelessness and coherence that could easily lure the casual observer into an idyllic assessment.[1]

The country was a loose aggregation of central government, provincial territories, and dependencies, occupying nearly 300,000 square miles of Southeast Asia. Total population was not known, but five to six million persons seems a likely estimate.[2] Settlement was sparse. Some regions that had contained thriving communities during the grand era of the ancient Khmer empire had long since reverted to jungle. A subsistence-type agriculture produced more than a million tons of rice a year, as well as cotton, tobacco, silk, sugar cane, coconuts, and a lavish supply of excellent fruits.[3] Perhaps 95 per cent of the people lived in small villages scattered across the land, some linked with the larger world by rivers and irrigation canals, others along the great Gulf of Siam by the sea, and still others by trails which had been trod for centuries by warring armies and traders who roved between South China and Burma and Thailand.

Time was measured in seasons and years and cycles of years. Nature was usually not unkind, the Theravada Buddhist ethic was not onerous, and specific temporal concerns were seldom compelling in an ageless universe where man was governed by his karma in an often languid quest for nirvana.

Life in the ancient kingdom, however, was not entirely idyllic or unchanging. Thailand had barely survived the sack of its capital by the Burmese in 1767. The military leader who had driven out the enemy and ascended the throne had become insane and had been deposed. At the turn of the nineteenth century a new dynasty had established itself in a new capital, and the kingdom was faced by its usual vicissitudes. The threat of rebellion in outlying areas and attack from over the borders, of treachery from officials—these persisted, along with occasional drought, epidemic disease, and other endemic difficulties.

Military operations during the first forty years of the nineteenth century demanded the services of thousands of conscripts for ranging campaigns. But, with the exception of the Wiangchan (Vientianne) rebellion of 1826–1827, in which the Laotian vassal armies drove to within fifty miles of Bangkok before they were destroyed, the fighting was in border areas and tributary states, and the people at home were free from wartime pillage.

There was an impressive integrity in the socio-political system of the kingdom. The society incorporated all of its members, nominally at least, into a matrix of places and relationships that were legitimized by a shared cosmology. The earthly order of things was thoroughly explicit, generally tolerable, and directly linked with the supernatural.

In this world there were from time to time disasters—to individuals, to communities, and to the leaders of the society itself. War and disease were as much parts of existence as the changing seasons, and, like the seasons, they were accepted as such. Threats to the social system could be perceived, and usually met, within the existing frame of reference. Even those whom it disadvantaged invariably sought to improve their lot by working within the system's bounds, and not by attacking it.

In short, Thailand was a traditional society, although its traditions were by no means simple, nor were they entirely unchanging. Its institutional apparatus was ancient. Between the institutions and a widely shared world view lay no gaping inconsistencies. The patterns of society were largely justified by their seeming fitness and by their antiquity. But in the nineteenth century Thailand was challenged by outside forces that it could neither comprehend nor accommodate, except by radical change. This study is concerned with the bureaucratic aspect of the changes which occurred in Thailand in response to the impact of the West. But let us first examine the central characteristics of the traditional system, for a point of departure is a necessary bench mark for the study of change.

The chief features of the traditional society included the general social structure, religion, the kingship, and the bureaucracy. These facets of the Thai social system were intimately interrelated; they are separated here to provide a manageable set of foci.

The Society

It has been said that the population fell into two broad classes—the rulers and the ruled.[4] In the broadest sense, the rulers included the king, the princes, and a stratified hierarchy of officials extending down to the level of the commoners and slaves. In addition, the Buddhist order comprised a separate, or at least semiseparate, class of society. Males from all levels of secular society moved into and out of the order. Young men traditionally spent a short time in it, but one could also make a career of the priesthood.

In addition, in the middle of the nineteenth century the number of Chinese in Thailand was estimated at several hundred thousand, and it was growing at the rate of about 15,000 per year. But the Chinese as a group had a limited impact upon Thai society, and "absorption of Chinese into the class of ordinary Siamese was constant throughout the reign [of Rama III]."[5] Groups of relatively primitive tribal peoples were also scattered through the more remote portions of the kingdom. Some of these peoples occasionally came into conflict with the Thais, but otherwise they did not much impinge upon the society with which we are concerned. Some Burmese tribal groups also lived within the nation's boundaries but had no great impact upon the general pattern of Thai society, nor did the Muslims in the tributary areas of the south.

The Thais themselves were a relatively homogeneous people. Those of the central basin of the Menam Chao Phraya did draw a distinction between themselves and the Lao of the north and northeast, and there were some differences in language and culture. But these differences were not so great as to constitute a fundamental barrier to communications, or to the gradual emergence of a sense of common identity as Thailand became a nation.

The Thai society was predominantly a village society, in the sense that nearly all the people lived in villages and practiced a relatively simple and stable kind of agriculture. But the culture was not a village culture.

Thai culture accounted for a cosmos including a real world not bounded by the village.[6] Admitting the animistic inclinations of the villagers and their eclectic practical Buddhism, they were far beyond cultural primitivism. Even in the village a man was consciously a member of a larger society. Its governmental aspect involved downward efforts at control and exploitation within the framework of a grand rationale, and the concomitant upward flow of some of the fruits of production. Its religious aspects gave satisfactory answers to all the basic questions about existence and afforded a wide range of outlets for worship, intercession, propitiation, and play. Tradition and religion together legitimized the social structure.

A man's place in the system was not immutably fixed. The circumstances of his birth largely determined his status and his prospects, but status at least was not simply ascribed by heredity. There was a possibility of personal movement within the society, with its encompassing structure which potentially, and to some extent in practice, linked outlying villages with the very center of the system. A few commoners achieved positions of power and honor in the society.

Perhaps one-fourth or one-third of the population in the middle of the nineteenth century consisted of "slaves," the great majority of them deliberate subjects of voluntary servitude based upon indebtedness.[7] The term "slave" is misleading, although it occurs in all the Western literature covering the Ayudhyan period. To the Westerner slavery connotes a state of degradation, a condition in stark contrast to that of freemen or commoners. But in mid-nineteenth-century Thailand all "freemen" were subject to onerous *corvées*.

Free common males who were not officials were required to pay a head tax, or, as an alternative, to serve the government for three months a year, each under the direction of an official "patron" to whom he was responsible. Earlier, the required service period had been four months, and before that six.[8] Theoretically, men had the right to choose their patrons, and to some degree this was true in practice. "Slaves," the full-time subjects of their masters, were exempt from the *corvée* and from the head tax of six baht (about U.S. $3.60) per person per year, payable in lieu of *corvée* service in the nineteenth century.[9] "Slaves" could possess and inherit property and establish their own families. In most cases, they were redeemable upon payment of their debts. They were sometimes freed to enter the Buddhist priesthood. As a result, their condition was often better than that of the so-called freemen, provided they were subject to mild masters. In this setting there was little or no stigma in slavery, and men readily sold themselves to those who could protect them.

Commoners typically held small farms from which they obtained their subsistence. Land was plentiful, and a freeman could claim up to 25 *rai* (10 acres) for his own use. In the Ayudhyan kingdom, status was not measured in land, and there was no important land-holding aristocracy—a fact of no small significance for modern Thailand. Status was more related to control over the critical factors in production—men—and over a portion of their labor and their produce. Giving common men free access to productive land was quite compatible with the aims and characteristics of Thai society, and it established a valuable productive base. For three, four, or six months—occasionally longer in time of a drawn-out war—a commoner might not be "his own man;" but at least he had his own small domain and was dependent upon his own productive efforts for his sustenance. In a tropical climate he did not have to work very hard to acquire enough to meet the needs of his family and his other obligations. Beyond this, there was little point in producing a surplus. So the Thai commoner might tend to be indolent, but he was also self-reliant. Given these conditions, the emergence of the legend that the word "Thai" means "free" was not wholly inconsistent with the existence of an elaborately hierarchical social system.

Other circumstances reinforced the rare combination of deference and independence characteristic of Thais. They included religion (see below) and the limited efficacy of bureaucratic controls. All men were supposed to be registered so that they could be assigned to *corvée* labor or military service, and the legitimacy of this arrangement was unquestioned. But the system of registration was inefficient, and probably corrupt. Men could escape the *corvée*—and did, judging from the vexed tone of royal edicts ordering the officials to register the populace and granting leniency to those who had escaped in the past but were now willing to submit.

One way of escape in a thinly populated land was simply to flee into the jungle. In rural Thailand remoteness has not been an exclusive function of great distance. In 1954, out of 2,200 villages in an economic survey sample, three were inacessible because of high water, and two could not be found at all. In 1854, or 1754, or earlier, a group seeking to escape an oppressive official patron did not have to flee far to disappear completely. If legitimate and essentially unchallenged authority bore down too heavily a man could escape it, and men sometimes did.

In the more remote areas of the kingdom men and their families must have been relatively free from official interference. Official government did not exist within the villages. Each was under the direction of a headman, known traditionally, as at present, as the *pu ban* or *pu yai ban* (literally, "man of the village" or "big man of the village"), and under the influence of the abbot of the local temple, or *wat*. The village leader was supposed to control the people and to mobilize them as ordered. The abbot, if he filled his role well and properly, was a source of advice who shared in leadership on many matters. Official government reached the villages in the course of patrols, and the extent of contact must have varied with time and place. With care, caution, and a bit of what we would call luck, a man might live reasonably free from any undue burden of governmental demands, unless he happened to be in a fairly accessible area. Even then, he might have the choice between *corvée* work and flight.

From this distance it is not really possible to characterize the quality of village life in Ayudhyan Thailand with sureness and objectivity. It undoubtedly varied with proximity to governmental centers, and the impact of government must have been substantial in time of war. But, for the village-dwelling mass of Thai society, the king must have been more fabulous than factual, and his officialdom was probably more often remote than immediate.

From one perspective this society might be viewed as a large and relatively similar mass of village-dwelling peasants, surmounted by a small official hierarchy culminating in the kingship. But the structure of Thai society was not to be judged in terms of numbers. The peasants and "slaves" were important *to* the system; they were its manpower; but they were not important *in* it. And, to the ordinary villager, such abstractions as "society," "politics," "government," and "freedom" in the political sense of the word were meaningless. The common people were merely the subjects of the king, and his authority was manifested through an official hierarchy. The hierarchy and the kingship were profoundly more important than the peasants, for they gave meaning and direction to the society—they and religion.

Thai Buddhism

To gain any true insight into the culture and character of the Thai of Thailand, it is necessary to learn something of their religion. Here I mean the religion, not of the educated or of scholars, but of the people in general; for religion is the mainspring of behavior as manifested by the people.[10]

Thai Buddhism served as a socializing and acculturating force. It gave coherence to the society, and presented a teleology from which individual existence acquired a meaning that was entirely consistent with the structure of society.

Hinayana, or Theravada, Buddhism became an established part of the Thai culture prior to the establishment of the Ayudhyan kingdom in A.D. 1350. Later, when the sack of the Khmer empire led to the introduction of Brahmanic rites and concepts, Buddhism continued as the popular religion, supported by a monarchy which asserted both Buddhist and Brahmanic features.

The central premises of practical Buddhism included the idea that ultimate "salvation" consisted of escape from material existence into a nirvana in which one no longer existed as a sensate individual being. Earthly existence was a transitory time of trial and temptation, of reward and punishment. Good was rewarded and evil was punished in the world as well as outside of it, and in the simple, pragmatic view of the ordinary man, a person and his fortune were essentially the consequence of imperfection which bound a man to suffering and rebirth. But there were degrees of imperfection. The high and mighty deserved their state, just as did the lowly, for a man's progress toward the ultimate was roughly reflected by his immediate state.

In this system one might, to some extent, "make merit for another"—for one's parents, for example—but basically each man stood alone, in a condition produced by his own acts and will, within a vagaristic and ephemeral world in which "the path" was the basic prescription of proper conduct.[11]

In practical Buddhism the teachings of the Buddha were enhanced by many non-Buddhist features, to provide a "complete" religion which answered a host of personal and social needs. Ceremonies and rituals for many occasions, soothsaying, and the propitiation of the spirits which inhabit the world were among the services offered by the priesthood, along with lore of many kinds. "A young Siamese nobleman, bent on a military career, could hardly do better than first serve in the usual way as a novice in a Buddhist monastery. There the abbot would impart those important aids to military proficiency, the knowledge how to become invulnerable, how to employ discarnate spirits, and which were the right *mantras* [incantations] for sending people to sleep or rendering an opposing force immobile." [12]

The temple, or wat, was a source of advice and information on matters practical or esoteric. Accessible to all, it provided a smattering of education for young boys and served as the place of feasts, "theatrical performances, music, fireworks, and exhibits of artistic works." [13] This was the social center for practically all Thais. Finally, the local priests and temple were the instruments by which a participatory religion functioned as a vital acculturating force. Here ideas of right and wrong, of proper aims and means, of ways of relating oneself to society were spelled out, and the precepts were reinforced by a lifetime of temple-centered activities ranging from rites of passage to holiday celebrations. Every young man was expected to spend at least a little time—perhaps three months—as a monk, and many did so. Vella has estimated that in the second quarter of the nineteenth century at any given time perhaps 100,000 males were serving as Buddhist priests or novices.[14]

Buddhism, like the secular structure of society, was stratified, and status differences within the order were explicit. But the authority structure of religious organization was marked by looseness rather than by tight administrative hierarchicalism. There was a coherence of essential dogma and precept which must have been sustained by a fairly substantial flow of communications reinforced by status; but there was little occasion for command within the official religious structure, and the permissivity and tolerance of the society were reflected in, as well as sustained by, the religion.

Thai Buddhism was neither aggressive nor authoritarian. Instructive and benignly propitiatory, it did not seek to manipulate the broad conditions of existence. At least, it did not assert the power of control over them in any forceful way. For example, Buddhist ceremonies to invoke rain existed as early as the thirteenth century A.D. But, in a nation of rice growers who were periodically plagued by water shortages or inopportune rains, Buddhism developed no priestly caste on the basis of its ability to forecast or influence the rains. Rainmaking and fortunetelling were among its functions, but they were ever incidental to its prime concerns. And these were not worldly.

Thai Buddhism nurtured thematic social values and attitudes that were thoroughly compatible with the nature of Thai society. Given Buddhism, a highly stratified society was easy to accept. Yet within it a certain "looseness" or tolerance for autonomy was also sanctioned. However stratified the system, it must allow the individual freedom to follow the dictates of his conscience, to work out his own salvation. Because each person was largely responsible for his fate (and perhaps because interdependence among individuals occurred chiefly within primary groups), the society was characterized by an impressive degree of tolerance.

In accord with the concept of karma, one could accept his environment as "given," or intrinsically legitimate. Yet a person might also try to enhance his position within that environment through craft or cleverness, if karma did not otherwise decree. But to attack the environment, to try to change the *status quo,* was not sanctioned by the premises of Buddhism. It had no analogue of the Protestant ethic of the Western world.

Buddhism fostered stability. The king, commonly regarded as a bodhisattva, was implicitly identified with the popular religion, and the whole existing system of society was sanctioned by the faith. Yet individuals did matter in this system. Buddhism ascribed no immutable status to any man, nor did it preclude one from pursuing his own aims and interests. It nurtured social cohesion, but not secondary associations. It left none of the teleological questions unanswered, and its answers were compatible with social and physical reality, as these were perceived from a Buddhist perspective. It was—and is—an efficacious religion to its adherents, as the small success of Christian missionaries in Thailand has shown.

King and Country—"L'état, c'est moi!"

If Buddhism was the key to the universe, then the king was the key to the organization of its wordly aspect. The king was the center of the socio-political system, the "Lord of Lives." He was absolute and sacred, a charismatic ruler. The legitimacy of his position was beyond challenge.[15] In the simplest of terms, there was no "state." There was only the king's domain. He owned what was in it, and it existed for his aims and purposes.

In accordance with the theory of the *Dharmasastra,* the sacred law which had been introduced into Thailand by the fourteenth century A.D., the king's function was "to protect his people and preserve the sacred law." [16] But the king had both the right and the duty to give meaning and application to this fundamental law. Out of this emerged the *Rajasastra,* a large and periodically codified collection of royal edicts. In theory, the king drew his legitimacy from the *Dharmasastra.* In practice, he, rather than the law, was the keystone of the system, for there was no constitutionalization of the law.

The pre-Ayudhyan kings had resembled tribal patriarchs—leaders justified both by tradition and by the possession of immediate power. Ideally, they were paternal, and the legend of father-like ancient kings is revered in Thailand today.

In the adoption of the *Code of Manu,* or the *Dharmasastra,* and the Khmerization of the expanding kingdom, the monarch acquired characteristics of a bodhisattva and a devaraja—not a very logical conceptualization perhaps, but one quite acceptable in the system. Yet something of the older patriarchal tradition of the Sukhodaya era was retained as the kingdom grew larger and the kingship more formalized. The secluded absolutism of the Lord of Lives was never completely untinged with concern for the common people. In theory, and to some small degree in practice, a common man possessed the privilege of petition, a privilege recognized during the reign of Rama III in the nineteenth century by the installation of a new drum in the palace grounds to be struck by persons with petitions for the king.[17]

In the Ayudhyan era the people were dust beneath the king's feet, yet they were also his servants and children. Their well-being was his proper interest, justified in principle as well as by the fact that peace, order, and contentment contributed to the wealth and strength of the kingdom. Thus, a not atypical eighteenth-century Royal Edict on the Method of Provincial Administration proclaims: "Governors must keep the peace in their provinces. . . . The officials shall give their whole attention to their work, to keep the peace of the country for the sake of the happiness of the people. . . ." [18]

The objects of the king were the aims of the "state." In addition to the well-being of the populace, these included the defense and expansion of the domain; the acquisition of wealth; the supporting of

Buddhism; the construction of certain kinds of public works—chiefly canals; and the embellishment of the capital with temples, palaces, and other evidences of the splendor of the ruler and his kingdom.

Although wealth was a royal object, money revenues were relatively small by modern standards throughout the Ayudhyan era and into the nineteenth century. "Money . . . formed but a small proportion of the total resources which the Siamese kings had at their command. The greater part of their religious and other works were carried out by extensive forces of unpaid laborers and skilled craftsmen which . . . were at the disposal of the king." [19]

Wars were frequent, and the chronicles of Ayudhya are replete with references to battles, particularly with the kingdom's ancient enemy, Burma. Between 1488 and 1767, when the Burmese sacked the capital and nearly destroyed the kingdom, at least seventy different rebellions, campaigns, uprisings, and internal battles for succession involving military force occurred—an average of one notable military undertaking every four years. Yet the Thai king was not primarily a warrior king, nor was his essentially a garrison state.

Over the centuries, the central basin of the River Chao Phraya became crisscrossed with canals constructed at the king's initiative. As early as 1534, at the site of Bangkok, a *klong* was dug which is now occupied by the mainstream of the river. At least four waterways projects were completed between 1824 and 1850, including a canal thirty-three miles long, built in two years, at a reported cost of about $58,000 plus an unknown amount of free labor.[20] By the end of the nineteenth century there were several thousand kilometers of waterways. This utilitarian work stimulated the flow of wealth into the royal treasuries. The canals were also the chief means of internal transportation, useful for military as well as agricultural purposes.

The other public works activity, the construction of imposing structures in the capital, sometimes led Westerners to inflated estimates about the real wealth of the kingdom. Certainly, the central city of the kingdom—the only city of any size—enhanced any man's impression of the majesty of the king.

The kingship of old Siam was a complex institution, sustained by tradition, and achieved at times by guile and force. The king as ruler was surrounded by a cluster of officials, many of them half brothers or other relatives, for he could often—if not always—rely more upon close relatives than upon others. But it was as ruler that the king faced his greatest problems. His status isolated him from his officials and from most of his kingdom. His very power engendered fear and sophistry in those he dealt with. His absolutism was made almost ineffectual by the bureaucracy through which he sought to rule; yet that bureaucracy did not usurp nor undermine the inherent authority of the kingship, as the events of the Chakkri Reformation would show. But if the kingship of ancient Thailand was a wondrous thing, so was the bureaucratic apparatus which professed to serve the king.

The Structure of the Traditional Bureaucracy

Any institution which survives for four and a half centuries must have some interesting qualities. From the 1450s, when King Boromo-trailokanat reorganized the Thai bureaucracy, until late in the nineteenth century, when another great king reorganized it once again, there was a substantial continuity in its essential structure.[21]

The bureaucracy had a dual significance—functional and social. It was hardly a great, dynamic, productive machine, but it did perform functions essential to the continuation of the kingdom. In addition to doing certain kinds of work, the bureaucracy served as the framework of the strata of society between the king and the peasantry. It was the basic instrument for providing continuing social order and coherence.

The bureaucracy included an elaborate set of specialized royal staffs, in some ways reminiscent of the king's household in the monarchical states which emerged in the West. It also comprised organizations for territorial control, revenue production and retention, diplomacy, warfare, and defense. Finally, the religious apparatus might be regarded as one element of the bureaucracy.

The most impressive characteristic of this bureaucracy was its elaborate and explicit hierarchicalism. The status of each participant in the system was defined in great detail, essentially in terms of the position he happened to occupy in the bureaucracy. The reasons for this overweening hierarchicalism, and the characteristics which went along with it, will become clear in the following discussion.

THE DEVELOPMENT OF THE AYUDHYAN BUREAUCRACY

The foundations of the bureaucracy were laid by King Boromo-trailokanat (hereafter Trailok), who ascended the throne of Ayudhya in A.D. 1448 at the age of seventeen, and reigned until his death some forty years later. King Trailok inherited the apparatus of Khmer government which had been acquired in the sack of Angkor in 1431, including a retinue of Brahman officials and advisers who were brought to Ayudhya following the Cambodian conquest. With the evident assistance of this staff, Trailok spelled out a pattern of socio-bureaucratic organization whose forms persisted for more than four hundred years. In its broadest sense, this pattern encompassed every person in the kingdom. Its essential characteristic was a structure of ranks or statuses which designated every conceivable level in the society, from common men and slaves to the senior princes of the realm. A key feature of this ranking arrangement was the quantification of status designations through the use of *sakdi na,* or "dignity marks."

Sakdi na means, literally, "power over land," and the dignity-mark system was refined rather than created by Trailok. Earlier, *sakdi na* numbers had indicated the amount of land over which a noble or commoner possessed nominal or actual jurisdiction. Thus a *sakdi na* of 10,000, the rank of a head of an important department, implied control over 10,000 *rai* (4,000 acres) of land. The commoner had a *sakdi na* of 25, while a prince who headed one of the major agencies of the government might have a *sakdi na* as high as 100,000. Following the Khmerization of the kingdom, the *sakdi na* numbers lost their territorial connotation and came to indicate hierarchical position in the society. Not until 1932 were *sakdi na* designations abolished.

The bureaucracy was differentiated from the populace at large in terms of status as well as function. The levels of officialdom extended upward from a *sakdi na* just exceeding the 25 marks of the common man. Officials with ranks above 400 might be called the "commissioned officer" group; they were appointed by the king. Below the 400 level existed a host of petty functionaries appointed by ministerial and provincial officials. At the broad base of the pyramid were the commoners, with less status than any official.

Additional means were used to define systematically the rank and status of officials: *yasa,* a series of honorific titles, some of ancient Thai origin and others derived from Khmer terminology; *rajadin-nama,* elaborate names assigned by the king, which became the names of the incumbents of official posts; and *tamhnen,* or terms indicating the grade or rank of a particular office. For high-ranking officials other status symbols were also used, including royally conferred betel nut boxes, palanquins, and so forth.

It appears that all these indications of rank and status, or *sakdi,* were carefully correlated. Detailed records *(damniap)* were maintained, stating the offices and titles of officials from the highest to the lowest in each central department and in each of the provinces. Other *damniap* specified the ranks of the Buddhist order.

Through this precise and elaborate hierarchical plan officialdom and society itself were fused. Officials were identified by the names of their positions, and the status of each was defined, essentially in terms of his relative hierarchical "distance" from the king.

In this scheme, as it was spelled out in the 1450s, there was one additional classifying arrangement: the entire population was divided into two parts, the civil and the military; and at the levels of officialdom, two parallel hierarchies actually existed (or two facets of the same hierarchy)—the civil and the military. Finally, the duties and the privileges of the major officials in the system were spelled out in a royal edict, or "law."

ELEMENTS OF BUREAUCRATIC ORGANIZATION

Trailok's encompassing hierarchical pattern was one aspect of his successful effort to provide a governmental structure for his kingdom. This structure had two essential parts—a headquarters and a set of provinces. In addition, the domain of King Trailok and his successors included a varying group of vassal states or tributaries, whose remnants were not fully incorporated into the kingdom until the modernizing efforts of the late nineteenth century.

The headquarters organization of the kingdom included, in addition to the king himself, two great ministers, or *argamahasenabodi,* the heads of the civil and military divisions of the populace. The civilian side of the headquarters included four major departments, or *kram,* headed by ministers known as *senabodi,* who were the king's councilors. A parallel structure presumably existed on the military side. Wales implies that the *senabodi* were under the jurisdiction of one or the other of the great ministers, and through these to the king. But one of the civilian ministers was in charge of the Palace, and it seems likely that he received his commands directly from the king.

In any event, the two great ministers, who have been treated in some Western writings as prime ministers, were responsible for the registering and mobilizing of the population of the entire kingdom in the scheme of King Trailok, and they must have been among the most

powerful subordinates in the kingdom. An interesting potentiality for
jurisdictional difficulties was inherent in the fact that each great minister was expected to exercise power over the same territory. Later,
this problem was to be resolved by dividing the area of the kingdom
between the two (and giving control over a choice portion to a third
minister). Not until 1892 were the great ministers abolished.

The four civilian ministries in this structure were the *Kram Wang*
(Palace Ministry), *Kram Phra Klang* (Treasury), *Kram Nakarnban,*
or *Kram Muang* (which might be called the Ministry of the Capital),
and the *Kram Na* (Ministry of Lands).[22]

The Palace Ministry contained many elements of the king's personal staff, including his bodyguard, harem, and personal treasury.
This organization and its subordinate units became responsible for
royal ritual, communications and records, property, and oracular
functions. A Royal Scribes Department (*Kram Phra Alaksana*)
evolved, to write royal edicts and preserve documents. It also contained the court poets, royal pandits, and astrologers. A *Kram
Bhusamala* was responsible for royal wardrobes, insignia, weapons,
and ceremonial equipage—items whose importance stemmed from
the fact that they came in contact with the royal person. As Minister
of the Palace, the *senabodi* of the *Kram Wang* became responsible for
a share of the administration of justice and for making certain provincial appointments.

As a matter of speculation, it would seem that the judicial responsibility of the palace minister evolved out of the pre-Khmer patriarchal tradition of the privilege of petition to the king. Access being
the key to any effective attempt to petition, and the control of access
to the king resting with his palace minister, it must have been logical
to make this minister responsible for seeing that justice was meted
out in cases which came before the throne.

The Ministry of the Capital, responsible for law and order within
the capital area, and probably for various related matters, also performed judicial functions. The head of this ministry became the ranking criminal judge of the *wang rajadhani,* as the central territory of
the kingdom was called. He was known as *Chao Phraya Yamarat,* or,
in appropriate translation, "Lord of Hell."

The *Kram Phra Klang,* or Treasury, developed from the fifteenth
century into what eventually became a Ministry of Trade, Treasure,
and Foreign Affairs. The head of the ministry acquired responsibility

for royal trading ventures and dealings with foreign merchants. In Thailand's seventeenth-century contacts with the larger world, this function was extended to the reception of foreign embassies, and the head of the ministry was described variously as *Phra Klang,* or as *Chao Da*—"Lord of the Landing Stage."

Actually, the treasury of the *Kram Phra Klang* was but one of several. The ministries, and probably most departments of any consequence that evolved within them, had treasuries of their own, just as various units of the government evolved judicial and penal facilities of their own. "Law enforcement" and control over resources were thoroughly dispersed in this system.

The fourth of the civilian ministries headed by a *senabodi* was the *Kram Na,* or Ministry of Land. It was supposed to urge a somewhat indolent people to cultivate the fields at the proper season. Using *corvée* labor, it cleared jungle within the *wang rajadhani,* developed and maintained canals, and collected rice, fodder, ivory, leather, and eventually agricultural taxes. The ministry also ruled on cases involving land, cattle, and boundaries.

In the cluster of agencies at the center of the kingdom was also a *Kram Dharmakara,* or Department of Religious Administration. It was the instrumentality through which the king appointed high church dignitaries. The department also supervised the Buddhist order to some degree, and tried monks accused of serious offenses. The royal Brahmans were in a separate department.

Not much is known about the specific pattern of military organization. It did contain a number of specialized agencies, including a department of royal elephants.

THE PROVINCES

The *wang rajadhani* (central territory) comprised a relatively small part of the total domain of the Thai king. Its outer area was arranged into provinces, or districts, for purposes of control, and these were supervised by one or the other of the *senabodi.*

The greater part of the kingdom—outside the *wang rajadhani*—was also arranged into provinces. These provinces provided manpower and a flow of wealth into the capital, as well as manpower for defense. But some of them were also treacherous regions, with potential for revolt, perhaps even for assault on the capital.

By the beginning of the seventeenth century the provinces had been

An Idealized Sketch of Governmental Organization Under the Khmerized System of King Trailok

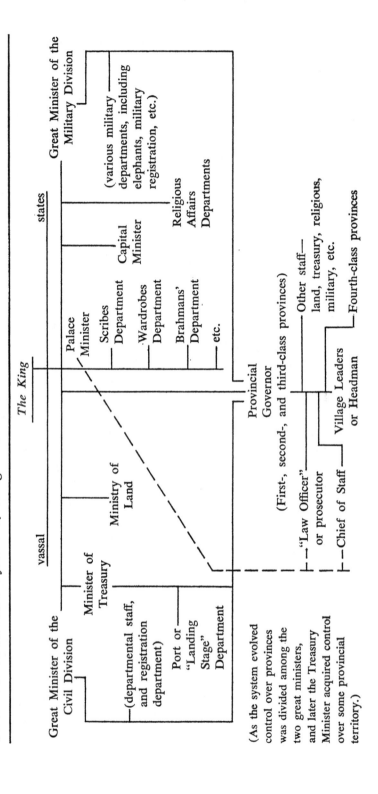

(As the system evolved control over provinces was divided among the two great ministers, and later the Treasury Minister acquired control over some provincial territory.)

grouped into four classes. The two first-class provinces of this time, Phitsanulok and Nakorn Srithammarat, were relatively large frontier regions of importance to the defense of the kingdom. Some of the seven second-class provinces were also strategically important. Eight third-class provinces were of less consequence. Finally, there were some fourth-class provinces *(muang noi)* subordinate to major provinces rather than to the central government.

A typical province was a town with its surrounding territory, an area which could be crossed in two or three days when travel was feasible. Provinces varied in size according to terrain, communications, stability, and the existence of suitable sites for provincial headquarters. The basic functions of their governments were to maintain peace and order; to collect information on manpower, elephants, and other resources; to mobilize military conscripts upon request and use *corvée* labor; and to collect a share of the area's wealth for provincial use and transmission to the capital. The provincial governments were supposed to encourage agriculture. They also appear to have kept records of land titles.

The provinces were organized as lesser replicas of the capital. A major province would normally include a garrison command, a treasury, officers responsible for land and agriculture, ecclesiastical officials, a law court, a bodyguard, physicians, astrologers, craftsmen, bargemen, and scribes. Numerous *kramakan*—minor officials with *sakdi na* of less than 400—included petty judicial officers and registrars, as well as the staffs of fourth-class provinces appointed by the governor of the supervising province.

The provincial governors, appointed by the king, were normally responsible to him through the great ministers. Masters of their domains, commanders of provincial armies in time of war, the provincial rulers were powerful men. In concept, they served at the pleasure of the king. In practice, their offices, like others in the system, not uncommonly became semihereditary.

CENTRAL GOVERNMENT–PROVINCIAL RELATIONS

As time passed, relations between the provinces and the central government became more complex.[23] Central government ministries acquired jurisdiction over certain kinds of provincial affairs. Officials of the Ministry of Land were assigned to provinces to register titles, promote water control works, and encourage production. The Ministry also collected land and garden taxes which were levied as early as the eighteenth century, along with saltpeter, tin, sapanwood, ivory, elephants, and other monopolized products for the king's treasury. As Thai kings became engaged in international trade these collections grew, along with the bureaucracy responsible for them.

Officials under the ostensible control of the central Department of Registration were established in the provinces to conscript persons for military or civil work and to maintain the records needed for this purpose. But the provinces were never locked into a complex network of integrated government. The amount of functional interdependence between provinces and center remained quite limited, and provincial control was a persistent problem for Thai kings and their ministers.

The duplicated jurisdiction of the two great ministers over the provinces inevitably created difficulties. Following rebellions in the provinces of Nakorn Srithammarat and Korat, and in the northern tributary of Luang Prabang during the seventeenth century, jurisdiction over northern territories was given to the chief civilian minister (*mahadthai*), while the south was placed under the control of the military minister (*kalahom*). For the next two hundred years parallel organizations at least nominally controlled the northern and southern provinces. With the expansion of trade, the maritime provinces at the head of the Gulf of Thailand came under the jurisdiction of the *Phra Klang,* on the ground that this was necessary to his work of controlling trade, commerce, and the treasury.

The king sought to control the provinces and enforce his aims by installing checks and balances in the provincial hierarchies. Within a major province, the governor personally controlled the key members of his staff, and, in turn, was responsible to one of the great ministers (or in some cases in the latter part of the Ayudhyan era to the *Phra Klang*). Early in the eighteenth century the *yokrabat,* in charge of provincial law and order, and the *luang wang,* governor's chief of staff, were made appointees of the Palace Minister, to whom they also reported.

If the governor sits in judgment on legal cases he must have the *yakkrahpatra* [yokrabat] to try the case with him. . . . If it is found that the people have their property taken away by officials when the latter are going among them on duty, the *yakkrahpatra* shall make inquiries. . . . In case of misbehavior on the part of the governor, the *yakkrahpatra* must report; in the case of the *yakkrahpatra* the governor must report, or if both misbehave the other officials must report.[24]

This was an unusual example of an effort to modify the basic pattern of provincial administration, and to supplement exhortation with a division of responsibilities so that different officials would act as checks upon each other—a device which, incidentally, is endemic in contemporary Thai public administration. How well the arrangement served its aim is unknown. If the *yokrabat* and *luang wang* asserted their independence of the governor and upheld the values of the king, they might impose substantial limitations upon the governor's independence. But these officials were closely associated with the governor and were linked with Ayudhya only by a thin line of communications. They all depended upon provincial resources for their sustenance. So it is doubtful that this particular arrangement produced any basic change in the character of provincial government.

Patterns of Action in the Traditional Bureaucracy

The elaborate, encompassing, persisting structure of the traditional bureaucracy was as impressive in its fashion as any of the physical features of the old kingdom. The remains of temples and palaces and the evidence of earthworks tell us something about life in the Ayudhyan era. So does the structure of the bureaucracy. But the relation between the bureaucratic framework and the action which occurred within it was paradoxical.

For example, the bureaucracy—the entire society—was formally organized on the premise that it existed to serve the king, the source of all authority. Yet to a great extent the bureaucracy served itself, and there were other forms of authority in the system than the legitimate power of the monarch. In appearance, too, the bureaucratic system was one grand monolithic structure linked by a comprehensive chain of command; in practice, it was a loose collection of enclaves, some of them sometimes knit together in an *ad hoc* fashion. Finally, one might assume from an examination of the structure of the bureaucracy that it was continuedly energized by a flow of royal edicts and commands. In a sense it was—but, at the same time, inertia was probably the commonest impetus to action in the bureaucracy.

Like most pedagogic paradoxes, these have the sharp clarity of mirages. They are not real; contradictions between the expected and the actual are only apparent.

How did the traditional bureaucracy "work"? What did it actually do, and why did it do it? The answers to these questions explain the persistence of the bureaucracy, help reveal the nature of the late nineteenth-century administrative reform efforts, and provide a clue to the outcome of those efforts.

AUTHORITY IN THE TRADITIONAL BUREAUCRACY

Power is a central element of any system of organization, for it is the key to action. The traditional Thai socio-bureaucratic system was based upon one sweeping principle of authority—the authority of the king.

In theory, the king possessed all legitimate power. To exercise authority within the bureaucracy was to make use of the power of the monarch, presumably for his purposes. In theory, too, there was a limit to the authority of the king—the limit inherent in his obligation to uphold the sacred law. But this limitation-in-principle, not sustained by any effective constraints, was not enforceable.

Yet the king was not unbounded. First, his power was to some extent limited by "influence"—by certain ideas and expectations in the social system. Ameliorating influences diluted the stark theoretical authoritarianism of the king. The subtle, pervasive influence of Buddhism also must have tempered the authority it did not explicitly challenge. Finally, the sheer force of tradition—the patriarchal element in the image of the kingship and the idea of a privilege of petition, for example—regulated aspects of royal behavior, producing expectations that were not lightly denied. Thus, once the king began making annual gifts to certain officials he was constrained to continue the practice even when it proved financially inconvenient.

Second, a countervailing force effectively offset much of the power of the king. This was the "authority of self-interest," which resulted from the innate character of the socio-bureaucratic system. In principle, there was no such authority; in practice, it existed only on sufferance, subject to challenge from above. But, in practice, such intervention was limited by the inadequacy of the king's means for exercising his own inherent authority.

The actual play of power in the socio-bureaucratic system was interesting and complex. The authority of the king required no justification; it was inherent in this culture which had no need to rationalize its institutions. Tradition, the possession of instruments of force, and charisma upheld the kingship as the center of the Thai social universe. The formal monolithic structure of society expressed and reflected the prime premise of royal absolutism. No effective, legitimate competing power centers were acknowledged.

Charisma was an important source of royal authority. Charismatic omnipotence was asserted in a number of ways—by the symbolic procreational potency of the polygamous king, for example, and by a rich variety of rituals acquired in the Khmerization of the kingdom.[25] These ranged from the prostration of officials before the monarch to the requirement that no ordinary man might look upon his face and live. Under the palatine laws, even to damage the king's boat accidentally was punishable by death. Ritual made the king a shadowy symbol, an object of awe and grandeur, and this helped sustain the myth of his charismatic omnipotence.

Charisma was used to exact obedience and proper behavior from officials. The semiannual lustral water ceremony was the most vivid example. Twice a year each official of the king was required to drink holy water and swear a mighty oath of allegiance.

We, the slaves of the Lord Buddha, beg to offer to His Majesty . . . our personal oath, pledging our loyalty, in the immediate presence of the Buddha, the sacred teachings and the sacred priests.

If we, the slaves of our Lord Buddha, are not firmly fixed in true natural gratitude . . . , or if we disclose our minds to the people or rulers of other regions which are hostile, and plot that others do evil to . . . the King; if we see with our eyes, hear with our ears, or know that others are about to do evil to His Majesty, and do not bring forward the subject for investigation, so that it may be specially brought to the knowledge of His Majesty, but delay with evil intent, with ingratitude, and lack of honesty, and with evil purposes . . . :

We pray the deities of lands and forests; the guardian deities; the atmospheric deities; the goddesses who care for the earth, especially the powerful deities who are located where is the great white Umbrella, emblem of royalty, may plague us with evils, destroy our lives, effect our destruction and death by breakage, by serverance; cause our death by lightning and thunderbolts, by royal weapons, the powerful royal sword, by poison, and the power of land and water animals; let there be some opportunity for the destruction of the perfidious ones; let swift destruction come; let us not escape all great disasters. . . . We beseech the power of the deities to plague with poisonous boils, rapidly fatal, and all manner of diseases, the dishonorable, perverse, and treacherous; plague with untimely, wretched, and appalling deaths, manifest to the eyes of the world. When we shall have departed this life from earth, cause us to be sent and all to be born in the great hell, where we shall burn with quenchless fire for tens and thousands of ages and limitless transmigrations. And when we have expiated our penalty there, and are born again in any world, we pray we may fail to find the least happiness in worlds of pleasurable enjoyments. Let us not meet the Buddha, the sacred teachings, the sacred priests, who come to be gracious to beings, helping them escape misery. . . . Should we meet them, let them grant us no gracious assistance.

If we remain firmly established in gratitude and honesty, and do not contemplate rebellion . . . , we beg the land, the forest, and the atmospheric deities, and the four great guardians of the world . . . , and the guardian deities that protect His Majesty by night and by day, and the deities that protect the palace, and the deities stationed to protect the twelve royal treasuries, and all the deities, the armories, and ministers, and great royal property; we entreat you all to assist, and protect us who perform all official duties faithfully; grant us prosperity and happiness in this and in other worlds. . . .[26]

The sanctions which might be brought into play by violating this magnificent oath could not be regarded lightly. Note, however, that the main object of the oath-and-water ceremony, which was used until 1932, was to deter mendacious and treasonable conduct.

Lesser oaths were used as instruments of control, somewhat as modern governments require employees to sign affidavits when they complete expense vouchers. Officials assessing gardens and farms for tax purposes in the *wang rajadhani* were assembled in the royal chapel on the Buddhist holy day (*wan phra*) *after* they had finished their work, and made to swear that they had done it honestly.[27] In a modern administrative system, the oath is seldom if ever regarded as the prime mechanism of control. In traditional Thai administration, where the charismatic power of the king was assumed, a greater potency was ascribed to oaths.

Reward and *punishment,* more immediate temporal sanctions, were also used to sustain the power of the king. At his slightest whim or displeasure his majesty could have an official seized, flogged, banished, or flung into prison—a reminder that the offender, and all other officials, were mere slaves of an omnipotent majesty. Rewards might be dispensed just as summarily and arbitrarily, although to be favored also had its dangers, for it made one vulnerable to whispered attacks by others. No lasting stigma attached to punishment. An official, having been punished, might (if he lived) be restored to his prior status or something akin to it.

The inherent power of the king was also expressed in *edicts* and *orders*. The system of ranks and statuses was promulgated and from time to time modified by edict. The palace was regulated by edicts. Jurisdictions of officials were changed and departments were created by royal order. Seals were used to evidence the source, and thus the legitimacy, of royal edicts, and no man might properly challenge or question an order of the king.

But the absolutism of the monarch was by itself insufficient to cope with the relativism of the world, and Thai kings did not hesitate to use methods for exercising power which were not particularly consistent with the idea of omnipotence. The installation of checks and balances as a feature of provincial government has already been mentioned. The regular use of spies and informants implied that there were very real limits to the potency of royal edicts and semiannual oaths.[28] The need for such devices suggests that the bureaucracy, which derived its form, its legitimacy, and much of its substance from the kingship, must have violated persistently the principles that all power was from the king, and that all action was to serve his ends.

In short, the authority of the king was in practice limited and incomplete. Yet it was vital. The over-all hierarchical structure of the socio-bureaucratic system derived its existence and meaning from the kingship. Many actions which occurred within this structure stemmed directly from royal orders. The king could—and did—intervene in the system.

Effective royal intervention in the bureaucracy was personal and particular. When the king desired a specific concrete action he could usually get it. Canals, temples, palaces were built; campaigns were fought. The king's elephants were cared for, and the appropriate rituals were performed.

When the king prescribed an organizational arrangement, it was adopted, to remain until another king changed it. When the king summoned an army, it was almost instantly mobilized. Yet an almost endless flow of exhortations echoed across the Ayudhyan centuries to indicate the limits to monarchical power. Orders not to oppress the people, not to be disloyal, not to be dishonest, flowed forth, as if to imply that such exhortations were self-enforcing—and by their number and frequency to show that they were not. "Inability rather than lack of desire . . . prevented the king from protecting the people." [29] Obviously, other factors than royal power helped determine the patterns of action of the traditional Thai bureaucracy.

THE "AUTHORITY OF SELF-INTEREST" IN THE TRADITIONAL BUREAUCRACY

The bureaucratic behavior which systematically flouted aims and commands of the king was not based on a rejection of his legitimacy. Nor did it stem from a nonchalant attitude toward the Lord of Lives and his power. The tacit pattern of actual authority governing day-to-day administration was largely the consequence of several characteristics of the bureaucratic system, which reinforced each other to produce a stable, inertial apparatus responsive to specific and explicit commands from above, but otherwise highly responsive to values which were not promulgated by the king.

The phenomenon can be summed up in one statement: The bureaucracy functioned as a social system—more precisely, as *the* social subsystem which included all the secular strata of society between the king and the commoners. The formal framework of the system was the matrix of official ranks and roles which derived their meaning and legitimacy from the king. But no social system is merely a matter of an explicit, formal framework; and in the Thai case the formal framework itself helped produce values that were often more meaningful than the aims and orders of the monarch.

The normal behavioral characteristics of the bureaucracy were largely the product of these factors: the hierarchical system for defining and differentiating status and role, the diffuseness of the goals in the system and of the roles of its participants, and the arrangements for procuring and motivating and organizing them into units of action. "Normal" behavior consisted of a broad range of activities, of which the performance of specific tasks or functions was but one part—and often a small one.

The Behavioral Consequences of Thai Hierarchicalism. Traditional Thailand was, if not a planned society, at least an outlined society. In intent, although by no means in practice, it was a totalitarian society, with a single authority-principle and an inclusive, explicit, even quantitatively expressed structure of roles and statuses by which the authority of the king might be exercised.

Personal identity was largely determined by reference to this hierarchical matrix. One might move within it, but not beyond it (except into Buddhism, or into the jungle). The emphasis in the system was profoundly vertical; the hierarchy identified superiors and subordinates, and "defined" relations between them in terms of status. A superior was entitled to deference and obedience; a subordinate was expected to defer and obey.

In theory, the official as a person was meaningless; his meaning, or his identity and status, derived from his office with its hierarchical rank. But the attributes of office were not explicitly limited in scope. There was no real distinction of official and office. As a result, the norms which governed personal action in this system were diffuse. Behavior toward superiors consisted largely of the fulfillment of sweeping obligations of deference and compliance, and what was an obligation in an upward relationship became a right in relation to subordinates. But the lateral range of these rights and obligations was not bounded. From the perspective of a Weberian conception of bureaucracy, there was a profound incompleteness to the traditional Thai system. It did not limit hierarchical relations to matters of "official duties and responsibilities." The absence of a differentiated economic aspect of society was matched by the absence of any distinction between official and nonofficial roles (family and religious roles being the only significant exceptions). Thus the essential quality of an effective personal relationship in this system was "pleasing a superior" rather than "doing a good job."

The somewhat ironic result was to personalize the ostensibly depersonalized bureaucracy in which an official had no nominal identity save his official title. Immediate personal relations were the most compelling in the system. One might be the "king's man" in principle—one might owe ultimate fealty and allegiance to the monarch—but one's well-being in the encompassing socio-bureaucratic system was essentially a result of relations with immediate superiors, and to some extent with immediate subordinates.

Kin muang; the Remuneration of Officials. Kin muang was a premise which derived from the theory of the kingship, and a principle which controlled much bureaucratic behavior. *Kin muang* literally means "to eat the place." The phrase has also been translated idiomatically as "to govern."

The king was entitled to eat the kingdom. It was his. Officials, who obtained authority and status from the king, acquired the privilege of *kin muang* within their particular jurisdictions.

This arrangement was not without its logic and legitimacy. Like everyone else, the officials existed in a subsistence economy; the level of subsistence to which they were entitled was a function of their status, which presumably reflected the king's judgment of their merits and their value. In traditional Thailand, economic activity was not differentiated from other kinds of effort by specialized concepts or theories of production, distribution, the rights of labor, or anything of the sort, and there was no conceptual basis for questioning *kin muang*. Besides, the arrangement had the advantage of simplicity, given a bureaucracy with limited performance capability. No elaborate apparatus was needed to collect and redistribute resources with which to pay the bureaucrats. Access to income was built right into the job. *Kin muang* enhanced the personal quality of relationship within the bureaucracy. A bureaucrat's rights often extended not only to deference but to support as well. A superior might be concerned with the productivity of those below him, but not merely in the Weberian sense of the term. *Kin muang* added a significant dimension to the personal hierarchical relations already discussed: it gave superior and subordinate a reciprocal set of material interests.

In the seventeenth century, the Thai monarch began the practice of systematically giving *biawat* (annual gifts) to his major officials. These were based upon the status of the recipients as well as the pleasure of the king. To some extent *biawat* came to resemble "pay." In theory it was a gift, but in practice it became an implicit, traditional obligation sanctioned by the expectations of the officials. In the latter part of the era of the traditional kingship, *biawat* payments came to be made in money. In the nineteenth century, when the king was sometimes short of funds, he acknowledged his obligation by making gifts in kind. But *biawat* supplemented rather than supplanted *kin muang,* and the bureaucrats generally derived their support from the exploitation of subordinates.

Procurement of Personnel for the Bureaucracy. The traditional Thai bureaucracy was a careerist system, marked by characteristics which contributed to the emphasis upon personal relationships.

"Managers" were produced by the institution of the royal pages, or *mahatlek,* the training school for an Oriental administrative class.[30] Sons of important officials were presented to the king at an early age, perhaps eleven or twelve. Treated as members of the royal family, they lived, played, and studied together. Pages were instructed in the royal language and ritual and assigned to perform small services for the king. As they grew older, the pages attended his councils and learned the workings of the center of the governmental system. The king advanced his pages in dignity marks, presumably on the basis of merit and competence as well as age, and assigned them to subordinate posts in the headquarters of his ministries. From here they might rise to positions of great power. Because of their background—and their prospects—the pages possessed a special status within the bureaucracy. Because of their background, too, they formed a coterie.

Elsewhere in the system, governors groomed sons to succeed them. Sons of commoner officials observed the work of lesser offices, and moved from such apprenticeships into official positions.

No man had any right to retain his post or to prepare a son to succeed him. In theory, the status, authority, and continued existence of officials was in the hands of the king, except at the lowest levels of official society—below the 400 *sakdi na* grade—where myriad petty officials depended upon their bureaucratic patrons. In practice, a man's standing with his immediate superiors much influenced his future and his prospects for bringing one or more sons into the ranks of officialdom. The king himself supervised only a miniscule part of the system.

Arrangements for training and procuring officials was entirely compatible with the needs and values of the bureaucratic apparatus. They afforded some—if not much—social mobility. They made for continuity; the bureaucracy reproduced itself as it went along. New officials brought no novel ideas from alien backgrounds; they entered the system at an early age, literally grew up in it, and absorbed its procedures and norms into their own shaping personalities. This did not create any great propensity for change, but the environment made no substantial demands for adaptation. And the bureaucrat entered one particular component of the system and normally stayed in it throughout his career.

From the lofty level of the royal pages to the strata of clerks and menials, the induction and training of careerist bureaucrats was a diffuse process, a broad and implicit exercise in socialization, in which no sharp distinction was made between the acquisition of technical skills and the absorption and expression of a broad array of appropriate values. The process both reflected and sustained the diffuseness of the socio-bureaucratic system and its emphasis upon close personal associations. New bureaucrats were not "brought into the system" so much as they were absorbed into an existing structure of immediate personal relationships for which the over-all bureaucratic system formed a background or a framework.

SELF-CONTAINMENT OF BUREAUCRATIC UNITS

The grand pattern of the Thai social system was distinguished for its elaborateness, and, in a sense, for its sophistication. The same was not true of the pattern of administrative organization within the socio-bureaucratic system.

The typical administrative organization was an enclave—a largely self-contained universe, whose dependence upon other organizations was as limited as possible. A *kram,* or province, procured and trained its own personnel, collected taxes and other resources to sustain itself, enforced its own laws, administered justice, and operated its own prison. Its officials had status identities which enabled them to relate to other persons both inside and outside the organization. But there was little need for external relationships, except with superiors.

The relatively large administrative unit was a "secondary association" type of organization to only a small extent. Business was probably transacted on a highly personalized basis. The top level of the enterprise rested upon a set of substantially self-contained subordinate units, each of them functionally discrete and tradition-sanctioned, but also responsive to specific orders from above. There were no complex patterns of persisting interdependence among the major units of administration. Given the limited technology of the time and place, there was little need for complicated work flows and scant means for complex flows of information. Given the hierarchical emphasis of the society, lateral relationships were incidental and almost irrelevant unless they were the personal relations of men in close association. The absence of complex patterns of interdependence among units of administrative organization was a corollary of the grand hierarchical pattern of society.

This simple arrangement made much sense. It was compatible with *kin muang.* It did not tax the communications capacities of the system or create needs for elaborate management to continually keep the elements of the administration system suitably meshed. It minimized the extent to which a breakdown in one unit of the administrative apparatus could jeopardize the whole thing. It even concentrated responsibility: disasters could not be blamed upon "the system"; there was always a department, a unit, or a person responsible for whatever happened to evoke displeasure.

Finally, the arrangement was wholly consistent with the intrinsically personal basis of bureaucratic behavior. The primary unit of action in the system was likely to coincide with the prime unit of organization—the informal group consisting of patron and clients, intimately related by the legitimate status system *and* a diffuse set of shared or reciprocal interests. In short, the formal pattern of organization, whose major feature was self-containment, both reflected and sustained the pattern of organized personal relationships within the society.

Of course, a self-contained unit existed to "do something"—to perform some function. But little pressure for performance was exerted by insistent claims of other units, physically remote but functionally interdependent. And no unit was constantly being judged and juggled in terms of performance criteria by some outside source of responsibility. A relatively stable environment, characterized by slow, almost imperceptible change, made no incessant demands for accommodation through frequent adjustments in organization or performance. An order from above might lead to frenzied action, followed by a return to tranquil equilibrium, in this universe of self-contained organizations linked more by a status structure than by substantive production goals and functional interdependence.

PERFORMANCE AND THE PURSUIT OF PRODUCTION GOALS

Functional skills were not lacking in the traditional bureaucracy. Records were kept and reports were made. There were patrols and investigations. *Corvée* labor was mobilized and put to work. Buildings were built; canals were dug. Taxes were collected and commodities were stored and transported.

The pace was usually far from frantic, and the utilitarian aspects of the bureaucratic culture never became highly sophisticated. Simple but not uningenious works were devised for water distribution. Practical skills evolved in surveying, as well as in building and decorating. But artisanship, an activity usually associated with persons of relatively low status, never led to powerful and systematic abstractions. No mathematics emerged from surveying, nor did construction produce any great architectural innovations.

The most comprehensive efforts of officialdom occurred in the event of war, when the king and his generals controlled action in a rather large sphere.

. . . Van Vliet was probably not far wrong when, referring to the middle of the seventeenth century, he said that though there were few soldiers in actual service, within two days 60,000 to 80,000 could be raised; while in time of war it was rare to mobilize more than 100,000 men and usually only 20,000 to 60,000 were called on to serve on military expedition. There were more than 3,000 war elephants. . . .

Apart from the food supplied by the government for the first two or three days' journey, the local authorities were ordered to make their people provide sustenance for the army. Supplies were brought to the camps by convoys of women, as well as in the requisitioned carts.[31]

Wars, if frequent, were brief, being largely limited to the dry season of the year. They required no intricate logistics, communications, planning, or control. The two chief bureaucratic elements of military power were the elephant cavalry and the top command structure.

The ability to wage war at least as effectively as the other parties to the combat was a critical requirement of the kingdom, and one which was met until the Burmese victory of 1767. In the seventeenth century the Thais even sent a group of trainees to France to be instructed in European military practices, and in the sixteenth and seventeenth centuries some Portuguese mercenaries served in the king's forces.

But the form of specialization which warfare took was ritual-centered as well as achievement-oriented. By the time of the reign of Ramathibodi II in the early sixteenth century, a treatise on the art of war (*Tamra phichai songkram*) was produced. An edition of 1793 still exists, apparently more elaborate and more refined than earlier versions, but showing little evidence of significant change in strategy and tactics.[32]

In military matters, as in others, the bureaucracy was not without an obligation to accomplish specified tangible purposes. The bureaucracy *was* responsive to explicit and specific impetus from above. The extreme example of such response was war, which produced an *ad hoc* integration of aims and efforts, and a burst of focused energy within parts of the bureaucracy.

The lack of innovation or evolving creativity in the military facet of the bureaucracy and elsewhere reflected the absence of any pressing environmental demands for these qualities. The strategy, tactics, tradition, and rituals of war, for example, were common to Thailand and her military opponents, as well as compatible with the qualities of the Thai socio-bureaucratic system. There was little impetus to significant change.

The bureaucracy was *inertial.* A practice or pattern, once established by legitimate authority or made a matter of habit, generally persisted. Officials responded to orders from above—orders to do some specific thing. But orders which had the intent of changing abiding patterns of bureaucratic behavior were not effective when—as usually—they conflicted with the diffuse and implicit aims of that behavior. To order the officials to stop oppressing the people or to devote their full time to their work were, in a sense, absurd in a socio-bureaucratic system with *kin muang* as a central premise and with no real differentiation between being an official and living one's life.

Diffuse hierarchical relations and *kin muang* together nurtured exploitation as an object of bureaucrats—sanctioned it, necessitated it, and to some extent regularized it. The intake and training arrangements of largely self-contained organizations socialized bureaucrats in terms of the *status quo;* and the environment within which the socio-bureaucratic system existed did not threaten to destroy it.

The result: an encompassing, comprehensive, explicit hierarchy, which served as the essentially static framework of bureaucratic behavior centered in clusters of related primary groups. The values that governed normal behavior in these groups were the shared—or reciprocal—values of participants in a diffuse set of personal relationships. Subordinates depended upon a superior for rewards, or access to them. Superiors depended upon subordinates for loyalty and support, the latter term often applying in the literal as well as the figurative sense.

The group existed within a system of groups, linked by the hierarchy, but an official patron and his immediately subordinate official clients—they also perhaps patrons at a lesser level—comprised the primary unit of organization in the bureaucratic system, the unit in terms of whose values normal behavior occurred.

The interests of the patron dominated the interests of the group, but there was, as we have seen, a reciprocity in patron-client relations. Maintaining his position in the system, the patron could hold his subordinates. They, in turn, found security in their relationship to their superior. Together, the group advanced its values—survival, identity, and some degree of well-being. From time to time there were orders from above. But working in this system did not consist chiefly of responses to such orders; it consisted in the much more diffuse set of group-centered activities which were legitimized by the over-all system.

The static integrating network of hierarchy and the limited dynamic of royal power could not offset the dis-integrated, group-centered patterns of behavior prevalent in the traditional bureaucracy. Judged by the criterion of system survival, this was no critical problem. If the socio-bureaucratic system could do anything, it could maintain itself, with little or no energizing from above, in the context of its traditional environment. In the language of sociology, this was a "system maintenance" bureaucracy, not a "goal attainment" bureaucracy.

With time, it gradually grew more complicated, as units and functions were added to the once simple structure of King Trailok. The administration of justice within one of the *kram* of the traditional bureaucracy during the nineteenth century illustrates the way the system worked.[33]

The work was broken down into an impressive array of separate functions performed by separate units or individuals. Civil and criminal cases were handled by the same court, but most cases involved criminal law violations, for few men would wittingly submit themselves to this justice as a means of settling personal differences. Besides the judges and advisers, there were innumerable court officials, all of them dependent upon fees, fines, or presents for their incomes. Each court had its prosecutor, its recorders, its interpreters of the law, and its deliverer of judgment. Fees were levied for every conceivable act, and borne equally by both parties to the action in civil cases. During the Ayudhyan period, when trial by ordeal was permitted, there was even a "fee for pressing down under water the necks of the contenders—1 tical." [34]

As the system had evolved, innumerable procedural forms and observances came into use; these, along with the division of duties among the various officials, were intended to check corruption by making it impossible for any one individual to control the outcome of a case. "The system had all the appearance of a thorough and comprehensive machine, but was unfortunately quite unworkable . . . ," and "the corrupt state of the judicature was notorious." [35]

Appeals could be taken to a high court at the capital, the *Luk Khun,* which nominally controlled the work of the *kram* and provincial courts, but the number of cases which found their way here was small. The king, supreme judge and lawgiver, sometimes participated in the proceedings of this court of appeals. But, with his complete power over life and death, he could not effectively control the content of the judical process as it actually operated.

The Beginnings of Change and the Traditional Bureaucracy

Over the centuries that followed the establishment of the traditional bureaucracy some changes did occur. New functions were occasionally added, along with organizations to perform them. The pattern of provincial control was modified. But the basic characteristics of the system were not much changed.

In the nineteenth century, however, Thailand's relations with its environment began to change. The king began to engage in extensive trade and to be increasingly concerned with monetary matters. Meanwhile, the steady influx of Chinese produced a new labor supply, one which in some ways was more attractive than *corvée.* At the top of the socio-bureaucratic system an interest was beginning to emerge in goals which were quite incompatible with traditional bureaucratic behavior and with the central premises supporting the socio-bureaucratic structure of society.

Perhaps one of the earliest significant impacts of the West upon the Thai administrative system occurred early in the nineteenth century, in the form of a suggestion supposedly made by an English ambassador. He proposed the farming out of tax collection to private enterpreneurs.[36] During the reign of Rama II (1809–1824) the practice was adopted. It proved thoroughly oppressive, but produced substantial increases in revenue. But the tax-farming operations were conducted under the control of, and for the benefit of, the existing tax-levying governmental elements. (As late as 1872, ten agencies of

Thai government were responsible for collecting taxes—after some consolidation of this work.) [37]

Under the tax-farming system, the privilege of collecting some particular tax (*bhasi*) in a specified area for a single year was put up for bid; the Chinese bidder agreed to pay a stipulated sum of collected taxes into the appropriate treasury.[38] The high bidder paid one-sixth of the annual amount in advance and the rest in monthly installments.[39] For the duration of their appointments, the collectors were considered as public officials with *sakdi na* of at least 400. They could confiscate property and enslave defaulters; and they were usually supported by ranking officials of the *kram,* who relied upon this work for their incomes. "Rarely if ever did a tax-farmer fail to realize the money which he had agreed to pay, and he usually contrived to make a very comfortable profit from his lease." [40]

During the reign of Rama III (1824–1851) tax-farming was expanded to cover thirty-eight objects of taxation.[41] A lottery was also established on a farmed basis; at its inception in 1835, it netted the government 20,000 ticals (about $12,000). This grew to 200,000 ticals within twenty years.[42]

In the farming of taxes, the king and the bureaucracy "contracted out" a goal-attainment function which experience had shown to be beyond the performance capabilities of the administrative system. And tax-farming was followed by the hiring of Chinese labor to undertake the royal public works previously performed by *corvée* labor within the *wang rajadhani.*[43]

The immediate response to the need for greater revenue was simple enough. So was the supplanting of *corvée* labor by hired help. But underlying these specific changes were subtle and portentous shifts, whose full implications were undoubtedly not apparent: the adoption of an alternative to *corvée* for royal public works was tantamount to a change in the relationship of commoners to king. The motive of the change was pragmatic—labor was hired instead of being requisitioned because a new source of hired labor was available, and it did the work better than conscript labor. Therefore, let the king's subjects pay taxes; let them satisfy their obligations in this limited, regularized fashion, instead of being vassals. In a small, tentative fashion, the abolition of the royal *corvée* (it was not abolished in the provinces generally at this time) represented a break with tradition, a shift from a diffuse, encompassing relationship between monarch and subjects toward a more specific, circumscribed relation.

It would be easy to read too much into this occurrence, which presaged no revolution in the status of common Thais, nor any shattering of the myth of the absolute god-king. But the diminution of *corvée* did indicate that the tradition-sanctioned system was not totally the prisoner of the basis of its legitimacy. At the king's behest, patterns of action could be established which were at variance with tradition. This was important: it indicated a capacity for accommodation which would be vital to the survival of Thailand as an independent country in the last half of the nineteenth century.

At midpoint in that century, Thailand stood on the verge of an era of shattering interaction with the West. It was an ancient, stable, and integrated society, with its broad base of village-dwelling Buddhist farmers who lived off the fruits (and the rice) of their labor and produced small surpluses; with its charismatic potentate, in theory the source of all power; and with its bureaucracy, organized according to the principles laid down some four hundred years earlier, linking king and country after its fashion, and claiming the rewards to which its sheer existence entitled it.

Chapter 3

WESTERN IMPACT AND THAI RESPONSE: THE BEGINNINGS OF MODERNIZATION

NOW, IN THE nineteenth century, the old order of things in Thailand began to erode. The nation was bombarded by a profusion of Western forces and influences; and the ancient, traditional system of government could neither deny them nor cope with them. Change or perish as an independent nation—these were the alternatives confronting the country in the latter decades of the 1800s.

The sheer perception of these grim options was the least probable facet of nineteenth-century Thai history. Fortuity produced a heroic king at just the right moment; he laid the groundwork for a national future through his own efforts and by preparing a talented son to succeed him as ruler.

The Western impact, so ably portrayed by Walter Vella, ran in two broad streams: (1) Sharply focused political and economic forces —the trade-oriented imperialism of Britain and France in particular —jeopardized the kingdom through military force and by undermining its fiscal integrity. (2) A more diffuse pattern of Western impact consisted of knowledge, technology, and perspectives on the nature of reality. Slowly, quietly, unevenly, and sometimes almost imperceptibly, these Western influences began to penetrate Thai culture. One of the eventual effects of this penetration was, quite literally, revolutionary. This phase of Thai-Western relations has not run its course; its broader effects transcend the limited scope of our concern. But Western skills and knowledge became essential instruments of national survival during the nineteenth century, although their full cost was not known until long after they had been committed to use.

The first effects of Thai-Western treaty relations in the mid-nineteenth century were to open the country to foreign trade on terms which wiped out the royal commercial monopolies. Extraterritoriality provisions of the mid-century treaties obliterated the jurisdiction of the Thai government over thousands of residents who later claimed protection from the French or the British. Involvement with the West also led to changes in the scope and effectiveness of some Thai governmental activities—by importing Western talent and creating enclaves of modernized, production-oriented administrative organizations within the central bureaucracy. Finally, the drive for survival produced an anxious effort to integrate the nation's territories—as an alternative to losing them.

Western impact led to a deliberate, systematic effort to replace the traditional Thai bureaucracy with administrative mechanisms committed to the pursuit and attainment of explicit organizational goals, goals deemed essential to national survival.

Western imperialism did not suddenly burst upon an unknowing nation in the nineteenth century. Thai contact with the West had occurred as early as the beginning of the sixteenth century.

Don Affonso d'Albuquerque had sent ambassadors to the court of Ayudhya in 1511.[1] Within a few decades Portuguese adventurers were serving in the Thai army. In the sixteenth and seventeenth centuries, Dutch and British trading ventures involved Thai rulers in their earliest efforts at balance-of-power politics in Western relations. As early as 1609, a Siamese embassy was received at The Hague, the first recorded visit of Thais to Europe;[2] and Thai embassies were sent to France in 1684 and 1685.[3] In the 1680s, a European adventurer, Constance Phaulkon, had become the most powerful minister of King Narai, had led the king to accept French troops to garrison Thai forts, and might have succeeded in bringing the kingdom under French control had he not been killed at the direction of General Phra Phetraja, who shortly succeeded to the throne.

The seventeenth-century experience was sufficient to cause the Thai court to be wary of dealings with Europeans, and for more than a hundred years after the assassination of Phaulkon in 1688 relations were almost nonexistent. The Dutch maintained a trading post, and a few French missionaries were active; but Burmese wars, Cambodian adventures, and Chinese trade bounded the international concerns of the nation into the nineteenth century.[4]

The Background of the Crisis of the Nineteenth Century: Themes and Patterns of Western Impact

Thai isolation was not based upon an insularity of the type which proved so disastrous to China; the posture of the Thai court in the early nineteenth century suggests that the nation's ruling power had no comfortable illusions about Western power or purposes. The king felt no need to trade with the West at Bangkok, and was reluctant to entertain diplomatic relations.[5] Regular trade took place in Siamese junks—and under Rama III in Western-style sailing vessels—plying between Bangkok and Penang, Malacca, Singapore, and Canton, through which European and Asian products were obtained.[6] Munitions were procured from the Portuguese, with whom the Thais resumed direct trading in 1818 without benefit of any treaty.[7]

Trade, however, was one of the main themes of developing relations between Thailand and the West, from about the second quarter of the nineteenth century. Militant Western imperialism and American Protestant missionaries, also militant in their fashion, constituted the other significant themes.

THE MISSIONARIES

The significance of the missionaries lay in the Western knowledge, technology, and values which they brought with them.

The first Protestant missionaries arrived in 1828; by 1860 perhaps forty of them had labored in the field; among the Thais they made perhaps ten or twenty conversions in this time.[8] But the first publication printed in Thailand, in 1836, was printed by American missionaries.[9] In 1837 the first modern surgical operation was performed by an American mission doctor who amputated the shattered arm of a Buddhist monk.[10] In 1838 smallpox inoculation was introduced by a missionary physician, Dan Beach Bradley.[11] In 1839 the first government document printed in Thailand, a Royal Edict banning opium, was printed by Dr. Bradley, who also inaugurated an English-language newspaper.[12] In 1851, at the invitation of King Mongkut, an informal school was established in which missionary wives taught English to women of the palace. The typewriter, the sewing machine, a definitive Thai-English dictionary, Western dentistry, Western med-

ical education, and some of the foundations of a school system—
these are among the contributions of the missionaries, chiefly
American, who began pouring into Thailand around 1830.[13]

Thus, in many ways the missionaries "brought the West" to Thailand, making few converts but giving some impetus to reforms in
Buddhism.[14] They contributed substantially to the education of King
Mongkut, and thereby helped lay an all-important foundation for the
successful accommodation to the nascent West in the last half of the
century.

KING PHRA NANG KLAO AND EARLY TRADE AGREEMENTS

King Phra Nang Klao, commonly referred to as Rama III, who
reigned from 1824 until his death in 1851, reopened limited diplomatic relations with Europe, but he was essentially a traditionalist
who failed to appreciate the mounting significance of the West.[15]

The beginning of his reign was marked by the Anglo-Burman war of
1824–1826, a step in the establishment of Western control of Thailand's traditional enemy, which produced a radical change in the
concerns of Thai diplomacy. Burmese-Thai incidents came to an end,
but a familiar devil was replaced with a strange and possibly hungry
tiger. The conclusion of the Anglo-Burman war led to an Anglo-Thai
treaty, the first modern treaty of friendship and commerce between
Thailand and a Western nation—a most moderate and limited arrangement which provided for not even so much as the establishment
of a British consultate, let alone a solution to the problem of extraterritoriality, which was later a grievous incubus to the Thais. The British treaty was followed by an American trade agreement in 1833, and
until about 1840 direct Thai trade with the West grew appreciably.

In the 1840s the expansion of tax-farming and the substantial
growth of direct Thai government trading produced increases in the
local prices of export commodities available for purchase by foreign
traders, and other impediments to orderly commerce, thus driving out
most of the British and all of the American trade. The aim of the
monarch seems to have been to minimize Western contact and with it
the threat of interference; but it was restrictive trade policies which
finally produced a Western reaction.

The United States vainly sought a new trade treaty in 1850, as did
the British. King Nang Klao resisted. He and his court were fearful of

treaty developments which would impose economic restrictions upon the crown by liberalizing trade.

During Nang Klao's quarter-century reign, the wall against the West was but slightly breached; only a trickle of Western power and influence appears to have penetrated the kingdom—the missionaries and the now discouraged Western traders. But with Burma humbled by Britain and with British authority established at Penang and the Straits Settlements, with the China ports smashed open, the surge of Western activity posed a growing threat to the security of Thailand.

KING MONGKUT AND THE BASIS
FOR SUCCESSFUL WESTERN ACCOMMODATION

Before King Nang Klao succeeded his father in 1824, he had been active in military affairs, in the conduct of the traditional Ministry of Port and Foreign Affairs, and in other matters. A mature man of thirty-seven, able and experienced in the concerns of the day, he was chosen king by the leading princes and ministers in preference to Mongkut, a prince of higher rank, who was not quite twenty years of age at the time. It was apparently felt that Nang Klao was more suited to protect the country from external dangers, particularly the Burmese threat.[16]

Mongkut, temporarily serving in a Buddhist monastery in accordance with the custom of the land, discreetly remained in the temple. He did not emerge from the priesthood until a quarter of a century later, when he succeeded his elder half brother. Meanwhile, in ranging studies the prince laid a fortunate foundation for his reign.[17]

With Bishop Pallegoix, the French prelate of Bangkok, Mongkut studied Latin and, in return, aided the Bishop in the compilation of his dictionary of the Thai language. Mongkut studied science, and developed an impressive competence in mathematics and astronomy. He met a variety of foreigners—traders, shipmasters, and the American missionaries. Mongkut came to appreciate their medical work and the Western knowledge and technology which they brought. He began the study of English, first under Dr. Bradley and then under the Reverend Jesse Caswell.

A glimpse of Mongkut at this period [about 1845] is found in the diary of Dr. House, another medical missionary, who recorded the details of his first call on the prince-priest at Wat Pawaraniwesa: "I looked around the room," he wrote, "Bible from A. B. Society and Webster dictionary stood side by side in a shelf on his secretary, also a Nautical Tables and Navigation. On the table a diagram of the forthcoming eclipse in pencil with calculation. . . . His manners were rather awkward at introduction, and his appearance not prepossessing at first, though we became more interested in him as we saw him more. . . . He understands English when he reads it, but cannot speak it well yet." [18]

Mongkut also studied geography, physics, and chemistry, as well as the histories and contemporary characteristics of the major Western nations. He acquired Western books and devices, even installing a printing press in the temple—"the first press outside the Catholic and Protestant missions and the first to be operated by Siamese." In April, 1851, this able, mature, and intelligent man became King Rama IV, the most broadly educated Oriental monarch of his time, uniquely equipped to cope with the West when the need for such talent was great.

King Mongkut's perception of the position of his nation was aptly summed up in an observation made near the end of his rule:

Being, as we are now, surrounded on two or three sides by powerful nations, what can a small nation like us do? Supposing we were to discover a gold mine in our country, from which we could obtain many million catties weight of gold, enough to pay for the cost of a hundred warships; even with this we would still be unable to fight against them, because we would have to buy those very same warships and all the armaments from their countries. We are as yet unable to manufacture these things, and even if we have enough money to buy them, they can always stop the sale of them whenever they feel that we are arming ourselves beyond our station. The only weapons that will be of real use to us in the future will be our mouths and our hearts, constituted so as to be full of sense and wisdom for the better protection of ourselves.[19]

Pursuing a course of *realpolitik*, Mongkut encouraged the opening of Thailand to the West by accepting a drastic revision of treaty relations, and managed to cope for the time with the ominous expansionist drive of France into Thai vassal territory.

The Bowring Treaty of 1855 with Great Britain marked a radical realignment of the Thai posture of the 1840s. It provided for a great extension of British trading rights and included extraterritoriality provisions. It was followed by similar agreements with the United

States and France in 1856 and, in a short span of years, by treaties
with most of the other European nations—eight of them by 1868, the
year of King Mongkut's death.[20]

This treaty pattern had revolutionary consequences for the Thai
economy, eliminating Thai control over taxes and duties on all of its
trade commodities and putting an end to the state trading which,
under King Nang Klao, had been a major source of royal revenues.
As Bowring himself observed:

It was clear that my success involved a total revolution in all the financial
machinery of the government—that it must bring about a total change in
the whole system of taxation,—that it took a large proportion of the
existing sources of revenue,—that it uprooted a great number of privi-
ledges and monopolies which had not only been long established but
which were held by the most influential nobles and the highest functionaries in the state.[21]

The significance of the treaty lay not only in its provisions but in
their willing enforcement over the years by King Mongkut and his
successor.[22] The net effect was to catapult Thailand into the Western
world economy as a supplier of food and raw materials, such as tin
and teak and as a buyer of an ever-growing quantity of manufactured
products. The Thai role in this economic relationship somewhat resembled that of a colony, but there was a significant political
difference—the nation was not brought completely within the sphere
of interest of any single Western nation. Pursuing a shrewd and
effective strategy, Mongkut extended the Bowring Treaty pattern to
every receptive Western nation.

The treaty network stabilized the economic aspect of Thailand's relations with the West and greatly reduced the threat of economically
motivated conquest. The impact upon royal revenues and the domestic economy, the broadening range of contacts with Western society,
and the gradually mounting reaction to extraterritoriality helped lay a
foundation for bureaucratic reform, although no notable efforts at
administrative rationalization occurred during Mongkut's reign.

Economic accommodation did not entirely allay the threat of conquest, particularly from the French who, in the 1860s, established
ascendancy over Cochin China and the old Thai tributary of Cambodia.[23] By treaty of 1867 Mongkut surrendered all asserted rights
over Cambodia in return for French disavowal of all claims, for itself

and for the Cambodian vassal king, Norodom, to the provinces of
Battambang and Angkor (Siemreap) which, "according to the
French interpretation of Cambodian history, Siam had held 'irregu-
larly' since 1795." [24] But the French were clearly on the move,
exploring the possibility of penetrating China via the Mekong River,
consolidating their position in Indo-China, and failing rather miser-
ably in their Thai trade under the treaty of 1856 in the face of British
competition. On the east, Thailand was now confronted by an aggressive Western nation in a hurry to build an empire.

Meanwhile, the British followed a policy of nonintervention in
Malaya, but thousands of Chinese tin miners were pouring into the
area, the feuding Malay chiefs were patently unable to maintain
order, and rich resources promised lucrative trade. In Burma, in
1862, Arakan and Tenasserim (annexed in 1826) were united with
the Peguan territory conquered in 1852 to form an amalgamated
province of British Burma. Rangoon, the capital of this jurisdiction,
was developing rapidly as a thriving center of trade and colonial government. Old Burma, the great enemy of centuries past, was no more,
and British eyes too were beginning to turn northward to Yunnan and
visionary prospects of great trade.

Such was the ominous state of affairs in 1868 when Mongkut died.
King Mongkut had done "all that he could to make his country
known and understood abroad and to ensure respect for its sovereignty. He developed and carried on throughout his reign a voluminous correspondence with heads of state and influential men in other
countries. He even initiated an exchange of letters and gifts with Pope
Pius IX. He saw to it that Siam played a conspicuous part in the Paris
Exhibition of 1867." [25] He had no illusions about the stakes involved in his diplomacy, and he assiduously exploited all available
devices for strengthening his position.

Domestically, he modernized the coinage, expanded the system of
water transport, established an official gazette in which the edicts of
his government were published, substituted paid labor for the traditional *corvée* labor on royal public works, and exhorted his people to
improve the health, safety, and sanitation of his kingdom and its
capital.

King Mongkut's efforts modified the quality of the Thai monarchy.[26] This, along with survival in his time and the adequate

preparation of his successor, was perhaps his greatest contribution, for it was the key to all that later followed. His immediate predecessor had left the palace perhaps once a year to participate in temple ceremonies; to look upon his face had been forbidden.[27] In 1855 King Mongkut had acquired a steam yacht of his own, and he made much use of it. In his statutes he expressed not only awareness of his people but genuine concern for them. "He sought equal justice for all before the law and curbed some, at least, of the nobility. . . . He took the first steps to eliminate slavery. He enacted laws to improve the status of women and children. He authorized the common people to look at the king!" [28]

He chose Thai ambassadors to represent the nation on important missions, and sought to offset their inexperience with long and charming personal letters,[29] and he began the practice of using Western advisers and administrators. Eighty-four Europeans served the Thai government during King Mongkut's reign, including military officers, a palace tutor, and various Western technicians.[30]

Beyond all this, King Mongkut laid a foundation for continuity in the reconstruction of the governmental system. In 1861, when the son who was to succeed him was about nine years of age, he sought an English governess to introduce the boy and other young princes to Western ideas and knowledge:

We wish the School Mastress to be with us in this palace or nearest vicinity hereof to save us from trouble of conveying such the Lady to & fro almost every day; also it is not pleasant to us if the School Mastress much morely endeavoured to convert the schoolars to Christianity than teaching language, literature, etc., etc., like the American Missionaries here because our proposed expense is for knowledge of the important language & literature which will be useful for affairs of country. . . .[31]

For five years Mrs. Anna Leonowens served at the palace as teacher and foreign-language secretary to the King. After her departure, for a year and a half the Crown Prince was under the authority of an English tutor, Robert Morant. These arrangements had their sometimes painful limitations, but they comprised one vital part of the road to survival through comprehension of the West.

In these ways, rather than through any systematic reform of the administrative machinery of government, did the great King Mongkut help insure the future of Thailand.

King Chulalongkorn and the Foundations
of Bureaucratic Reform

Without a Mongkut there could have been no Chulalongkorn. Yet the epochal developments under Rama IV were but a beginning—a commitment to great change in the governmental system as a means to survival. One of the most pressing needs was a renovation of the machinery of government, for in 1868 there was "no fixed code of laws; no system of general education; no proper control of revenue and finance; no postal or telegraph service. . . . The opium laws were badly administered; there was no medical organization. . . . There was no army or modern railways and almost no roads." [32]

At the root of these conditions was the untouched pattern of traditional bureaucracy. A major theme of the reign of Rama V (Chulalongkorn) was the reformation of this administrative system. This reconstruction went forward, not serenely but at least persistently, despite dominating problems and great crises in international relations. [33]

Not until the closing years of Chulalongkorn's reign was stability achieved in international relations; and in the process Thailand conceded 90,000 square miles of territory, or nearly a third of her domain—admittedly, most of them peripheral territories, whose loss in some ways was small. But twenty years of international tension and crisis were beyond all doubt the greatest stimulus to an impressive reconstruction of the governmental system.

There is no better index of the significance attached to this transformation than the statement made by King Chulalongkorn only eighteen months after French gunboats had ascended the Menam Chao Phraya:

The greatest difficulty of the present day is the protection of our territory. . . . Today we have Britain at our left and France at our right. . . . We can no longer live in isolation as once we did. In our protection of the country three measures can be taken: friendly diplomatic relations, the maintenance of defensive forces, and orderly administration. We will administer the country well if we foster opportunities for the people to earn livings so that they are benefited by the government. Then they will pay the taxes which are the economic foundation of the government. Consequently, an effective administration and a fostering of the ways of providing for the livelihood of the people are the most important, the final purposes of the Kingdom.[34]

By 1895 much had been done to restructure the bureaucracy. The first steps toward reform began in the 1870s, when the King, who had governed under a regency until 1873, assumed the full powers of the monarchy. Near the end of the regency period, in 1871 and 1872, he made two unprecedented foreign tours, during which he examined methods of administration in Java and then in India, returning from Calcutta in 1872. King Chulalongkorn was eighteen at the time. By 1910, when he died at the age of sixty-three, his reign, the longest of his dynasty, had been marked by the administrative reconstruction called the Chakkri Reformation.

The First Phase of the Reformation

The first phase of the bureaucratic reformation by King Chulalongkorn ended in 1892 with a sweeping reorganization of the governmental structure.

This period was marked by a variety of specific developments. Some elements and requisites of a performance-oriented administrative system were established in a relatively unsystematic fashion. New agencies were created and a few long-established ones were modified. Some of the operating characteristics of the ongoing administrative system were changed and environmental resources, such as educational and communications facilities and managerial talent, were developed or acquired. All of this took place over a fairly long period of time—about twenty years.

FISCAL REFORM

Fiscal reform was one of the earliest administrative matters of the King's attention. In 1875, two years after Chulalongkorn had superseded the regency, he established a new office called the "Revenues Development Office." Its functions were taken from the traditional Ministry of Port and Foreign Affairs, which, with the growth of foreign trade, had accrued considerable power over finances.[35]

Revenue was a critical problem of the kingdom. The abolition of state trading and the treaty-imposed limits on duties had serious fiscal consequences; the kingdom was heavily dependent upon tax-farmers, and the administration of finances was both corrupt and confused. A fundamental reform in the administration of finances was needed. During the entire reign of King Mongkut, only one official estimate was ever made of the revenues of the kingdom—in 1868; the figure given was eight million baht (slightly less than five million dollars, the baht having an official value of $0.60 during this time).[36]

Establishment of the Revenues Development Office was, however, more of a commitment to reform than an achievement. It was the beginning of a change which slowly gathered force; not until 1892–1896 did a thoroughgoing rationalization of the fisc occur. Meanwhile, dependence upon tax-farmers was somewhat reduced, and the revenues actually received by the King appear to have increased gradually. They were reported as fifteen million baht in 1892.[37]

BEGINNINGS OF REFORM IN PERSONNEL ADMINISTRATION

The Revenues Development Office was, in the words of Prince Damrong, "the first to adopt Western methods of work." The director-general of the Office, the Palace Minister, continued the tradition of performing his functions in his home, but the officials received regular pay and their daily working hours were fixed.[38] This did represent a small break with the Ayudhyan tradition, a step beyond *kin muang*.

The Revenues Development Office was made responsible (at least in part) for payment of the stipends of various civil and military officials of the central government, and with the creation of the Office there came also some expansion of the practice of paying officials at monthly intervals instead of annually, and some further standardization of pay rates.[39]

The traditional *kin muang* system had always been supplemented to some degree by other forms of remuneration.[40] By the reign of King Mongkut, *biawat* payments to court officials had become standardized to some extent. The King's concubines, actresses, pages, and certain others received more or less fixed annual stipends, and it is possible that some of them received *ngoenduan,* or monthly wages.[41]

At the beginning of King Chulalongkorn's reign, *biawat* was the primary method for paying royal officials of the *wang rajadhani* who were not dependent upon *kin muang.* Pensions were also granted by the King to high-ranking officials upon retirement, and these were geared to *biawat* levels. With the creation of the new Revenues Development Office came an extension of *biawat* payments, and the apparent conversion of some of these from annual to monthly stipends.[42] Some of the staff of the Army, Navy, Police, Mint, Palace Ministry, and Ministry of Port and Foreign Affairs now began to receive regular monthly pay, and these included not only ranking officials but also the *phrai,* or traditional conscript workers. Thus, in the central government, at least, a first step was taken toward a modern system of bureaucratic inducements to personnel. Throughout most of the government, *kin muang* persisted, as it would for decades to come; but tradition was no longer to be its own justification, as it had been in the past.

COMMUNICATIONS: THE POST AND THE TELEGRAPH

Telegraph construction in Thailand began in 1875, marking one of Chulalongkorn's early efforts to integrate the nation and link it with the outside world. Construction and operation were viciously hampered by natural obstacles, the lack of technical skills, and the inadequacies of the administrative system. In 1883 Bangkok was linked to Saigon and Tavoy, and some interior lines were also constructed.[43] In 1881, the telephone was introduced in Bangkok.[44] In that year a Department of Posts was also established, with which the Telegraph Department was combined in 1883. From the beginning, European technicians were used in the effort to develop communications facilities.[45] Surveys for telegraph lines were made by the Royal Survey Department, headed, and in effect established, by James McCarthy, and from the 1880s into the twentieth century the Post and Telegraph Department was under the direction of German officials.

Effective communications, the key to an integrated system of domestic government, was, however, a long-term development. In the 1890s and early 1900s wild elephants persisted in knocking over poles "against which they delight to rub themselves," while insects, jungle, and a monsoon climate further conspired to wreck the system.[46] Yet, in the 1880s none of these problems was perhaps as great as were the administrative inadequacies.

MAPS AND SURVEYS

Boundary questions had created a need for surveys as early as the reign of King Mongkut, but when his son acceded to the throne no definitive map of the kingdom existed. The first step toward the establishment of modern surveying and mapping occurred in 1875, when improvements were being undertaken in the city of Bangkok. At the direction of King Chulalongkorn, some of the officers of his body-guard were constituted a special company of military engineers, to be trained and directed in survey work under the command of Henry Alabaster, a royal adviser.[47]

In 1878 the great trigonometric survey being conducted by the British government in India reached the western border of Thailand; by 1880, with the consent of the King, a chain of triangles was carried across into Thai territory, under the direction of James McCarthy. In 1881 McCarthy was hired by the Royal Telegraph Department to survey a line between Bangkok and Moulmein. About this time Prince Damrong (then known as Pra Ong Chao Disawara Jumarn) conceived the idea of forming a Survey Department, and, upon the completion of the Bangkok-Moulmein survey in 1882, engaged McCarthy for that purpose.

A survey school was established, with thirty men assigned from the royal bodyguard. "About twenty of these, however, were found to be utterly useless, and had to be got rid of." [48] In the closing days of the year, McCarthy, with the rank of captain in the royal bodyguard, and his party "began to prepare the way for a general map of Siam." It was published in 1897.[49] Compiling the needed data took fourteen years and the lives of several Thai and British surveyors. Meanwhile, in 1885 a royal decree established the Royal Survey Department,[50] which, under McCarthy, rendered invaluable service in boundary surveys, mapping, surveying projected railway lines, and establishing a foundation for the systematic description and registration of land titles.

RAILWAYS

Railway construction did not begin until 1891, although the initial concern with the development of a rail network arose in the 1880s, as a response to British and French intentions. In the early 1880s British interest in a back door to Yunnan led to a desire to connect Burma and Thailand with China, and a concession was requested from the Thai government for a line across northern Thailand.[51] A certain amount of exploration went forward under this projected venture before the whole matter was dropped, and this led to King Chulalongkorn's concern with railway construction. In 1889 a tramline was constructed in Bangkok by a Belgian group; by 1891 it was about to be electrified. The same year saw the development of a rail network, which in a few decades linked the major sectors of the country.

FOREIGN AFFAIRS

A variety of other changes in the governmental system occurred, including the beginning of the modernization of the naval and military forces. More important, however, was the initial effort to establish a modern ministry of foreign affairs—with the creation in 1885 of a Department of Foreign Affairs.[52] Prince Devawongse, a half brother of the King, the first Siamese foreign minister to speak European languages, began his service in the new Department at its creation, only a few years before the critical troubles with France. And in this Department the pattern of monthly pay and regular working hours which had been adopted in the Revenues Development Office was also established.

EDUCATION

These varied and specific movements toward comprehensive reform gathered scope and momentum as time passed, and as the time of great crisis in international relations loomed larger. Meanwhile, another part of the foundation for reform and development was laid through efforts to establish a modern system of education. In 1887 King Chulalongkorn established a Department of Public Instruction under the direction of Prince Damrong, asserting a commitment to the systematic development of a public educational system.[53] But many years passed before this became possible.

Concern with education stemmed from the needs of the royal service; interest in Western education was understandably utilitarian. The beginnings of educational development trace back to Mongkut's reign, but it was under Chulalongkorn that a systematic pattern was first conceived, beginning in 1878, when the king authorized the establishment of the King's School, or *Suan Anand,* under the direction of an American missionary, the Reverend Samuel G. McFarland.[54]

In this school the sons of princes and nobles were to be educated, although other students were also to be allowed to participate in the five-year program designed by Reverend McFarland. The initial enrollment of 130 included 12 princes and many sons of officials.

The venture was less than a success; few government students re-

mained in the program, and, by 1883, 102 of the 120 students were
private pupils. Even before the first class graduated, in 1883, the
King had established a second royal school, *Suan Kularb* (the Rose
Garden), also known as *Raja Kumara* (Royal Children's) College,
under an Indian headmaster.

In 1891 Suan Anand School became Sunandalaya College. At the
time, it had 278 pupils (the sons of princes, nobles, middle class, and
commoners), 13 teachers, a library of several hundred volumes, and
perhaps 1,500 alumni employed in government offices and Bangkok
business houses. Meanwhile, Raja Kumara College had grown to an
enrollment of 200. [55]

In 1893 Sunandalaya College was abruptly converted into a girls'
school by the Department of Education as the consequence of the
opposition of Robert Morant, *de facto* headmaster of the English-
oriented Suan Kularb or Raja Kumara College, educational adviser to
the government, and tutor to the crown prince. Suan Kularb now became the first government school planned specifically for the education of the sons of commoners.

A foundation for medical education was established in the 1880s,
with the creation of Siriraj Hospital in 1888 and the opening of a
medical school under the auspices of the Department of Education in
the following year. In 1891 Dr. George McFarland, a son of the Reverend Samuel McFarland, an American missionary renowned in Thailand, was engaged as superintendent of the hospital and principal of
the medical school.

The 1880s also saw the beginnings of administrative training in
schools conducted by the Royal Survey Department, the gendarmerie,
the military, and the various other departments emerging under the
leadership of the King.[56]

As Thailand moved into the final decade of the nineteenth century,
the traditional bureaucratic pattern was far from overthrown, but at
the center of the government a series of specific variations had occurred. Also, a number of new organizations had been established,
Western in functional character and often in management. Between
these organizations and the traditional bureaucracy lay an unbridge-
able gap.

By the late 1880s a few hundred Thais were involved in the work
of a new type of administrative organization, in which regular salaries

were paid, regular hours were worked, duties were specified and often supervised by foreigners, and the immediate objective was the accomplishment of some definite set of tasks. Thousands of other Thais continued on as king's men of the old style. Justice was dispensed as it had always been. And the provinces continued to be ruled and run as lesser kingdoms, in the tradition of *corvée* and *kin muang*. If anything, the gradual monetization of the Thai economy during the period since the 1850s had increased the oppressiveness of provincial government. Governors and their subordinates were becoming participants in entrepreneurial activities, and they exploited their subordinates more than before.

Yet it was the provinces that were vulnerable. Tin in the south, teak in the north along the Burma border, and contiguity to French Indo-China in the east and northeast made the border areas attractive to Britain on the one hand and to France on the other. In these areas thousands of persons claimed to be subjects of France or England by the end of the 1880s. The hinterlands had to be quickly integrated into the kingdom if they were to remain part of it, and none of the developments of the first half of the reign of King Chulalongkorn had significantly expanded the compass of the king's government. To this central strategic problem King Chulalongkorn turned his attention.

The Radical Reorganization of 1892

In 1887 Prince Devawongse went to England to represent the King at Queen Victoria's Diamond Jubilee. He was under orders to study the cabinet and ministry structure of British government.[57] The report he filed after his return in November, 1887, served as a basis for the King's planning of a broad reorganization of the bureaucracy.

A tentative plan of ministerial reorganization was made as early as 1888, but Chulalongkorn experimented cautiously with the new arrangement before placing it in effect. That year he began a series of weekly meetings in the Grand Palace, "in order to try those who would be appointed new ministers."

Both the current and prospective ministers attended these sessions, at which the King presided and various affairs of state were discussed. From 1889 Prince Damrong Rajanubhab, the energetic, intelligent young half brother of the King, participated in the deliberations as Minister of Education. In 1891, he was sent abroad on a joint diplomatic-study tour: to return the visit of the Russian crown prince (later Czar Nicholas II) to Bangkok early in that year and to study educational systems in Europe, Egypt, and India. Seven days after Damrong's return in March, 1892, the King announced a reorganization, and the transfer of Prince Damrong from the post of Minister of Education to Minister of Interior. The work of the Ministry of Interior, said King Chulalongkorn, "was more important than the work of the Ministry of Education" at that time. Foreign aggression was coming, and "if the administration could not be modified and developed into a modern system the country would be in danger; or worse, we might lose our independence and freedom. So to protect the country by changing and developing the administration of the provinces was much more important than the work of the Ministry of Education, because the provinces were to be subject to the Ministry of Interior."

With the appointment of Prince Damrong came the development of a new pattern of provincial government in Thailand, and the foundations of the new bureaucratic system as well, for the Ministry of Interior was the creative center of domestic governmental development under Prince Damrong until his retirement in 1915.

On April 1, 1892, King Chulalongkorn issued the reorganization edict which changed the basic structure of the government.[58] Immediately prior to the reorganization, the government had been arranged in six traditional ministries, plus a miscellaneous collection of agencies including those established during the first half of the reign. Two of the old ministries—Defense and Interior—were headed by the great ministers of the right and left hand. The others were in the charge of lesser ministers (*senabodi*)—the ministers of the Capital, the Treasury, the Palace, and Lands. These were the formal effects of the edict:

A new *Ministry of Justice* was created, ultimately (but not initially) to control the entire judicial system of the nation.

A new *Ministry of Defense* was established, to control the old Ministry of Military Strategy as well as the Marine Department, the Elephant Department, and the Armament Department.

A new *Ministry of Lands and Agriculture* was established, responsible for agricultural taxes. The previous responsibility of the Ministry of Lands for export and import duty collection was transferred to the Ministry of Finance.

Responsibility for finance had been completely removed from the traditional Ministry of Port and Foreign Affairs in 1885. The financial apparatus developed during the first half of the reign was now designated the *Ministry of Finance,* and in it the responsibility for the collection and disbursement of revenue was eventually to be centralized.

In 1890, a *Ministry of Public Works* had been created, including the Department of Post and Telegraph; this ministry was retained as part of the new structure.

The traditional Capital Ministry, under the control of a committee of royal and common officials as well as a minister, was superseded by a new *Ministry of the Capital (Nakornban)* under a single head.

The old Department of Clerks and Scribes, whose functions had enormously increased, was elevated to the status of the *Ministry of the Privy Seal (Muratathon).*

The *Ministry of Education* had been initiated earlier, in 1889, when the Department of Education (established in 1887), the Hospital Department, the old Department of Morals and Religion (or Ecclesiastical Affairs), and the Bangkok Museum (established in 1878) were combined. This Ministry was retained in the new plan of organization.

The *Palace Ministry,* or *Ministry of the Royal Household,* was continued, although it was no longer to be responsible for the administration of justice.

Foreign Affairs, actually established in modern form as a department prior to 1892, was designated a ministry in the new structure.

The heads of the ministries plus the head of the older Department of Military Strategy, who retained ministerial rank, were constituted a twelve-member *Council of Ministers (Look-khoon na sala)*, to replace the traditional six-minister council. Under the new system, there were to be no great ministers; all would possess equal rank, and the duties of each would be set forth in law.

As in the past, all of the ministerial posts were filled by members of the royal family, but some of the incumbents, notably the six younger brothers of the king, brought unique educational backgrounds to their posts. Prince Damrong, Prince Devawongse, and Prince Rabi (The Prince of Rajaburi), who became Minister of Justice in 1896, made historic contributions to the development of the government; others rendered extraordinary service.

The significance of this reorganization, like many of the developments which preceded it, lay in its promise as much as in its substance. It augured the end of the Ayudhyan bureaucratic tradition.

"Self-fulfilling" was the one thing which the great organization ordinance of 1892 could never be. Its fundamental premise ran counter to the basic values of the ancient and time-honored bureaucracy. The aim of reorganization was to create a comprehensive set of performance-oriented administrative organizations. They would devise and administer laws to capture the respect of the Western nations and thus enable the abolition of extraterritoriality. They would develop the resources and collect the revenues to finance the modernization of the kingdom. And they would link the nation's farthest outposts into a coherent network of government in which the king's writ would run. The new organizations would do these things if and as the new plan succeeded.

One key to its success would be the modernization of the Ministry of Interior, under a thirty-year-old prince who had already demonstrated a rare combination of genius and discipline. This was the critical ministry because it was to be the ministry of domestic government, the trunk upon which other modernized civil governmental functions would depend if they were to exist outside the capital area. It was the critical ministry, too, because its task was not merely to build a modern system of purposive administration, but to supplant the most deeply rooted traditional administrative institutions of the kingdom. Thus the story of administrative development in Thailand after 1892 becomes the story of the building of the Ministry of Interior and, with it, a new national bureaucracy.

The Beginnings of Administrative Modernization: An Assessment

Against the long background of Thai tradition, there is something almost preposterous about the events of the reigns of King Mongkut and King Chulalongkorn. The perceptivity, the pragmatism, and the effectiveness of these kings could not have been anticipated.

The thrust of the West transcended both the containment capabilities and the world view of traditional Thai society. The continued existence of the kingdom was threatened by imperial forces so great that, as King Mongkut observed, they could not be met by any power which the Thais might muster. More than this, the impact of the West was to undermine some of the very premises in terms of which Thai society had been traditionally ordered. Fortunately, at the time, this aspect of the Western onslaught was latent rather than visible.

When the West began to exert a persistent, spreading, deepening impact (through missionaries and other carriers of Western art, science, and technology, and through diplomats, armies, and traders), the ancient fused society—in which neither officialdom nor economics was differentiated from the rest of social organization—began to lose its relevance. The old order, whose simple central premises were elaborated in a thoroughly sophisticated way, began to be inadequate to the needs of survival. To be what one was and to serve the king and one's patron in the diffuse, unquestioned, time-sanctioned fashion —this could no longer be the *raison d'être* of society.

The self-justifying quality of the traditional, charismatic kingship was not explicitly denied. But the concept of the kingship was challenged by an expanding range of knowledge in a gradually growing number of persons who came to know other patterns of society with other goals, other processes, and other sources of legitimacy. It was challenged also by disruption of supporting elements in the social system. A system-maintenance bureaucracy, saturated with diffuse roles and relationships based on status ascribed by the king, was no longer adequate, nor did it continue to encompass all important activity as traders moved into the society to undertake specialized economic activities.

If the impact of the West was shattering in its portent, the Thai response was amazing and improbable. In the first place, there *was* a deliberate and perceptive response. It was both shrewd and pragmatic. As specific needs emerged, concrete actions were taken. Some achievement-oriented administrative organizations were established, and Western talent was brought to set them up and run them. Out of this experience evolved a commitment to convert the whole bureaucracy into a functionally effective, productive set of Western-style administrative agencies.

In a more general, abstract sense, the Thai response to the West was deliberately to differentiate sectors of the traditional socio-bureaucratic system. Even before the mid-nineteenth-century treaties some economic differentiation began to appear in response to the trading proclivities of Thai monarchs and Western merchants. In the

1870s and 1880s, a similar differentiation was started in the bureaucracy. Official roles were more clearly separated from the diffuse totality of personal existence in a small but growing number of organizations. And, in 1892, a commitment was made to extend this arrangement to the whole bureaucracy, in order to make it productive, in order to integrate and preserve the nation.

The response to the West was to move beyond tradition in order to survive. Yet the immediate impetus to this sweeping change came from the central institution of all Thai tradition—the kingship. On April 1, 1892, the questions were simple, but the stakes riding on the answers were vast and not entirely clear: *Could* the administrative apparatus be changed enough to enhance the kingdom's chances for survival? And what form would that survival take?

Chapter 4

ADMINISTRATIVE DEVELOPMENT FROM 1892: THE EMERGENCE OF A NATIONAL BUREAUCRACY

THE REORGANIZATION of the Ministry of Interior was the means by which the provinces were integrated with the capital. The Ministry became the breeding ground for new administrative agencies to carry out functions reflecting new conceptions of the role of government. And a new system of administration evolved in the Ministry of Interior, in place of the Ayudhyan pattern of bureaucracy.[1]

The Old Ministry of Interior

The old Ministry of Interior epitomized the Ayudhyan tradition.[2] The minister performed his functions at his home; his income was from judicial fees, other Ministry revenues, and *biawat;* his contacts with the work of the Ministry were limited to the papers and visitors who came to him. He did not initiate, but, rather, sat detached in judgment on matters brought before him, or he passed them upward to the king.[3] Only a thin flow of paper united the Ministry with the provinces and their semi-autonomous, quasi-feudal governors.

Ministry headquarters was split into two parts. Judicial officials and the staff of the Ministry's prison were outside the palace grounds, the judicial officers serving the minister at his home. The other headquarters units, under the deputy minister, were located on the grounds of the royal palace. This was the "working office" of the Ministry of Interior, staffed by officials who were receiving monthly salaries by the time of Prince Damrong's accession.

At the time of Damrong's accession to office, the "working office" staff under the deputy minister consisted of four *sanyabat* officials (i.e., "commissioned" or designated by the king, with ranks ranging from *phra* to *luang*). These officials had several assistants. The balance of the staff was comprised of clerks.

Also attached to the central office was a Revenue Department *Krom Ngern Suai*) responsible for collecting capitation taxes in the territories under the jurisdiction of the ministry. Officials of this Department, an outgrowth of the traditional *pan* function of recruiting men for the royal service, received monthly pay.

The *sanyabat* officials of this small and largely traditional organization had initially come into the royal service as pages. Through their service in the palace they had come to know the procedures of the top level of the government. The clerks, or noncommissioned officials, were the sons of Bangkok commoners who had begun their careers in traditional clerical apprenticeships and had thus acquired experience in the details of administration. Between the commissioned and noncommissioned ranks was a seldom-bridged status gap.

Such was the organization in 1892. The Ministry of Interior (called the "Ministry of the North"), sharing responsibility with the ministries of Defense and Foreign Affairs for territorial government of the nation, was staffed by a small group of tradition-oriented central officials who knew only Bangkok. "When it came to the border provinces, they had only heard the names, but did not know exactly where they were. So they did not know how the foreigners menaced the borders both in the east and the west and it was useless to discuss these events with them at that time." [4]

First Steps in the Reconstruction of the Ministry

On April 1, 1892, Prince Damrong Rajanubhab became Minister of Interior. With the abolition of the Great Ministers, general responsibility for regulating civil and military personnel was nominally transferred to the Ministry of the Palace, where it was to remain until the development of a specialized civil personnel organization in the last years of the absolute monarchy.[5] The new Minister of Interior possessed a definite and limited jurisdiction and an enormous set of responsibilities.

When Prince Damrong took office, the two top-ranking officials in the Ministry, including the deputy minister, had just been pensioned, leaving only Luang Paisan Silpasat, the head of the Revenue (*Suai*)

Department, familiar with the general procedure of the Ministry. This man, Damrong's mentor in the early years of his Ministry, became Phra Montri Potchanakit, undersecretary, or chief administrative official, of the Ministry.

The first stage in the reorganization of the Ministry of Interior occupied about six years. By the end of this period the Ministry had acquired jurisdiction over all of the nation's territory save the capital and had established a national administration pattern set forth in legislation governing provincial administration. In this relatively short span, during which French aggression reached its apogee in 1893, a basic plan of village government was formed, and a premature effort was made to implement it; an integrating structure of provincial and regional government was devised and established in a few areas; a beginning was made in reorganizing the personnel system of the Ministry; central office work procedures were revised; and the Ministry made a significant contribution toward the improvement of the financial condition of the kingdom.

In this work Prince Damrong was aided by two able men. One was to become his right hand in the conduct of the affairs of the Ministry, Seng Wiriyasiri, who, in 1892, possessed the name and position of Luang Tesachit Pichan in the Royal Survey Department. Ultimately, he became Phraya Maha-ammarathyatibordi (deputy minister). The other aide, Luang Paisan (Phra Montri Potchanakit), was responsible for the revision of the correspondence and communications procedures of the Ministry, work to which Prince Damrong attached great importance.[6]

Luang Tesachit (the former Nai Seng) had graduated from the reverend McFarland's Suan Anand School about 1883. He had served under Prince Damrong when the latter was an officer with the Royal Bodyguard. When the Royal Survey Department was established, Nai Seng was assigned as the student and interpreter of James McCarthy. Guided and taught by this able man, young Seng developed valuable skills and knowledge: he learned cartography, traveled widely and assisted in the mapping of the frontiers, and developed a full command of English. Over the years, he acquired both wisdom and administrative ability. In April, 1892, he was in the north at Luang Prabang when Prince Damrong requested that he join the staff of the new Ministry.[7] He was given the title of Phraya SriSahatep, and his assignment was the reorganizing of the pattern of control over villages.[8] Phraya SriSahatep's study and experiments at Bang Pa-in, a royal country seat about thirty-five miles up the Menam Chao Phraya from Bangkok, later proved useful, but in 1892 there was no adequate larger structure to which a revised pattern of rural local government could be attached.

PRINCE DAMRONG'S INSPECTION TRIP

Meanwhile, Prince Damrong spent six months familiarizing himself with the work of the Ministry of Interior, making no important changes for the time being. By September he felt that he had a grasp of the operations at Bangkok, and he undertook an inspection trip through the northern territories under the Ministry's control.[9] From October 7 until sometime in December, 1892, he and some of his officials traveled through the provinces, inspecting, observing, and creating consternation.

At Nakorn Sawan, Damrong discovered that his was the first general inspection ever made by a minister; in the past the Minister of Interior would go to the north only in time of trouble—to recruit soldiers or suppress uprisings. For all the twenty-three years of his ministry, Prince Damrong continued his periodic inspection trips, as part of his effort to integrate the nation through effective provincial government. This integration was the basic aim of the Ministry and the prime concern of the King—"to dissolve all dependencies and half-dependencies in order to make them 'inner provinces' and to make all the people Thais, not Lao, not Malay at all." [10]

The inspection tour gave Prince Damrong full appreciation of the problems he faced. He saw at first hand the workings of *kin muang,* and noted the effects of the interaction of this traditional system with the monetary economy emerging in the nation.[11] The provincial governors and authorities were planters and traders, exploiting their positions for personal profit and obtaining favors from the tax farmers. They were practically a hereditary aristocracy.

"The authorities of the towns were rich men in the towns"; and the system was often quite perverse in its operations. For example, "the governors tended to appoint thugs as authorities" in order to suppress robberies. In Ayudhya, the governor had appointed a rich man named Chang as *Luang Bantaotukrat,* the local authority in charge of peace and order. Luang Bantao was a man of fame and dignity, and persons under his protection had no fear of bandits. But robberies of strangers in the district were numerous; Luang Bantao was the head of a band of discriminating dacoits.

On his tour, Prince Damrong met a number of these sometimes charming and able predators. He came to recognize that "the rearing of thieves to catch thieves does not work," and that the system of maintaining order was fundamentally inadequate. To suppress banditry in a particular district by limiting it to the robbery of strangers entering the district or to dacoitry outside the district was in effect to regularize crime and disorder.

The Prince had many hours to think and study, as his entourage moved up the river in its three launches. He came to the conclusion that:

The purpose of public administration is the maintenance of the peace and contentment of the people. This new concept is different from the old one. The old concept was that the country should be free from danger, such as the danger of robbers. This was called "to be in peace," and can be traced in the law. Thus if the governor was able to maintain order and peace so that no robbery occurred, he would be regarded as achieving his purpose. If there was much disorder, Royal Commissioners would be sent to suppress the evils, or the minister himself might even go if conditions were sufficiently serious. There had thus been no inspection in peaceful times.

The concept that the country must be improved even in time of peace is a new one. It seemed to arise in the reign of King Rama IV, and was strongly emphasized as a principle of public administration from the reign of King Rama V.[12]

The genius of Prince Damrong lay in an exquisite appreciation of both the abstractions and the practicalities. For example, one of the most acute needs of the new ministry—and the kingdom—was money, and the good Prince returned from his northern trip with loaded ships.

In discussing finances with the Minister of Finance before his trip, Prince Damrong was told that large quantities of *suai* (capitation or poll taxes) had not been collected in the provinces. Damrong was asked to obtain the money. This the Prince was reluctant to do because of the possible ill effects upon his own position. In exploring the matter with Phraya Woraput Pokai, head of the Department of *Suai,* an ingenious scheme was devised—a discount on taxes in arrears. When Damrong went north, he took with him the records on delinquent taxes, and meeting with the responsible officials offered them the extraordinary opportunity to settle their delinquent accounts at 50 per cent of the indebtedness. Some even borrowed money to take advantage of this chance, and Prince Damrong collected 200,000 ticals (about $120,000) during his inspection, without incurring grievous ill-will. All of this was in coin, as paper currency was not yet in use, and his launches were heavily laden upon his return to the capital.[13] The money was turned over to the Ministry of Finance, and the King cautioned Damrong to be economical.

ESTABLISHMENT OF A PATTERN OF TERRITORIAL GOVERNMENT

The minister returned from the north committed to the abolition of *kin muang* and the establishment of a structure of domestic government based upon trained, salaried officials working within a framework of effective direction and control, superimposed upon a base of thousands of villages whose residents would share in the responsibilities of peace, order, and the collection of taxes.

A basic need was for a framework of territorial government to link the outlying areas and regions with the capital. The system devised was a simple and logical hierarchy of regional, provincial, and district jurisdictions. Below the last of these lay the *tambol* (communes) and the villages. The provincial towns, in which a small portion of the populace resided, were mostly governmental centers; regional and provincial headquarters would be located in them.

This pattern, whose key was the *monthon,* or region, developed from 1892 into a network of general government blanketing the entire nation, responsible for peace and justice, and serving also as the skeleton to which a growing number of functionally specialized activities could be attached in an orderly fashion.

The *monthon* pattern of territorial government was a logical response to the circumstances of the time: the creation of a group of responsible, competent power centers at key points across the nation was a direct attack upon the quasi-autonomous, quasi-feudal Ayudhyan pattern. Given the communications and transportation conditions of the time, neither full centralization of power in Bangkok nor the creation of a large number of provincial power centers was feasible.

Communications was the *sine qua non* of any network of organization that would actually integrate the nation's territories. Without it there was no real alternative to the traditional pattern of provincial self-containment.[14]

Between 1892 and 1894 the effort to "centralize through decentralization" began, and the first of a series of regional governmental centers were placed in operation. The heads of these regions, high-ranking officials (often princes) appointed by the king and responsible to the Minister of Interior, were salaried. They conducted their business in government-owned offices. They had explicit functional and jurisdictional mandates. And they were incorporated into an expanding, integrated bureaucratic system whose goals were based upon policy rather than tradition, and whose effective center was the Ministry headquarters and the Crown.

As with many of the elements of the Chakkri Reformation, the form of *monthon* organization did not involve a complete break with tradition. From ancient times, the King, in case of trouble, had appointed *kha luang yai,* great commissioners, to take command of a particular territory. The new *monthon* commissioners were identified with this tradition.

As early as 1874 King Chulalongkorn had sent a royal commissioner to control the important northern vassal state of Chiengmai,[15] and the success of this step led to the extension of the arrangement. Five prototypes of the *monthon,* each headed by a great commissioner, had been established prior to 1892, to meet specific needs for territorial control in the face of the threat of aggression or rebellion.[16] In practice, this arrangement was complex and confusing; the great commissioners were responsible to the Minister of Interior, but the fortified towns within the *monthon* were under the direction of the Minister of Defense. The great commissioners were charged with protecting their territories rather than governing in the sense that Damrong came to conceive of this. Only with the emergence of the modern Ministry of Interior did this use of commissioners become an element of a complex, rational *system.*

In December, 1892, Prince Damrong proposed the creation of four *monthons,* each organized to take advantage of waterways for communications.[17] By the end of March, 1893, two great commissioners, the heads of Monthon Phitsanulok and Monthon Prachin, had been appointed. The Ministry was having difficulty in finding suitable persons.

Both hampered and stimulated by the French crisis of the 1890s, the development of the *monthon* network continued, quickly expanding beyond Damrong's original plan. By April 1, 1895, the Phitsanulok and Prachin *monthons* had been supplemented by the transfer of the Korat region from the Ministry of Defense to the jurisdiction of the Ministry of Interior, along with former territories of the ministries of Defense and Foreign Affairs, which were arranged into Monthon Rajaburi (Ratburi). In the following year, the originally planned *monthons* Krung Kao (Ayudhya) and Nakorn Sawan were installed, Bangkok was designated a *monthon,* Puket was taken over from the Ministry of Defense and made a *monthon,* and former territories of the Ministry of Foreign Affairs were incorporated in Monthon Nakorn Chaisri. By the end of the nineteenth century, much of the nation was blanketed by fourteen *monthons,* a number which grew to seventeen by the time of Prince Damrong's retirement in 1915.[18]

THE TESAPIBAN SYSTEM

The significance of the *monthons* lay in their contribution to a new system of government, the *tesapiban,* which means "the system of territorial (or local) government." The *monthons* were an essential first step in a reconstruction which necessarily began at the top. Not only did they link the center with the towns and provinces, they imposed an authority over traditional provincial government to which there could be no effective resistance.

From the outset, the development of the *tesapiban* system was marked by the caution, realism, and balanced concern with traditional form and modern purpose which were the hallmarks of Prince Damrong's ministry.

When the *monthons* were first created as elements of the *tesapiban* system, the only immediate modification of traditional arrangements consisted in the placing of the provincial governors under the *monthon* commissioners.[19] The commissioners, however, were carefully chosen and systematically instructed in their basic responsibilities. In January, 1894, Prince Damrong summoned the first of a series of annual meetings of *monthon* heads. Five commissioners attended this first meeting, a carefully planned training conference with a detailed agenda, spread over most of a week.[20] To this unprecedented meeting the King addressed a message, which was read by Prince Damrong, stressing the importance of the *monthon* system to the preservation of the nation, and the need for the commissioners to foster peace and the development of the nation by directing and controlling provincial and local officials, "irrespective of difficulties both physical and mental, and of personal interests."

From the beginning, the *tesapiban* system was based upon a salaried officialdom, although limited financial resources were a persistent problem, partly because of a need for constructing official living and working quarters as well as paying regular wages. At the end of 1892, Prince Damrong had secured agreement from the King and the Minister of Finance that initially quarters would be provided and salaries paid only to the new *monthon* commissioners and their staffs, with a gradual downward extension of the system of remuneration as the finances of the kingdom permitted.[21]

PROVINCE, DISTRICT, AND VILLAGE GOVERNMENT

One basic feature of the *tesapiban* system was the establishment of a systematic administrative structure *below* the level of the provincial governor, a combination of official district government plus a formalization of the system of village government. The provincial governors were bracketed within the new administrative system. They lost much of their former power in the process, and their assimilation was furthered by the conversion of the governorships into salaried posts. In time, these came to be filled by civil servants rising from the district level of the governmental system. The traditional governors first were bracketed and then gradually supplanted. In such manner was the Ayudhyan tradition transcended.

The plan of the district level of government traced back to Prince Damrong's first inspection tour, and to the studies of Phraya Ammat, who was sent to observe the local government systems of the British in Burma and Malaya in 1894. These systems were based on a hierarchy of high commissioner, district officers, and village leaders. They resembled the traditional Thai pattern in their structure, and undoubtedly influenced the plan of district and village government proposed by Prince Damrong, a plan eventually set forth in the Regulations Governing Local Administration issued in 1897 and the Provincial Administration Act of 1898.[22]

As the *monthons* were established, each contained a division responsible for the development of a system of village government. Small groups of households were designated as *muban,* or villages, under *pu yai ban* (big man of the village), and villages were grouped into *tambon* headed by *kamnan* responsible to designated governmental officials, the district officers.

The form of this arrangement was consistent with tradition. The old laws of the kingdom had instructed the governor to "select a man of honesty and appoint him to be *nai ban* [equivalent to *pu yai ban*] in each district in consideration of his ability to supervise the inhabitants." [23] Under the *tesapiban* system, the substance of village government was to be different; the villages were to be integrated into a governmental system which would no longer be merely exploitative, and they were to be positive participants in the effort to achieve peace, order, increased productivity, and better revenue collection. In keeping with this change in orientation, the villagers were to designate their own leader, and a group of village leaders were to choose a *kamnan* from among themselves, for official appointment by the governor.

The ancient form of governor-appointed village leadership had long been abandoned in most places, and the first efforts to re-establish it met with distrust and resistance. In one of the early attempts to get villagers to designate a leader at Monthon Ayudhya, the people of one village elected as *pu yai ban*—the *monthon* commissioner who happened to reside in their area. Meeting this canny move with shrewdness of his own, the commissioner, Krom Mun Marubhongse Siribhad, a half brother of King Chulalongkorn, accepted the designation and performed his functions in such a manner as to encourage the trust of the villagers and help secure acceptance for the effort to order and improve village government.

THE PROVINCIAL ADMINISTRATION ACT OF 1898;
THE NEW PLACE OF THE PROVINCIAL GOVERNOR

Six years after the great reorganization of 1892, the initial phase in the development of a new system of domestic government ended with a basic statute defining the structure and responsibilities of the elements of the *tesapiban* system, supplemented by an appropriate set of rules and regulations. Twelve *monthons* were in existence by 1898.

In the 1898 enactment, the position of the provincial governor in this new system was regularized. With the creation of the *monthons,* the governors were no longer the lords of their territories. The salaried governor was also flanked by two provincial boards whose purpose was to advise and assist him in the conduct of his duties, and by implication to cause him to function as a responsible governmental official rather than a semiautonomous ruler.[24]

One board consisted of three senior (*sanyabat*) and five junior provincial officials: the deputy governor, public prosecutor, and finance officer, and the provincial clerk, registrar, assistant prosecutor, assistant finance officer, and the governor's secretary. Given the emphatically hierarchical character of Thai society, this board had little significance as an entity, though its statutory establishment indicated that the governor was to engage in a certain amount of consultation among his officials in the administration of his province.

The other board (*krommakan nok tamnieb*), appointed by the Minister of Interior on advice of the governor and the *monthon* commissioner, consisted of wealthy and influential residents of the province; they received honorific titles but no pay for their service. The aim of this arrangement was to increase and systematize communications between the government and wealthy leaders in the community, and to advise the governors "concerning the ways in which the livelihood of the provincial people could be improved." [25] These provincial consultative boards, a new departure in Thai public administration, reflected the fact that during the latter half of the nineteenth century the economy of the provinces had developed. Provincial centers contained important economic elites engaged in trade, fishing, forestry, commerce, agriculture, or mining, who were in a recognized position to contribute to the pursuit of the governmental goals of King Chulalongkorn and Prince Damrong.

These special boards, consisting of ten eligible persons appointed for three-year terms, were required to meet twice a year to consider the provincial annual report before it was sent to the *monthon*. Other meetings were called at the discretion of the governor, but board members were authorized to initiate and submit to the governor for consideration "any measure to be taken which would foster the earning of livings." The board members also participated in an annual *monthon* meeting to consider the economic affairs of the provinces of the *monthon*.

Members of the board might be given the simulated rank of either noncommissioned or commissioned officials, and half of each board appears to have consisted of members who were granted permanent rank or title.

These advisory "citizen" boards were abolished by the Provincial Administration Act of 1922, but for two decades some of them appear to have made a contribution to the evolution of the new governmental system. Phraya Rachsena observed that "the special officials were of great benefit. . . . Their positions were not obtained by flattery. They were positions of prestige and honor. The officials were induced into service not by any monetary remuneration but rather by dignity and prestige." [26]

It would be unwise to attach too much importance to the existence of these boards. They must have functioned in varying fashion as devices for communication and co-operation. But, in some cases, they formed a link between government and economically powerful leaders of individual communities, most of whom were Chinese. Their very existence amounted to a recognition of the importance of these groups, and implied, too, that they were more than mere subjects of an authoritarian regime. The boards represented an attempt at co-optation; they afforded the most meaningful rewards of the Thai system—official status and the prestige that went with it—to co-operative members of a blossoming provincial economic elite. The boards, established on the basis of pragmatic concerns rather than anything more, may have helped inspire the ideologically motivated provincial boards created in 1933 as an intended step toward the democratization of provincial government.[27]

Under the *tesapiban* system the governor was no longer the chief judge of the province. He no longer possessed power to remove provincial officials of commissioned rank. While he continued to be formally subject to royal appointment and removal, his office was no longer quasi-hereditary. From *chao muang* (lord of the place) the governor had been reduced to *pu warajakarn changwad* (man in charge of the province for the king).[28] And the change was symbolic of the basic modification which was under way in Thailand.

By the end of the nineteenth century—specifically, by 1898—the main outlines of the new Ministry of Interior had been drawn, and a new pattern of domestic government was in the making. The achievement, incomplete as it was, was stupendous. Meanwhile, significant changes occurred in the administration of justice and in tax collection —changes which were inseparably linked with the reconstruction of the Ministry of Interior.

JUSTICE

The *monthon* initially included a justice division, a court with jurisdiction over appeals from the more or less traditional provincial courts, with the *monthon* commissioner serving as judge. Coping with the exquisite procedures of traditional provincial judicial administration quickly proved hopeless; this led to the appointment of special commissioners to establish courts at *monthon* headquarters.

The reformation of judicial administration in the provinces was part of a thorough reconstruction of the system of justice stemming from the 1892 reorganization. Judicial reform was a prime concern of King Chulalongkorn, for it was a key to an attack upon the extraterritoriality which reflected Western lack of respect for Thai governmental institutions. The Ministry of Interior played a vital role in this effort, furnishing a framework by which, for the first time in Thai history, a coherent national approach to the administration of law and justice was possible through systematic interministry co-operation.

Judicial reform involved a radical revision of the substance of law as well as judicial administration. In 1893 King Chulalongkorn had established a Legislative Council comprised of the ministers of state, six members of the royal family, and a number of other persons nominated by the King. The Council was empowered to introduce and discuss new laws and regulations.[29] In 1896 and 1897 it approved and submitted to the King a series of measures which marked the beginning of a new legal system.[30]

A Law of Evidence, repealing the ancient Manuic Law Concerning Witnesses, was enacted in 1895,[31] and a Civil Procedure Act, a transitory Law of Criminal Procedure, and a Provisional Court Ordinance were adopted in the following year.[32] These were forerunners of a comprehensive codification effort that was made the responsibility of a Codification Commission in 1905; its first product was the comprehensive Penal Code of 1908.[33]

The enactments of the 1890s were the joint products of the reorganized Ministry of Justice and the government's foreign advisers, notably Monsieur Rolin-Jaequermyns and his assistant, Mr. A. J. Kirkpatrick. And it was the reorganization of the Ministry under a brilliant and able young minister of justice which, with the contribution of the Ministry of Interior, gave meaning to the enactments.

In 1894 H. R. H. Krom Mun Rabipattanasak, the Prince of Ratburi, commonly referred to as Prince Rabi, returned from England, having graduated from Oxford with honors in Law. A son of King Chulalongkorn, Prince Rabi, born in 1874, had been sent abroad at an early age. In 1897 [34] he became the minister of justice, having participated in the planning of judicial reforms from the time of his return to Thailand.

In 1896 three judicial commissions with extraordinary powers were appointed to dispose of more than two thousand criminal cases long pending on the dockets of the Bangkok courts; about 10 per cent of the persons being held pending trial were released on the basis of the commissions' findings that they had already fulfilled their sentences.[35]

This Herculean house cleaning established a basis for the reorganization of the capital courts, and attention was turned to the provinces at the suggestion of Prince Damrong. At the end of 1896, a new five-member judicial commission was appointed, including Prince Rabi as chairman, the commissioner of Monthon Ayudhya, Mr. Kirkpatrick, and two high-ranking Thais. Armed with full powers to try cases, inspect prisons, gather information, and even try and punish provincial judges, this commission had a field day. It formulated recommendations which became the basis for the administration of justice under the *monthon* system. It also ordered that a number of judges who had condemned innocent men undergo the sentences they had passed upon their victims, and it released hundreds of innocent or untried prisoners.[36]

The new system of justice was bolstered by the establishment, in 1897, of a law school to produce judicial officials for the provincial and *monthon* courts as well as the appeals courts of the Ministry of Justice at Bangkok. In 1909 the new judicial system was described as "the bright particular star in the administration of the country, a fact which doubtless counted for much in the determination of Great Britain to abandon extraterritoriality." [37] But without the reconstruction of the Ministry of Interior, the development of the *tesapiban* system, and the eager co-operation of Prince Damrong, the aims of law revision and judicial reform could not have been achieved.

With the spread of the *monthons,* Ministry of Interior officials served as provisional justices in *monthon* and provincial courts; these were gradually replaced by trained judges as law school graduates became available. Of course, the promise of the bold reforms of the 1890s was somewhat brighter than the actual practice. For years, the judicial system was impeded by "the want of enough intelligent, trustworthy and experienced men to fill the numerous judicial offices. . . ." [38] And after the retirement of Prince Rabi in 1910 and the death of King Chulalongkorn, the Ministry of Justice lost much of the *élan* which distinguished it in the early years. Even so, the change from traditional Thai justice was profound.

FINANCES, DIPLOMACY

In 1896, a British financial adviser was appointed to the Ministry of Finance, and a Comptroller-General Department was established within the Ministry. The Ministry of Interior, which shared responsibility with the ministries of Agriculture and Finance for tax collection in the provinces, was keenly aware of the need for increasing revenues, and was intimately involved in the revenue reforms which doubled the kingdom's tax collections between 1896 and 1903.[39] An Outside (Provincial) Revenues Department was established within the Ministry of Interior in 1896. The Ministry of Agriculture ceased to be responsible for land tax collection, and a foundation was established for reforms in provincial revenue administration, which continued with the development of the new system of government.

The reformation effort of the 1890s went forward in a most difficult setting. This was a time of great tension in the kingdom of Thailand. Relations with France reached their nadir in 1893, when French gunboats sailed up the Chao Phraya to anchor in front of the palace. Sick in body and spirit, the King retired to Sriricha on the Gulf and momentarily withdrew from the struggle to survive. It was Prince Damrong from whom he seemed to gain the strength and fortitude to return to Bangkok and resume negotiations with the French.[40]

During this period, the Ministry of Foreign Affairs, under young Prince Devawongse, was aided by Rolin-Jaequermyns, a Belgian international lawyer, who became general adviser to the government in 1892. Jaequermyns made many contributions to Thailand before his death in 1902, notably in the fields of finance and justice; but in foreign relations he placed perhaps too great an emphasis upon legality in seeking to deal with matters of force.[41] The French exacted important concessions, and were permitted to occupy Thai territory in the Cambodian border area. (Three eastern provinces were later ceded to France as a result of the aggression of the early 1890s.) But Devawongse and Rolin-Jaequermyns were building a Foreign Ministry, as Damrong was constructing the Ministry of Interior, in the midst of these fateful developments. Meanwhile, work was also going forward to begin a railway system, reorganize the military, regulate mining and forestry, improve public health in the Bangkok area, and develop the nation's water resources.[42]

By 1898 the greatest crisis in Thai foreign relations had passed, although a lasting and satisfactory accommodation had not yet been reached between Thailand and the Western powers. Now, after issuance of the Provincial Government Act, the Ministry of Interior moved into the second phase of its modernization, extending its organization and expanding its activities.

Twentieth-Century Development of the Ministry of Interior Under Prince Damrong

In the progress towards efficiency which began with the establishment of the Cabinet of Ministers, Prince Damrong's ability and energy enabled him easily to outstrip all competitors, so that the Ministry of the Interior soon developed out of proportion to the other great Departments. . . . Much work which should have been done by others devolved upon this hive of industry and enthusiasm. Indeed at one time the Bureau of the Interior so completely overshadowed most of the other Ministries that it appeared either to have swallowed them entirely or to be about to do so. . . .[43]

Before presenting important matters for discussion in the Council of Ministers, the King obtained the advice of Prince Damrong. . . .

The Ministry of Interior became the office of the Council of Ministers. . . . And any new department whose work was difficult, such as the Department of Outside Revenues, the Department of Forestry, the Department of Mines, the Land Department, the Department of Public Health, the Department of Municipal Public Works, the administration of schools and the establishment of courts in the provinces, was placed in the Ministry of Interior.[44]

The structure of the new administrative system was developed in full detail during the period which began with the Provincial Administration Act of 1898, and ended with the retirement of Prince Damrong in 1915.

In these years, the Ministry of Interior grew into a "Ministry of Domestic Government." This was a time of institution building, of careful, persistent development of a large-scale administrative enterprise. It was the Golden Age of administration in the absolute monarchy, the era in which the grand reforms of King Chulalongkorn reached their greatest degree of fulfillment. It was also a time when the burgeoning administrative system outran the long-run managerial capacity of its political setting.

Within the Ministry of Interior, the need for large numbers of competent district-level officials became critical by the turn of the century. The great impact of the expansion of domestic government occurred at the district level; it was here that the new administrative aims of peace and development had to be implemented.

In meeting these needs, a civil service system was built; characteristics of that system, the subject of the following chapters, remain a part of the foundations of the Thai civil service today. The idea of the civil servant as "the king's man" became a reality as an integrated bureaucracy supplanted the Ayudhyan administrative feudalism of the provinces.

By about 1910, the Ministry of Interior had evolved an elaborate formalized administrative apparatus.[45] Its central organization consisted of the Office of the Minister and the headquarters staffs of nine departments, each under a director-general. Its personnel were divided into a central office group and a field service. The latter was located in 16 *monthons,* 71 provinces, and 369 districts. Within the districts were 4,723 communes, or *tambons,* composed of 48,825 villages, according to the Ministry's census of 1912.

By this time, the total staff of the Ministry must have been at least 14,000 or 15,000 persons. The Provincial Gendarmerie alone contained more than 8,000 officers and men.[46] Provincial officials below the levels of *monthon* commissioner and *changwad* governor included 17 deputy *monthon* commissioners, 513 deputy provincial governors and district officers, 35 royal page reporters, 73 provincial secretaries, and about 1,400 other officers above the rank of clerk. The Ministry had 1,387 officers, plus clerks and other assistants, scattered across the kingdom and owned a total of 2,223 offices and official residences.

The vital center of the organization was the Ministry headquarters, where each day at 2:00 P.M. the minister, deputy minister, undersecretary, and departmental director-generals met to discuss and decide upon current problems and activities. Confidential matters were handled separately, in smaller, less formal meetings, but for more than two decades the daily management conference was a vital mechanism of central administration. A somewhat similar practice was followed in the provinces.

Ministry headquarters was supervised by the undersecretary who handled communications, was responsible for the effective performance of assigned work, and reported to the deputy minister and the minister himself. During Prince Damrong's tenure, Phraya Ammat, his deputy, bore many of the burdens of Ministry management. He had the full confidence of the Prince and of King Chulalongkorn, who one day told him that his competence merited a ministry but his work with Prince Damrong was too important to permit his advancement in rank.

THE DEPARTMENTS

The remainder of the central organization consisted of the managements of a varied group of departments engaged in specialized program activities, in housekeeping, and in control. One of these, the *Department of Public Health,* at a relatively early stage of development at the time, was responsible for the health of provincial officials and prisoners, as well as for providing some services to the public. Another, the *Department of Forestry,* organized in 1896, functioned chiefly in the teak forests of the north, regulating timber extraction.

In 1883 the British and Thai governments had entered into a treaty extending the principle of extraterritoriality to Burmese British subjects resident in northern Thailand engaged in teak extraction.[47] Previous to this, Burmese teak traders had been in frequent conflict with the governor of Chiengmai, which, in turn, caused diplomatic difficulties between Thailand and Great Britain. This led to the 1883 treaty, under which a British vice-consul was sent to Chiengmai to protect Burmese interests. This, however, did not resolve the disputes, nor did it improve relations with Great Britain at a time when international relations were a prime concern of Thailand. Consequently, about 1895, M. Rolin-Jaequermyns recommended the establishment of a State Forestry Department, and Prince Damrong and King Chulalongkorn concurred. A British officer was borrowed from the Imperial Forest Department of British India, and the department was established within the Ministry of Interior, in 1896. The Ministry of Foreign Affairs no longer found itself concerned with timber disputes; the competence of the new department and the fairness of the

Minister of Interior in handling issues presented to him had the effect, in Prince Damrong's words, of "taking the politics out of the forestry problem." [48] Existing timber leases were drastically revised, higher royalties were levied, and overcut areas were closed. By 1901, a conservancy policy was well established, a group of Thais was being trained for work in the department, and both the quality and quantity of teak production showed definite improvement. Effectiveness led to expansion, and in 1910 the jurisdiction of the department was extended to other forest products. [49]

Between 1899 and 1908, the *Department of Mines and Geology* was also a part of the Ministry of Interior. [50] This department had been created in 1891, as a consequence of an alarming influx of European gold prospectors and a concern over the regulation of tin mining. Much valuable ore land was lying idle, controlled by concession-holding speculators. The department sought to develop a systematic arrangement for granting and regulating mining concessions, and undertook some useful surveys of the nation's mineral resources. [51] Under Prince Damrong's direction, mining regulations were enacted in 1901; by 1902 an efficient staff of surveyors was being created, and a regular system was developed for the survey and issuance of leases. Sufficiently strengthened, the department was handed back to a new Ministry of Agriculture in 1908.

The Police, or *Provincial Gendarmerie,* another of the departments of the Ministry of Interior, was established in response to an unanticipated consequence of the erosion of the Ayudhyan tradition. In 1892, Prince Damrong had noted the undesirability of using criminals to maintain law and order. Yet the old system had to a degree succeeded in doing just that; the traditional governors did manage to restrict and regularize dacoitry within their jurisdictions. But as *kin muang* was undermined, "violent crime of every description increased to an alarming extent and very soon passed altogether beyond the control of the authorities." [52]

As a result of this unexpected effect of reform, the gendarmerie, a national body of military police, was organized in 1897. [53] It attained a strength, by 1908, of 270 officers and 8,000 noncommissioned officers and men (including 600 mounted patrolmen); it obtained its noncommissioned men at first from volunteers and later by conscription from the army recruiting list. The gendarmerie was separate from the civilian structure of *tesapiban* government but co-ordinated with it.

Police stations were located at *monthon,* province, and district head-quarters; and persons apprehended for law violations were turned over to civilian officials of the Ministry of Interior for interrogation, prosecution, and possible imprisonment.

Very soon after its creation, the police organization established its reputation by quickly suppressing Shan tribal uprisings in 1902, and by wiping out a band of border guerrillas whom a strong force of French *Tirailleurs Annamites* had been unable to capture during many months of harassment.[54]

The backbone of the Ministry of Interior was its hierarchy of *monthons,* provinces, and districts—each under administrators gener-ally responsible for the affairs of their respective territories—and the headquarters staff which supported the field service. One important element of this headquarters which had developed fully by 1915 was the *Department of Administration (Palumpung).*[55] This department was responsible for the appointment and transfer of *tesapiban* offi-cials, for a variety of registration activities, and, in general, for carry-ing out the established responsibilities of the Ministry in the field. It did not, however, superintend the *monthon* commissioners, who re-ported directly to the Ministry.

Another of the central departments, the *Department Concerned with the Northern Territories (Mahadthai),* retained the ancient name describing the traditional responsibilities of the old Ministry of Interior. It was at this time actually concerned with criminal investi-gation, prosecution, and prison administration.

An *Accounts,* or *Finance, Department* controlled the disbursement of funds, including the pay of ministry officials. As a result of numer-ous and persistent difficulties in financial administration, the position of "finance and supply officer" was established at *monthon* and province levels in 1913, and great stress was placed upon financial exactitude.

Temptations were considerable, and control was a problem. There was no bonding of officials. Stringent and detailed rules were issued in an effort to obtain fiduciary honesty. Money was to be kept only in safe and specified places. The maximum amount to be kept at any place was specified, a sum assumed to be within the means of those responsible for repaying if it were lost. And charming use was made of a rather typical Thai device for obtaining responsibility: wherever money was kept, a "committee in charge of keeping the keys" had to be established, composed of no fewer than two persons from different units of the particular organizational element.

A *Department of Registration* was also part of the headquarters organization, responsible for a variety of records and data, including the census which was begun by the Ministry of Interior in 1903. The census was conceived as a useful device for planning and administration—in the conscription of soldiers, for instance. Census taking by district officers was also related to revenue administration, for the census covered householders, dependents, vehicles, beasts of burden, and weapons. The 1912 census, admittedly incomplete, indicated the existence of 6,500 elephants, almost 87,000 horses, more than 2,000,000 water buffalo—and 24 cars. Peace-loving, tranquil Thais admitted to the ownership of 421,688 guns of various types, an average of about one weapon for each eighteen persons covered. As Phraya Ammat observed, "This census was only approximate . . . , but it was better than none."

The Registration Department also maintained basic personnel records on each official in the Ministry. A rather interesting device was used: for each official there was a book containing his name, qualifications, age, work experience, and appropriate comments upon his achievements and conduct. For provincial officials, two copies of the book were maintained, one in the provincial office and one in the Registration Department files.

This department also served as the archives of the Ministry. As record-keeping department, gradually it became a means for consolidating various recording activities previously scattered throughout the Ministry.

There was also a *"Survey" Department,* responsible for a mixed bag of functions—confidential matters of concern to the Ministry, including covert investigations of official conduct, plus correspondence, the care and maintenance of Ministry headquarters offices, and the issuance of passports within the jurisdiction of the Ministry of Interior.

Finally, there was the *Department of Outside (Provincial) Revenues,* distinguished by its reform of land, fisheries, capitation, and various other taxes, as a result of which "the revenues accruing from the rural districts were gradually and considerably increased, while the actual incidence of taxation upon the people was not noticeably heavier than formerly, the improvement being largely due to a better adjustment of the taxes and to a complete revolution in the manner of collection." [56] In the fiscal year 1908–1909, the Ministry of Interior produced tax receipts which exceeded the ministry budget by more than 20 per cent.[57]

The Ministry of Interior and the Emergence of a National Bureaucracy

The Ministry of Interior sustained an expanding pattern of activity outside its own sphere. The postal and telegraph system spread its services and facilities across the land. A network of railroads grew. Significant beginnings were made in the expansion of agricultural lands through water control. This, interestingly, was, in part, a modern bureaucratic response to the consequences of the earlier abolition of *corvée* labor. Down to the reign of King Chulalongkorn, canals had been dug and maintained by conscripted labor. With the abolition of *corvée* came an end to the maintenance of canals. Siltation rapidly reduced their utility, with harmful consequences for agriculture. In 1889, the government had chartered a private canal construction and land development project under which 500 miles of canals were constructed and almost half a million acres of jungle land were opened to rice production. Fifteen years later, about 1904, a Department of Irrigation was established, and in the following years at least a beginning was made in public water resource development in the central basin of Thailand.[58]

The Ministry of Lands and Agriculture, established in 1892, proved to be feeble and vacillating. It was abolished in 1897 and reestablished as the Ministry of Lands, Agriculture, and Commerce in 1899. It began the issuance of title deeds based upon modern cadastral surveys in 1901, and land record work was one of its most valuable functions in the pre-World War I era.[59]

The *tesapiban* system of the Ministry of Interior contributed to these developments by affording a secure and stable setting within which they could occur. It served as the supporting trunk of domestic government; its regional, provincial, and district offices were the points of attachment for field personnel in education, agriculture, justice, posts and telegraph, and so forth. Some administrative organizations such as the railways had self-contained field establishments, but these were exceptions. For most of the expanding governmental system, the Ministry of Interior provided the link between ministry headquarters and field personnel.

The *monthon* commissioner was responsible, almost literally, for everything within his jurisdiction; this was true for the provincial governor and the district officer. Functional specialists in agriculture, health, education, and other fields were attached to, and administratively subordinate to, these generalist officials. They were selected and assigned by the respective ministries which paid their salaries. They communicated with these ministries through the *tesapiban* chain of command. Their relationships with the Ministry of Interior hierarchy inevitably posed problems capable, in part, of only personal solutions; but the specialists were either supported by the *tesapiban* officials or likely to fail in their efforts.

A territorial basis of organization, coupled with an impressive growth in the scope of specialized governmental functions, produced complex administrative structures, as the following list of key *monthon* positions in 1915 suggests.[60]

MAJOR MONTHON OFFICIALS [61]

Monthon commissioner
Monthon deputy commissioner
Monthon prosecutor
Monthon penitentiary officer
Monthon police commander
Monthon public health officer
Monthon military assistant commissioner *
Monthon agricultural officer *
Monthon treasury officer *
Monthon revenue officer *
Monthon customs officer *
Monthon inspector of post and telegraph service *
Monthon educational officer *

With the exception of the customs officer, each of the above officers held the same official rank as a provincial governor.

At the provincial level, one again found a complex cluster of officials in three categories: line administrators of the *tesapiban* system and their assistants; line administrators of specialized departments of the Ministry of Interior, such as police and public health; and line

* Officials indicated by asterisk are those of other ministries attached to *monthon* organization.

officers of other ministries subject to a dual chain of control. With adaptations, the pattern was repeated at the district level of government.

The ranks of all these officials were related in an orderly fashion in accordance with the rules governing provincial administration, all posts being pegged to a series of hierarchical levels established by the ranks of the commissioners, governors, district officers, and deputy district officers.

No one has ever developed a completely satisfactory formal arrangement for combining territorial and functionally specialized patterns of organization, but the *tesapiban* arrangement was at least a logical one. It was consistent with a tradition of territorial organization. It supported the concept that the aims of the Ministry of Interior were not limited to law and order. It provided effective communications channels at a time when technical limitations alone were an impediment to effective communications. It encouraged decentralized decision-making, capitalizing upon the vast status and authority of the governor and the *monthon* commissioner and sustaining those attributes of office. Finally, the arrangement also reduced the costs of supporting multiple field organizations and afforded opportunities for co-ordinating various program activities in the field.

The success of this arrangement depended upon the competence of the generalist administrators at provincial and *monthon* levels, plus a persistent, active dedication to a broad array of purposes within the top levels of the Ministry of Interior. To the extent that these requirements were met, the *tesapiban* system constructed in the two incredible decades of Prince Damrong's ministry provided a viable, flexible, authoritative system of territorial government. At its best it functioned surprisingly well.

One might characterize this as a "tutelage" system. In principle, it was an administrative system whose power devolved downward from the king, the Lord of Lives. In practice, it contained some admittedly limited devices for encouraging "public" support and participation in the pursuit of broad governmental purposes. The two most important of these were the provincial councilors designated as "special officials" in a system where all status and power were official, and the social—but not consciously political—democracy of representative village government in a nation of villages. In practice, too, the administrative system of the Ministry of Interior developed into a stable institutional arrangement by which the daily conduct of hundreds of officials was more or less routinely directed, controlled, regularized, and rewarded.

In this system, the district officer was the lowest level of generalist, and an important man. The district officer and his deputies became the chief sources of higher administrative personnel in the *tesapiban* system. And it was at the level of the district that the official structure of government came into contact with the populace. From the beginning, the district officer was the local eyes and ears—and perhaps the nose—of the government, as well as the chief executive of a small domain, vested with symbols of authority in an authoritarian society.[62] He was the king's man.

The Emergence of a New National Bureaucracy: Some Implications

This brief summary of Thai bureaucratic developments in the two decades following 1892 is an outline of achievements in the construction of new organizations. It ignores the inevitable difficulties and occasional disasters. It omits the drama, and tends to convey an impression that in Thailand, between 1892 and about 1912, a rather simple, straightforward effort more or less inevitably produced a desired set of new administrative agencies.

The appreciation of problems and difficulties we leave to the reader. But a few comments upon the aggregate scope and implications of these developments are in order.

The bureaucratic reconstruction amounted to a substantial revision of the aims and purposes of Thai government. Damrong had mused during his memorable inspection trip in 1892 that "the purpose of public administration is [now] the maintenance of the peace and contentment of the people. . . . The old concept was [simply] that the country should be free from danger. . . ." He was right; but he understated the dimensions of change involved in the bureaucratic reconstruction in which he played so great a part. The old concept was essentially that the country should be free from danger in order to persist as a simple, stratified, exploitative system existing in principle as the king's domain. The old bureaucracy was a framework of social organization which gave order, meaning, and legitimacy to the existence of those who participated in it. It served its purposes; but its

immediate purposes were largely the fulfillment of reciprocal obligations inherent in personal statuses, defined by reference to the over-all
system. This might involve the performance of ritual activities, or of
some equally meaningful service such as the collection of taxes. Performance, in the sense of contributions to the production of goods
and services for a clientele external to the immediate group, was often
an incidental element of a diffuse set of behaviors. Bureaucratic
reconstruction proceeded to change this by seeking to supplant the
traditional structure with a set of purposive, functionally specific, performance-oriented administrative organizations.

The ancient bureaucracy had been a mechanism for the integration
of the kingdom—or, more correctly, of the society. It nominally incorporated all men and all things into an encompassing, legitimate
structure of social organization. But only spasmodically did large-
scale integrated action occur within this system (as in time of war).

The new bureaucracy sought to integrate the kingdom in new
ways—essentially by engaging in complex, coherent activities throughout it. And the elemental obviousness of this statement does not de-
tract at all from the enormity of the transformation involved in the
shift from the old to the new.

The new bureaucracy also began to perform some functions implicitly inconsistent with the *raison d'être* of the traditional kingdom.
The traditional myth that all things existed for the service of the king
had never been a fully adequate source of a perspective in reality. In
practice, the traditional system was largely dedicated to the service of
the congeries of interests that comprised it. But the new bureaucracy
was, to a substantial extent, geared to the service of interests—
however latent and inarticulate—outside the administrative system. It
was, in a sense, oriented toward the service of the kingdom, not just
the king and the bureaucrats.

It is easy to overstate or overstress this shift in orientation. The
welfare state did not come to Thailand between 1892 and 1910. But
a distinction was made between government and society, and the distinction had not really been part of the ancient rationale. This differentiation had been evolving through most of the nineteenth century; it
came to fruition during the Chakkri Reformation.

This hidden dimension of change was implicit in the various specific, relatively coherent activities which constituted the Reformation.
But the consequences of this aspect of transition in Thailand were

profound. The immediate, visible result of the Reformation was survival as an independent nation. The residual effects were changes in the terms of future existence for members of the society. The former was deliberately sought; but it could be had only at the price of the latter.

Within the bureaucracy a radical shift occurred in the norms governing behavior. Reciprocity as the primary basis for bureaucratic action within small, self-contained organizations was supplemented and supplanted by more complex patterns of action in large organizations responsive to productivity norms and program goals. These large organizations were marked by a greater degree of impersonalism than the old system had been, and by related reliance upon rules and rationalized routines as important, systematic determinants of action. Bureaucrats were now parts of a comprehensive system that was differentiated from the rest of society. The meaningfulness of bureaucratic status was hardly obliterated, but new requirements were imposed upon its acquisition, new obligations were attached to its possession, and the rights and rewards inherent in it were revised and restricted.

These changes in the quality of the bureaucracy resulted from three inseparable aspects of the Chakkri Reformation: the previously sketched construction of a new set of administrative organizations, the adoption of new processes for staffing them and controlling behavior within them, and the assertion of new values and norms as bases for bureaucratic behavior.

Chapter 5

NEW BUREAUCRATIC PROCESSES
FOR A NEW ADMINISTRATIVE SYSTEM

BUILDING the new bureaucracy was a many-sided effort. The establishment of new organizations was tantamount to the creation of rational systems of action for the pursuit of a variety of new purposes. Merely to establish organization structures was not enough; it was essential that the organizations should operate in certain ways.[1]

In abstract terms, the "ways" in which organizations operate can be examined in terms of the ways in which resources are procured, ordered (or allocated), and energized. Processes—systematic arrangements—for resource procurement, ordering, and energizing are generic characteristics of organizations in action. Here, they are simply called "bureaucratic processes." Of course, the particular content of these processes varies from organization to organization, or from system to system. This is exactly why a consideration of the bureaucratic processes which evolved during the Chakkri Reformation, and after it, is important. Administrative rationality is essentially a function of the relationship between bureaucratic processes and the goals to be pursued through organization; the aim of the Reformation was to construct a rational, productive administrative system.

One further comment about bureaucratic processes: they include both action per se and norms in terms of which the action is performed and assessed. It is possible, and for our purposes essential, to distinguish between these.

In the first place, the meaning of action lies in the norms which govern it. In the second place, actions which appear to remain unchanged when viewed narrowly may shift in their "real content" by becoming responsive to different norms. This is a somewhat jargonistic way of saying that, while forms may remain more or less constant, substance may not. In the Thai case, some ancient forms were adapted to the needs of the new bureaucracy, and the changes in the norms governing bureaucratic processes were in certain instances much greater than the changes in the manifest forms of action themselves. Later, after the Reformation had run its course, further changes of this sort occurred again.

In the traditional Thai bureaucracy, resource procurement, allocation, and energizing had taken place in relatively small, self-contained enclaves, in an intensely personal manner, through the intricate interplay of hierarchical status differentiations, implicit reciprocity norms, and an abiding concern with self-interest. Yet these processes were played out against an overarching background consisting of a status hierarchy stretching from cosmos and king to slave. There was an element of universalism in the system, which legitimized the power of officials and defined the content of status, but much of the action—most of it, in all probability—was controlled by particularistic norms. In practice, the traditional bureaucracy was a highly particularistic system. In its central tendencies, the old system *was* essentially traditional: it did not operate on the basis of *policy,* to any extent, either in establishing goals or in establishing effective bureaucratic processes for the pursuit of those goals.

This, of course, is something of an overstatement; and it ignores the fact that at one time early in the nation's history a great rationalizing effort had occurred, in which policies were laid down to establish a socio-bureaucratic apparatus to implement the aims of the "state." But what had once, perhaps, been rational became over the centuries utterly traditional. The Reformation was an effort to substitute rational, policy-based, competent action for tradition.

In the Chakkri Reformation, bureaucratic processes were deliberately established as matters of policy, to be carried into operation within bureaucratic organizations. The processes were shaped rather pragmatically in the course of building the bureaucracy; they were mandated as policies at the decision-making center of the governmental system; and they were implemented on a day-to-day basis in accordance with rules and regularized routines. During the Reformation itself, the shaping and adjustment of these processes for procuring, ordering, and energizing resources were of prime continuing concern of management. And management consisted of the king, his ministers, and their immediate aides and subordinates.

This aspect of bureaucratic reconstruction proceeded *ad hoc,* influenced by Western methods and techniques to a considerable extent, and by expediency as well. Because the Ministry of Interior and its minister occupied so central a position, the systemic processes of the new bureaucracy evolved to a large extent out of the Ministry's efforts and experiences. The result was a set of arrangements which seemed consistent with the aims of bureaucratic reform, but which also remained to an impressive degree identified with tradition. Empirically, the processes were a set of arrangements for procuring personnel, developing appropriate competence, accommodating personnel within the organizational system, and motivating and controlling behavior to elicit contributions to organizational goals. In the broadest sense, the bureaucratic processes also involved other resources used in the production of goods and services. Here we shall examine only the human aspect of the bureaucracy.

The Procurement of Personnel

The procurement of personnel involves all those activities and arrangements concerned with personnel recruitment and selection, including intake, promotion, transfer, discharge, and retirement. The process is common to all administrative organizations and groups of organizations; the techniques vary considerably with time and place.

In the ancient Thai bureaucracy, persons were "recruited" for *corvée* or military service, but little choice was involved. Official positions were filled on a preferential basis that included ascriptive norms. The sons or other dependents of officials generally had access to bureaucratic posts. Top positions were usually filled by members of the royal family. The society was never devoid of mobility, but the realm of officialdom tended to be self-reproducing. Such an arrangement was inadequate for the new bureaucracy. It needed new kinds of specialized personnel, and a growing number of literate junior officials and clerks.

The procurement of personnel involved, first of all, the establishment of sources. These included the royal family itself, foreign specialists who were used in great numbers, and the young men who came out of the temple schools, the new institutions of training and advanced education in Bangkok, and even overseas universities.

In the first phase of the Reformation the greatest need was for managers, for specialized advisers, and for technicians with the ability to make innovative contributions. The feasibility of enterprises had to be determined. Organizations to implement chosen objectives had to be planned and built through training, supervision, and management.

As administrative reconstruction proceeded, the demand for personnel expanded. Between the 1880s and about 1920 the new bureaucracy grew enormously. Rough estimates based upon Ingram's data on noncapital expenditures from 1892 suggest that the salaried bureaucracy more than doubled in size between 1892 and 1899, and that it probably doubled again between 1900 and 1905.[2] Between 1906 and 1918, the first year for which personnel statistics are available, noncapital governmental expenditures rose another 80 per cent.

The record implies more than a tripling of the size of the civil bureaucracy between 1900 and 1918. If so, the Thai bureaucracy must have contained somewhat more than 25,000 civil officials at the beginning of the present century. The next decades were marked by vast expansion, producing a civil service of 79,988 officials at the close of the fiscal year 1918–1919. By 1918 the great growth and most of the great changes had occurred. The Chakkri Reformation had run its course.

POLYGAMY AND PERSONNEL PROCUREMENT

Polygamy was not without its value as a source of personnel for the new bureaucracy. Members of the royal family had traditionally occupied important governmental posts. The upper levels of the system were integrated by the personal relations among princes, the major object being to assure loyalty. Thus, the governor of a particularly important first-class province might be the son or half brother of the king. Trusted members of his family also were likely to hold positions involving the control of military forces.

In the new bureaucracy, loyalty was no longer an adequate measure of managerial competence. But King Mongkut had laid well the foundation for staffing the top levels of the new bureaucracy.[3] His first child was born in 1823, his ninety-fourth and last in 1868, the year of his death. During his reign of seventeen years he sired eighty-two children in addition to the twelve he had fathered before beginning his quarter-century sojourn in the Buddhist priesthood. More than sixty of them were living at the end of his reign in 1868. In 1910, the year of King Chulalongkorn's death, at least twenty remained alive, including the ministers of Foreign Affairs, War, Interior, and Public

Works. Meanwhile, King Chulalongkorn had fathered about twenty sons, of whom two, H. R. H. Krom Mun Rabipattanasak, the Prince of Rajaburi, Direkridhi, and H. R. H. Krom Mun, the Prince of Chantaburi, Narunatr, were, respectively, ministers of Justice and Finance. Perhaps twenty additional princes, sons of Rama IV and Rama V, held official positions in the government. And at this time, three ministries—Capital, Public Instruction, and Agriculture—were under the command of commoners.[4]

The staffing pattern was no simple reflection of royal patronage and nepotism, although this was to be more nearly true under Rama VI. It was consistent with tradition, of course. But in planning the reorganization of 1892, King Chulalongkorn had placed great stress upon the ability of those who were to be in charge of the new ministries. The royal family was a universe from which a portion of a class of personnel was drawn. The arrangement had numerous advantages, one of them stemming from the fact that King Mongkut had begun the practice of systematically educating his male offspring, so that the royal family contained a sizeable number of young men of exceptional competence.

FOREIGN PERSONNEL

A second pattern of personnel procurement was the recruitment of foreigners. Foreign officials provided most of the expertise initially lacking in the Thai bureaucracy. This enabled the government to move along with its development efforts before Thais had been trained for a host of specialized jobs. It also facilitated training. The foreign officials developed new organizations, trained personnel, and generally prepared the way for Thais who were to follow them.

Foreign advisers were of great importance in the modernization of Thai government and the shaping of its policies.[5] In the use of advisers, "although there was no firm rule about it, there tended to be a correlation between post and nationality. Thus, the General Adviser [after Jaequermyns] was always an American, the Financial Adviser was always British, and the Legislative Adviser was always French. On the whole, however, the British tended to predominate." [6] But foreigners were by no means limited to the role of advising the king and his ministers. For every adviser there were several dozen foreign officials working as teachers, technicians, and administrators.

A careful study of the available records of the employment of foreign officials indentifies 549 persons who served the Thai government during the reign of King Chulalongkorn (1868–1910), most of them in the 1880s or later. In the aggregate, they furnished several thousand man-years of service.

These foreigners filled the gap between the commitments and the administrative capacities of the post-Reformation government. Foreigners actually dominated the managerial levels of many, if not most, of the new administrative agencies. They set the tone of administration, and their contribution to the central values of the new bureaucracy defies description.

Foreigners were recruited in a variety of ways. James McCarthy, the builder of the Royal Survey Department, was hired on the basis of contact when he was running surveys for British colonial government. M. Rolin-Jaequermyns was encountered by Prince Damrong in Egypt; the former had gone there to see about a post, which had failed to open up. Missionaries and members of their families were hired in some cases. There was no particular system for recruiting and selecting foreign officials. A need developed, advice was sought from those at hand, and someone was hired. This person might then serve as a recruiter of additional foreigners, until, in some cases, whole cadres were built up. Pay was generally subject to negotiation conditioned by precedent, and was often—but not always—generous.

In 1908 and 1909, about three hundred foreigners were in the employ of the Thai government.[7] More than thirty were teachers or educational administrators. Others occupied important positions in the Thai Navy. The director and deputy director of the Royal Survey Department were Australian and British, respectively, and the departmental staff included seventeen other Europeans. The director-general of the Royal Irrigation Department and the top management of the Posts and Telegraphs Department were also European. Except for a few engineering and medical posts, however, the Army was staffed entirely by Thais, although the military academy in which officers were trained had been developed by Italian Colonel G. E. Gerini, who was also an authority on the history and archeology of Southeast Asia.[8] (Other Thai officers were trained in Europe.) More than one hundred foreign officials held managerial posts in the Thai bureaucracy, and of these about a third were the directors or assistant directors of government departments or the equivalent. In the Royal

Foreign Officials of the Thai Government, 1909

General advisers, in foreign affairs, finance, agriculture, etc.	6
General financial agent of the government	1
Lesser advisers, in education, etc.	
Legal advisers, probationary legal advisers, and assistants	21
Director-generals of departments or equivalent	13
Assistant director-generals or equivalent	23
Foreigners engaged in administrative work at the level immediately below departmental management, including various inspectors	69
Architects and engineers, civil, mechanical, etc., not otherwise classified	51
Other engineering-type technicians	40
Educators not otherwise classified	14
Lawyers not otherwise classified	12
Naval ship captains	4
Assistants to naval ship captains	2
Naval engineering officers	2
Dredge masters	4
Harbor vessel captain	1
Medical doctors not otherwise classified	6
Sericulture specialists (Japanese)	3
Statisticians	2
Accountants not otherwise classified	2
Chemists not otherwise classified	2
Nurse	1
Veterinarian	1
Interpreter	1
Locomotive engineers	15
Embassy councilors	3
Embassy secretaries	5
Embassy attaché	1
Consuls general	8
Total	319

SOURCE: Wm. W. Fegen, *The Siam Directory*, R.S. 129 (1910) (Bangkok: Siam Observer Press, 1910).

Railways Department, foreigners worked at jobs ranging from loco-
motive engineer to top management.

Three implicit policies governed the use of foreign officials: they
were expected to be able; they were not to offer any threat to the
sovereignty of Thailand; and they were not to have final control over
major policies of the nation.

Of course, some of the advisers and officials had much influence
on policy, as competent and creative administrators always do. They
did not establish ultimate organizational goals, but they set the real
content of many of those goals. And they largely determined the administrative values to be sustained—efficiency, honesty, accuracy,
speed, and so on. They sometimes piqued their Thai associates; they
were perhaps as often frustrated as challenged by the conditions
which prevailed. But they were usually supported at the uppermost
levels of the government.

Generally, the foreign officials were accepted and respected. They
were regarded as serving the government, rather than running it. But
in a few cases, high-ranking foreign advisers exerted great influence
over the central policies and aims of the state.

After the thrust of the Reformation was spent, in the mid-1920s,
Francis B. Sayre, the foreign adviser, and Prince Traidos Prabandh,
the Minister of Foreign Affairs, jointly negotiated treaties with
France, Britain, the Netherlands, the Scandinavian countries, Italy,
Spain, and Portugal, under which these European nations abandoned
the extraterritoriality and other privileges established in the mid-
nineteenth-century Bowring Treaty and those which followed it.[9] In
these negotiations, Sayre exercised vast authority with great deftness
—but within clear policy lines.

During the Chakkri Reformation and afterward, the British financial adviser, W. J. F. Williamson, who served from 1903 to 1924,
exercised great influence over Thai fiscal policy. His conservativism
may have retarded the development of the nation's resources in the
first decades of the twentieth century, although it assured the soundness of the Thai fiscal position. Later, in the 1920s, the tenor of the
financial advice received by King Prajadhipok certainly produced no
boldness in dealing with the relatively moderate financial difficulties in
which the kingdom was then involved. In short, foreign advisers did
not formally control major policy, but their influence sometimes
verged on control.

In the first phase of the Chakkri Reformation, the foreigners were essential. The best of them made impressive contributions to Thai administration, and to the world's knowledge of Thailand as well. They were the secular missionaries of the late nineteenth and the twentieth centuries, who extended the efforts of their clerical predecessors to new fields—preaching and teaching and practicing, under official auspices, Western administrative art and technology rather than Western religion, albeit from different motives than those of the clerics. Most of them subscribed implicitly to productivity norms, and foreign officials in the aggregate helped shape and sustain the new bureaucratic processes to contribute greatly to the rationality of their organizations.

By 1910 significant progress had also been made in the production of a corps of Thai technicians and administrators. Apart from the Royal Railways Department, Thais occupied more than twice as many upper and top-level technical and administrative posts as did foreigners. The most critical need for foreign officials was beginning to pass.

Foreign officials were employed during the reign of King Chulalongkorn's successors, King Vajiravudh and King Prajadhipok, but the total number declined during the second decade of the twentieth century and dropped sharply in the 1920s.

THE ROYAL PAGES SCHOOL AND THE PROCUREMENT OF EXECUTIVES

One of the most interesting aspects of personnel procurement in the reconstructed bureaucracy was the adaptation of the ancient institution of the royal pages to fit new needs for qualified personnel.[10]

In a simpler era, high-ranking officials of the central administration had almost invariably come from the ranks of the royal family and from among the royal pages. But by 1898 the royal pages formed an insignificant part of the upper structure of a growing bureaucracy. The traditional training of royal pages was by this time of limited value. It did not produce officials competent in the functionally specialized work of the new ministries.

Prince Damrong proposed an arrangement to retain the advantages of the tradition while adapting the training to current needs. He saw the institution of the royal pages as enhancing the position and power of the king in relation to the administrative system, as well as contributing to the loyalty and competence of officials. The royal page "would be able to enter society and . . . to learn the customs and good manners of high dignitaries . . . , and also to make friends with other royal pages."

Damrong suggested establishment of a school in the Royal Pages Department of the palace "to teach the rudiments of work in the various ministries, to enable the students to become known to the king and to allow them to learn the customs of the court." Following this training, the pages could be sent to work in the various ministries, and if satisfactory would be commissioned officers in the king's service. King Chulalongkorn concurred, and asked Damrong to manage the school. The prince countered with the observation that the school should be independent of the various ministries. The following year (1899), when Prince Damrong's former secretary, Phraya Visutsuriyasak (later Chao Phraya Prasadet), returned from Europe where he had been instructor to the King's sons, he was appointed dean of the new school, which until 1902 was attached to the Ministry of Interior.

Admission was limited to males between the ages of fifteen and twenty, "of notable families or of means suitable to permit them to become royal pages." According to the initial plans for the school, numbers were to be restricted to the estimated needs of the ministries —from fifty to one hundred persons at most. Training would be divided into three successive parts, each of a year's duration. Students successful in their study of the initial phase (basic knowledge required of public officials) would be presented to the king and designated royal pages. They were then to study the organization and activities of his court. Finally, they would be trained in particular ministries.[11]

As the school evolved, the training program was modified. Several years elapsed before the number of students reached the upper number initially envisioned. Contemplated training in the work of the various ministries actually became training in the work of the Ministry of Interior, whose staff needs were great and whose appreciation of the values of these students was acute.

The first year's course came to consist of the study of clerical practice in the civil service; duties of royal pages and royal page reporters; Thai, Pali, and English languages; history; geography; mathematics; and ethics.[12] The intermediate term became a practical study of governmental policy and administration, using documents borrowed from the Ministry of Interior. The third year included a rigorous three-month course in field training and physical development, suggestive of the basic training of modern military organization. Students hiked and camped in the field, even learned to cook. They jumped fences and ditches, rode and cared for horses, were trained in the use of arms, learned to make maps, and were sent out at night on cross-country trips in which they were required to carry a document to an assigned point, have it stamped, and return within a specified time.

Six students were graduated in the first class of the school and sent out to work in the provinces.[13] They were placed under the supervision of the *monthon* commissioner and his deputy, and designated as "royal page reporters." In this capacity they were responsible for inspecting the various provinces. In these ways they became intimately familiar with the country and the people. The Ministry of Interior established two positions as royal page reporter for each *monthon,* and these became the posts into which products of the Royal Pages School moved without further examination before advancing into higher level administrative duties.

The Royal Pages School became the Civil Service School in 1911, and an element of the newly formed Chulalongkorn University in 1916. Under King Vajiravudh, the royal pages once again became the personal servants of the king and were detached from the mainstream of administration. But in the first years of the twentieth century, the institution of the royal pages was an invaluable means of procuring personnel for the *tesapiban* system—as well as an apt and charming adaptation of the resources of tradition to the needs of a new era.

THE GENERAL PATTERN OF PERSONNEL PROCUREMENT

The Royal Pages School was relatively small. It could meet only one part of the new bureaucracy's personnel needs. Foreign officials were vital, but their use was considered a transitory arrangement for helping to staff the administrative agencies. Royalty, even in a polygamous kingdom, could not begin to meet personnel needs at the upper levels of the bureaucracy.

The personnel needs of the Chakkri Reformation ultimately had to be met by recruits from the population at large. By the turn of the century, the civil service was staffed by several thousand clerks, artisans, and semiskilled and unskilled laborers, and was only beginning to expand. The procurement of these bureaucratic laborers was greatly facilitated by the tradition of Buddhist education. In 1908, for example, there were known to be 13,049 Buddhist temples in Thailand, with 94,000 priests and more than 150,000 novices and pupils. More than a thousand temples had regular classes for teaching young boys, and 336 had organized schools.[14] Temple education was, at best, basic. But it afforded the fundamentals of literacy to a small army of future clerks and officials, and it became the foundation of a national system of mass education in the twentieth century.[15] Meanwhile, advanced educational institutions in Bangkok were beginning to turn out a growing number of professionally and technically specialized officials.

Patterns of intake developed and became standardized in the course of the administrative reformation. The principle of a career service was adopted unquestioningly from tradition. Along with it came the idea of a bureaucracy with two broad classes of permanent officials—those of *sanyabat,* or commissioned, rank, and the lesser officials, some of whom might rise to commissioned rank. In addition, there was a third category of officialdom—the *wisaman,* or non-status employees—casuals, probationers, and others who had not qualified for ranked positions.

From the outset of reform, personnel intake tended to occur at or near the bottom of promotional ladders (except, of course, for the limited number of high-level positions filled by royalty or by foreigners). The promotion ladders were generally expressed in the terminology of the ancient hierarchy of ranks, adapted more or less pragmatically to particular organizations. Tendencies quickly developed to link entry levels with educational attainments. With the rapid expansion of the bureaucracy, upward movement was often rapid and opportunities were numerous.

PERSONNEL PROCUREMENT IN THE MINISTRY OF INTERIOR

The practices that developed in the Ministry of Interior are worth examining: the Ministry was the largest civilian unit of government, and its methods tended to spread throughout the bureaucracy.

Large numbers of low-level officials were hired directly in the provinces; *sanyabat* officials were appointed to the bottom levels of a well-defined hierarchy of administrators on the basis of prior education; and training and experience requirements for advancement were explicit. Examinations came to be used to determine eligibility for promotion and were extended to use in initial selection.

The process evolved in a simple, practical fashion in response to a concern at the top level of the organization with the effective accomplishment of results. Periodic assessment of the selection process occurred at annual *tesapiban* conferences, where past experience was assessed, current problems were examined, and new procedures were determined. Within the organic limitations imposed by the environment, there was much freedom to experiment and modify.

The great problem of the Ministry of Interior in the first two decades of its reconstruction was to find competent persons willing to work in primitive provincial surroundings far away from the capital. Various incentives were used to overcome this resistance—the provision of housing, preferential pay rates outside the capital (allowances of certain kinds were paid to officials outside Bangkok), the requirement of field experience as a basis for advancement in the service of the Ministry (many of the best opportunities for promotion existed in the field rather than at headquarters, in any case), and the procurement of field personnel as much as possible from the field rather than from Bangkok.

According to my observation it is difficult to acquire suitable and adequate personnel from Bangkok [for deputy district officer positions]. As a matter of fact, every monthon has sufficient personnel for its own use, both clerks and deputy officers. Monthon officials sometimes emphasize knowledge to the exclusion of intelligence in selection. They fail to recognize that an intelligent person can always acquire knowledge. Go to the schools and temples. In making their inspection, governors and district officers should search for persons of courtesy and intelligence and persuade them to be trained.[16]

By 1904 a definite career pattern had been established in the *tesapiban* system. At district office level the various clerks were under the supervision of the two deputy district officers. In 1903 these two deputies had been designated "the deputy of the left hand" and "the deputy of the right hand," the lesser-paid former being responsible for the routines of the district office, including clerical supervision. A vacancy in this post would be filled by the most suitable clerk. The deputy of the left hand would be eligible for promotion to higher-paid deputy of the right hand, whose work entailed inspection and patrol.

District officer positions would be filled from among the right-hand deputies. In 1904, after a year's experimentation, Prince Damrong commented that this pattern "proved quite satisfactory, in contradiction to original expectations." [17]

In 1904 it was also agreed that the general line of advancement for district officers would be to the position of head of the interior division of the provincial headquarters, and that either district officers or these division heads would be the source of appointments as provincial governors.

During the first decade of the twentieth century, selection and training were linked by a system of examinations. By 1907 four categories of officials had been established within the field service of the *tesapiban* system—clerks, "reserve officials," and second- and first-class officials.[18] Admittance to each category was by examination, and the examinations were based upon previous courses of study.

Clerks were grouped into two elements, first and second class. "Reserve officials" were clerks who had passed an examination indicating their competence to perform at least one specialized phase of provincial administration at the second-class level. These officials had become eligible for appointment to work in at least one particular functionally specialized facet of provincial government—prosecution of criminals, revenue administration, interior administration, treasury administration, and so forth. They constituted a "stand-by" group.

Second-class officials had established their competence, by examination or otherwise, in at least three of the above categories of work. This group consisted of assistant district officers and district officers but reserve officials might also be appointed to deputy-level posts in districts or provinces.

First-class officials were those with established competence in the same fields as second-class officials, but at a higher level of knowledge and evident ability. They served in some cases as district officer, but also as assistant governor, provincial or *monthon* prosecutor, provincial or *monthon* interior division head, or chiefs of such divisions as revenue at the provincial or *monthon* levels.

A series of regulations formally sanctioned this pattern of personnel procurement and ordering in 1907, and prescribed the examination arrangements to be used in personnel procurement.

For reserve and second-class positions, examinations were conducted by committees within the various *monthons*. The *monthon* commissioner or a provincial governor designated by him chaired each committee; the other members (not more than four) were comprised of such personnel as *monthon* division heads. *Monthon* commissioners were to arrange such examinations at their discretion. The examinations were to cover both "practical" and "technical" materials, the latter being defined as laws, rules, and regulations. Practical aspects of the examination dealt with particular facets of the work of the functionally specialized *tesapiban* system.

A system of registers was established on the basis of these examinations. Their use was generally confined to the particular *monthon* in which the selection process operated, but duplicates were maintained in the headquarters of the ministry. In appointment from the registers, knowledge as evidenced by examination was to be the prime criterion of selection. In cases of equal knowledge, seniority was to apply. Preference in filling the better posts was to be granted to those who had high examination scores and who had also demonstrated a wide range of knowledge—ideally those who had passed the examinations covering each phase of the functionally specialized administrative work of *tesapiban* government.

The 1907 regulations also applied to clerks. Each province was required to offer at least one clerical examination annually.

Examinations for appointment to first-class positions were placed directly within the jurisdiction of the Ministry of Interior, whose headquarters determined the dates, places, and content of examinations, evaluated the results, and maintained the resulting registers.

Thus did a series of techniques for personnel procurement quickly evolve into a complex process. From the beginning, the prime emphasis was to select officials on the basis of the available measures of competence. But all the regulations were qualified by provisions that "those who have special merit can be instated in any position in accordance with their merit." The Thai word for "merit" has a meaning sufficiently broad to cover the idea of "status," and even "connections."

Yet the general tenor of these selection provisions was quite consistent with the objectives of the Chakkri Reformation. During most of the first two decades of the twentieth century, when the chief problem of personnel procurement was finding a sufficient supply of able persons for an expanding service, the selection procedures seemed to work well. Later, as expansion tapered off while the available supply of personnel increased, the competition for appointment and promotion became intense. The stress upon knowledge as a basis for selection increased, and the emphasis upon the functional utility of that knowledge declined. Selection became more and more ritualized.

In the Ministry of Interior and elsewhere, personnel procurement was established as a "line" function of administration, and it has largely remained one to the present day. The eventual creation of a central personnel system produced no drastic shift in the methods of selection, and even now one can readily discern in the present pattern its antecedents.

New Skills and Knowledge for the Bureaucracy

In the last years of the nineteenth century the personnel needs of the reconstructed bureaucracy were the most significant stimulus of educational development. The traditional bureaucracy had been the means by which a man might advance in power, prestige, and wealth. Now the system was open as never before. And education was the key to access to the system.

High social status and the good fortune of residing in Bangkok enhanced access to education, but education was not regarded as the right of a privileged minority. It was perceived as intrinsically good, but the prime emphasis upon the development of educational facilities was to meet the needs of the expanding bureaucracy.

The Civil Service School, an outgrowth of the Royal Pages School, was established by King Vajiravudh to expand the array of talent available to the governmental ministries. In 1911 about one million baht remained from a popular subscription to construct an equestrian statue of King Chulalongkorn. King Vajiravudh gave the money and a large piece of land for the expansion of the Royal Pages School into "The School of His Majesty King Chulalongkorn for Civil Service Officers." Prince Damrong was appointed chairman of the directing committee of the school, and Phraya Sivoravongsa remained as dean, but the new mandate was clear: the enterprise should produce officials for all the civilian ministries.

Five years later, in 1916, the Civil Service School was abruptly incorporated into a new edifice, Chulalongkorn University, created by combining the Civil Service School with faculties of medicine, arts and sciences, and engineering drawn from existing institutions.[19] The sharp focus of the earlier pre-service training was blunted, but the school gradually overcame its early problems as the quality of primary education in Thailand improved beginning in the 1920s, and became a prime source of entrants into the commissioned officer ranks of the civil service until after the 1932 coup.

A College of Agriculture was established about 1907 to train officials for the Ministry of Lands and Agriculture. In 1908 it had thirty-two pupils, but with the death of the young European-trained prince who was to develop this important ministry, both the school and the ministry languished until about 1920.[20] The Royal Survey School, an outgrowth of the survey work of the 1880s, continued until its eventual assimilation into the Ministry of War. It was the source of the surveyors essential to the establishment of the modern land title registration system.

Other advanced schools for training civil servants grew out of the Chakkri Reformation, including the Post and Telegraph School and the Gendarmerie School. In 1908 all of these schools had a total of 231 students enrolled, of whom almost half (111) were in the Royal Pages School.[21] In the same year, a total enrollment of 1,130 was reported in the Royal Military College and the Royal Naval College, the majority of the students being enrolled in the cadet school of the Military College, actually a military prep school.

In 1908 the Teachers' College, nominally established in 1892, had about sixty students, and the Royal Medical College, founded in 1890, had an enrollment of 109.

By the beginning of the twentieth century, facilities for advanced education, most of it preparatory to bureaucratic careers, were not entirely limited to the above schools. There were several other "colleges" in Bangkok and one at Chiengmai.

The scope of education for the bureaucracy was enlarged when King Chulalongkorn began sending his sons abroad to study. His example was followed by others, and various of the new administrative organizations established from the 1880s also sent trainees abroad.

In 1896 His Majesty established an annual foreign scholarship competition, supplemented by the selection of additional students to study in particular fields.[22] Between 1898 and 1907, thirty-eight students returned from foreign scholarship studies, and only three were reported as having been unsatisfactory students. At the end of 1907, twenty-seven students were studying in England under the jurisdiction of the Ministry of Public Instruction, and the total number of Thai students abroad in any of these early years of the century was probably between fifty and one hundred.

Foreign study was well supported. Before World War I, the average scholar abroad received about $1,500 per year. Winners of the competitive scholarships were permitted to study in fields of their own choice, and the duration of their scholarships—nominally three years—was more often limited by the quality of their performance and the requirements of their particular programs. Students not uncommonly remained abroad for five years or more, and customarily returned to enter the bureaucracy.

During the reign of King Vajiravudh, superintendents of foreign students were appointed by His Majesty and attached to the Thai legations at London, Paris, and Washington to supervise overseas scholars.[23]

These efforts produced a small but growing supply of teachers, lawyers, engineers, military specialists, and other technicians. No less significant, and much larger in numbers affected, was the development within the bureaucracy of arrangements for service-related training.

TRAINING IN THE MINISTRY OF INTERIOR

In 1899, the shortage of qualified personnel for work at the district level of the *tesapiban* system became the chief impediment to the expansion of the new pattern of domestic government. As a result, a School of Amphur Affairs was established at Monthon Ayudhya, and various other experiments with the training of lower-level officials were inaugurated.[24]

The Ayudhya school was to train persons assigned by ministry headquarters as well as three students from each of the existing *monthons,* up to a total of fifty. Its program was composed of three phases—prep training for students whose general education was deficient, a course in the system of government, and a course in administration. The school was to issue a certificate making the recipient eligible for appointment to commissioned (*sanyabat*) rank.

Other *monthons* were given the option of establishing similar training facilities, and two did so—Phitsanulok and Prachinburi. These three *monthons* became known as "teaching *monthons.*" But they could not meet the needs for trained personnel.

Job rotation training was tried. Courses of study were set up at all *monthon* headquarters, and selected clerks and reserve officers were given work-study training in regular administrative posts of district government, with experienced district officers doing the training in addition to their usual duties. This program spread rapidly, but like all the innovations of the Damrong administration it was carefully assessed, and at the *tesapiban* conference of 1902 it was judged "not very beneficial. It was difficult to acquire satisfactory teachers. Those who studied . . . did not really *know* what they had studied . . ." and the whole arrangement was wasteful of time.

Meanwhile, in Ayudhya an effective program was emerging, focused upon training *seriatim* in the specific duties and responsibilities of each of the functionally specialized divisions of *monthon* organization, which were replicated at a lower level in the provincial and district facets of the system. Training materials were developed— outlines of functions, supplemented by citations of relevant rules and laws. These evolved into a famous volume, the *Golden Book,* containing, in addition to study materials, space for noting the time devoted by the individual student to each subject, and for attesting the results of his examination over the material. The students worked as clerks in the division under study, and thus gradually moved through a work-study course covering the basic functions of the *tesapiban* system. Upon completion of sectors of the program, one could achieve eligibility as a reserve officer or second-class official. Graduates usually became deputy district officers. Exceptionally talented students who had also passed a special section of the course dealing with the work of the public prosecutor became eligible for appointment as district officers.

Out of the Ayudhya school, and the Phitsanulok program which appears to have resembled it, came a training pattern which spread in the following years.[25] The *Golden Book* became the chief training device, given to students and clerical level officials and used as a basis for the examinations mentioned earlier.

The training pattern of the Ministry of Interior proved effective. It produced officials with the necessary skills and knowledge, and it was emulated elsewhere in the bureaucracy. Training, like selection, became established as a "line" function of administration, intimately related to promotion. A generation of officials was produced in this fashion during the era of bureaucratic expansion.

In 1921 the Compulsory Education Law was promulgated, leading to a great rise in the number of students—more than 600,000 outside of Bangkok by 1928. During the 1920s the civil bureaucracy, no longer growing, was meeting its needs for qualified personnel through its training programs and by the appointment of the small number of graduates of external educational facilities. An unfortunate problem of phasing inevitably arose: the scope of education had grown, and the number of those expecting bureaucratic careers, after the bureaucracy had stopped expanding. An impasse was inevitable: "In October 1932 it was found that the examination for junior civil servants had been passed by no less than 1,000 candidates, a number far exceeding that of the available openings." [26]

The Ordering of Personal Relations in the New Bureaucracy

The coherence of an organization requires that relationships among its participants be defined and controlled to conform to the agency's aims and instrumental values. Explicit formal arrangements for ordering personal relationships form an important part of the framework within which these associations take place in any persisting bureaucratic entity. Organizations classify jobs—and their incumbents—in various ways, and spell out patterns of authority, information transmission, and work flow, in an attempt to establish stable patterns of appropriate activity. A complex administrative system will include a variety of arrangements for ordering the relations among its various participants.

In traditional Thailand, the primary means by which relations were defined was the elaborate, encompassing hierarchical structure. The strategy of bureaucratic reform was to bend this traditional arrangement to new aims and values.

As the Reformation proceeded, an undeniable need for rationalizing the old status structure emerged, for it was substantially disrupted by the expansion of the bureaucracy. But continued reliance upon the hierarchical principle as the prime basis for defining and ordering relationships was unquestioned. Hierarchy was a "given," a central feature of the social system, a source of identity for the official participants in that system. The hierarchical structure reflected and expressed the authority of the king, which was the moving force behind the Reformation. And hierarchy is a basic device for defining and controlling relationships among participants in any complex administrative organization.

The hierarchical tradition facilitated bureaucratic reconstruction; here was an established, legitimate means for formally relating an unlimited number of participants and units of organization. But the old hierarchical arrangement had been more than a chain of command, and less than an administrative integrative mechanism. It had nurtured and sustained diffuse relationships among face-to-face groups, relationships not particularly compatible with the needs of complex, purposive organizations. And it had been the prime source of all status, to the exclusion of professional identity or functional competence.

A big question facing the architects of reform, then, was simply this: *Could* the traditional status-based hierarchical arrangement be adapted to the needs of a goal-attainment bureaucracy? The question was never asked, of course, but it was answered in the course of the Chakkri Reformation and its aftermath.

Bureaucratic reconstruction included an effort to redefine the terms by which status might be attained—to make it a reward for actual or potential contributions to the aims of an organization. To the extent that this actually occurred, status became a function of duties and responsibilities and the adequacy with which these were executed. In effect, this reduced the diffuseness of the ancient pattern of role relations by making them more job-centered.

To some extent, too, status came to be linked with functional and organizational identifications. To be a judge in the great days of Prince Rabi's ministry was to possess a sense of prestige that stemmed from the dignity of the position. To be an official of the Ministry of Interior under Prince Damrong was also to derive a sense of status from identification with the organization.

But no contrapuntal patterns for ascribing status developed during the Reformation to really offset the dominance of hierarchy. The tradition-sanctioned, still relevant hierarchical arrangement was both a tool and a limitation—a tool for patterning organizational relations, and an impediment to any patterns which were non-hierarchical. The old hierarchical status system was rationalized and adapted, but it was never transcended.

RATIONALIZING THE STATUS SYSTEM

The old status system was exquisitely complex. To determine the precise rank of a particular person in the middle or upper reaches of the society, one had to engage in an involved form of ratiocination, taking into account the following factors:

(1) *Yot,* or personal titles, such as *chaophraya, phraya, phra, luang, khun,* and *mun. Yot* distinctions were hierarchical, and personal. The title was held by the individual, who also had, in most cases, a *rajadhinnam,* or an official name bestowed by the king. The title was customarily granted, along with the name, in connection with appointment to a particular position. (Thus, Nai, or Mr., Seng Wiriyasiri was assigned to work with Mr. James McCarthy in the Royal Survey Department and given the title of *luang,* and the official name of Tesachit Pichan. Then, in 1892, he was transferred to the Ministry of Interior at Prince Damrong's request, upgraded to the title of *phraya,* and given the name of SriSahatep. Rising in the Ministry, he eventually became deputy minister, keeping the title of *phraya,* but acquiring a new *rajadhinnam*—Maha-ammarathyatibordi —indicating his high position and commanding great respect.) [27]

(2) *Tamnaeng,* or official position, to which a *sakdi na* number was ascribed. Rosters of positions had been maintained for centuries, and on these lists individual posts were related in terms of their *sakdi na* levels, which were, in turn, intended to reflect the powers and duties of the post.

(3) *Decorations.* Beginning in 1851, King Mongkut had adopted the Western practice of granting decorations. King Chulalongkorn had expanded the practice. Decorations were important and obvious signs of status, worn on uniforms which varied according to the *yot* and *tamnaeng* of the individual.

(4) *Seniority.* Given two persons of otherwise identical status, the older man in years at rank was senior.

By the end of the 1890s, the ancient status system was breaking down. Function and rank had come unglued; discrepancies between personal status and bureaucratic position had become numerous enough to be troublesome. It was sometimes difficult to ascertain the actual status of a particular official, because the relationship between *yot,* or title, and *tamnaeng,* or position, became chaotic as the bureaucracy expanded. Rank as indicated by title was no longer fully coordinated with rank as indicated by position in the bureaucracy.

In 1901 King Chulalongkorn attempted to bring some order into this situation by a royal decree governing titles and decorations.[28] A distinction was noted between *sanyabat* and *pratuan* titles, the latter being awarded by ministers and having less prestige. The King asserted that bureaucratic position and performance were to be the chief criteria of eligibility for a certain rank.

At the *tesapiban* meeting of that year, Prince Damrong laid down some rules for the award of titles to officials of the Ministry of Interior. "Titles," he said, "are something fostering virtue." Thus titles should not be granted to confer high rank upon a subordinate, reducing the authority of his supervisor. Further, titles should not be conferred upon officials unable to maintain a suitable degree of dignity in dress and manner. Finally, the mere fact that a particular position involved a rank for which a particular title was customary was not to mean that the title should be granted automatically; ability and suitability should first be determined, and then the title granted should be the lowest appropriate for the post.

Within the ministry a formal procedure for awarding titles was adopted. *Monthon* commissioners were to submit nominations to the minister, indicating in each case the compatability of the proposed title with the position occupied by the intended recipient, his qualifications, length of service, and the particular reasons for the nomination. An official was not to receive more than one "title promotion" within three years. Later, Prince Damrong ordered that any person nominated for title promotions must first submit to an examination at ministry headquarters. The effect and the intent of these efforts to regularize the issuance of titles was to eliminate confusion, and to make titles a motivating device as well as a means of ordering relations within the bureaucracy.

As the Reformation progressed, titles and positions were brought back into appropriate relation, as an encompassing rank-classification system emerged. King Chulalongkorn grouped all civil and military officials into three broad *yot* classes—first, second, and third. The status, or *sakdi na,* levels of practically all positions was standardized. Positions were divided between "commissioned" and "noncommissioned," to match the pattern of *sanyabat* and *pratuan* titles.

Noncommissioned personnel, appointed by ministry officials, included *rajaburut* officers, equivalent to noncommissioned officers in the military, and *samianphanak-ngan,* the lowest level of clerical and service workers.

In 1911 King Vajiravudh further clarified relations between titles, ranks, and positions. He created a series of twelve *yot* levels covering all but the lowest civil officials. These amounted to a structure of rank classification, which was equated with the existing military ranks as indicated in the following table:

Yot Levels Under the Acts of 1911

Level	Yot Designation	Military Rank Equivalent
1st	*maha-ammat-nayok*	field marshal
2nd	*maha-ammat-ek*	general
3rd	*maha-ammat-tho*	lieutenant general
4th	*maha-ammat-tri*	major general
5th	*ammat-ek*	colonel
6th	*ammat-tho*	lieutenant colonel
7th	*ammat-tri*	major
8th	*rong-ammat-ek*	captain
9th	*rong-ammat-tho*	lieutenant
10th	*rong-ammat-tri*	sublieutenant
11th	*wathi-rong-ammat-tri*	acting sublieutenant
12th	*rajaburut*	sergeant major

SOURCE: Chakra Hansakul, "A Study of Pay Policy and Administration in the Thai Civil Service" (Master's thesis, Thammasat University, 1959), p. 66

The former *yot,* or personal status titles, such as *chao phraya, phraya, phra, luang,* and *khun,* were now separated from positional status and regarded as expressions of personal dignity (*bandasakdi*). And the new *yot* designations, indicating hierarchical level in the bureaucracy, were treated as more important signs of status than the honorific *bandasakdi* titles. *Yot* levels were indicated by a standardized system of uniforms established at the same time.

Officials who retired from the civil service retained their *yot* and *bandasakdi*.[29] In 1931, when financial difficulties led to cutbacks in the civil service, pensioned officials were explicitly granted permission to continue to wear uniforms indicating their personal *yot,* suggesting that this was a matter of considerable significance to them.[30]

This rationalizing evolution was an inevitable consequence of the growth of the civil service as well as the change in its basic character. In the Ayudhyan tradition, "A man was his title and nothing more and his title rested upon royal pleasure." [31] Yet the depersonalized system was at the same time exquisitely personal. Title manipulation had been a means of controlling the old bureaucracy in a system which had largely functioned upon the basis of personal relationships. The king gave meaning to all things below him. He bestowed rank and perquisites, or withdrew them, and the actions were thoroughly personal. They were directed toward particular individuals, on the basis of particular assessments of them and their acts.

With the Chakkri Reformation this arrangement simply broke down. A large number of specialized organizations was not inconsistent with the old hierarchical principle, but sheer numbers of officials prevented the king from giving personal attention to details of official rank and status; he could no longer even know his own royal pages.

To accommodate the old ranking system to the new bureaucracy, it had to be made capable of more or less regularized, impersonal application. In the course of its adjustment, it did not lose its inherent potency. The appeal of status to the members of the bureaucracy remained great.

In this system the very phrase, "the ordering of personal relations," had a nuance of its own, a heightened emphasis upon the word "personal." The ranks and statuses bestowed by the system were obtained through the contingent possession of a particular office, but they were nonetheless personal. One continued to defer to a superior and to expect similar behavior from a subordinate. Superiority-subordination remained the essential basis for the posture of interpersonal relations.

Hierarchically defined status, the prime mechanism for ordering personal relations in the bureaucracy, was also a primary means of motivating the participants in the system. Analytically, it was multifunctional, as it had been for ages. But the way it affected behavior depended upon the kinds of performance which were rewarded or punished.

As the rank-and-status system evolved in the course of the Chakkri

Reformation, the Palace Ministry began to function as the prototype of a personnel agency. It maintained records of titles and decorations, reviewed proposals for conferring awards upon individuals, and prepared the commissions issued to *sanyabat* officials by the king.

The Ministry of Finance, as it acquired control over expenditures around the turn of the century, also helped sustain the system. By about 1901, when the first budget was published, detailed regulations began to be developed to govern pay, the establishment of new positions, and the granting of salary increases. Adjustments in the status of a bureaucrat which affected his position and his pay had to be approved by the Ministry of Finance. What had once been a grandly capricious arrangement for the personal manipulation of subordinates by an autocratic monarch was now reduced to a matter of forms and clearances. But it had not lost its meaning in the course of its modification. A deep and abiding tension persisted between personal drives to achieve status and the aim of using rank as a reward for functional contributions to the bureaucracy. This tension was controlled for a while by great administrators, but it was gradually eased as time went by, the reconstructed administrative system became routinized, and the great leadership of the reform era left the scene.

The Motivation of Participants in the Bureaucratic System

The Ayudhyan bureaucracy had resembled a somewhat tumultuous cluster of primary groups.[32] Achievement was rewarded, and behavior was guided by a thorough and precise definition of status, but "achievement was not seen as a function of ability and job performance but as a matter of observing formalities and possessing skill in gaining royal favor"—or the favor of a powerful superior.[33] Self-interest was not served by high dedication to productivity values.

The Chakkri Reformation sought to assert new norms and to enforce them by appropriate bureaucratic mechanisms.

THE SALARY SYSTEM

A high degree of standardization of pay had been achieved by the beginning of the twentieth century.[34] Between 1892 and 1898 the Ministry of Interior had evolved a comprehensive salary plan, and during the same period the Ministry of Finance had established control over governmental finances, including salary disbursements. In 1898 King Chulalongkorn established a committee to make a comprehensive survey of the duties, responsibilities, and salaries of all positions in the civil service. Tables of organization were drawn up and positions were allotted to specified rank-pay classes under the guidance of British financial advisers. The regularizing of salaries is evidenced by the following schedule issued by the Ministry of Interior in 1900 governing salaries in Monthon Phayap.[35]

Positions, Grades, Salaries, and Salary Increments in Monthon Phayap

Position		Monthly Salary (in baht) Minimum	Maximum	Annual Increment (baht per month)
Monthon governor	1st grade	1,200	1,600	200
Monthon governor	2nd grade	1,000	1,200	100
Monthon deputy governor	1st grade	900	1,000	50
" " "	2nd grade	500	600	50
" " "	3rd grade	300	400	50
Provincial governor	1st grade	700	800	50
" "	2nd grade	500	600	50
" "	3rd grade	300	400	50
Governor of area less than province	1st grade	500	600	50
" " " " "	2nd grade	300	400	50
" " " " "	3rd grade	200	300	50
Assistant governor	1st grade	350	400	25
Chief Judge	2nd grade	200	240	20
Provincial division chiefs (Interior, Justice, Agriculture, Finance, Military, Royal Court), Monthon Prosecutor, Monthon Inspector-General of Posts & Telegraph		200	240	20
Deputies of the above six provincial officials	1st grade	180	200	10
Provincial Prosecutor	2nd grade	150	170	10

Positions, Grades, Salaries, and
Salary Increments in Monthon Phayap (*continued*)

Position		Monthly Salary (in baht) Minimum	Maximum	Annual Increment (baht per month)
Inspector	3rd grade	100	120	10
Secretary to *Monthon* Governor	4th grade	60	80	10
Deputy District Officer	5th grade	40	60	10
Accountant	5th grade	40	60	10
Interpreter	1st grade	100	120	10
Chief Jailer	2nd grade	60	80	10
Chief Jailer	3rd grade	30	50	10
Clerk	1st grade	40	60	10
Deputy Clerk	2nd grade	20	30	5
Deputy Clerk	3rd grade	15	19	2
Jailer	1st grade	20	30	5
Messenger	2nd grade	16	20	2
Servant	3rd grade	10	14	2

SOURCE: Interior Ministry Regulation Governing the Administration of the Northwestern Region, R.E. 119, *Government Gazette,* July 22, 1901, pp. 174–194.

This particular Ministry of Interior regulation marked the end of *kin muang* within the *monthon* to which it applied. Not only did it enact a comprehensive salary structure; it also prohibited the levying of "taxes" by provincial governors and other salaried officials, forbade their engaging in trade, and limited the right of salaried workers to supplement their earnings by additional employment.[36]

The general level of these salaries is suggested by the fact that in 1901 slightly more than 17 baht equaled one pound sterling; in rough equivalents, the baht was worth about U.S. $0.30 at the time. In turn-of-the-century Thailand these stipends were relatively attractive except for the most menial posts. The spread between upper and lower salaries was substantial, reflecting the hierarchical character of the system, but also offering substantial rewards as an incentive to advancement.

Until the adoption of the Civil Service Act of 1928, each ministry maintained its own pay plan, subject to approval by the Ministry of

Finance. There were some variations in rates, but the above illustration seems representative of general practice.[37]

A pay plan is hardly a thing of beauty and a joy forever, but pay plans do have their undeniable importance in any nonvoluntary organizational system. The extent to which the Chakkri Reformation had proceeded by the beginning of the twentieth century is well demonstrated by the comprehensiveness of these formal inducements. Pay made bureaucrats out of what had formerly been little potentates, and bureaucracy permitted functional specialization, the use of policy as an effective device for governance, and the centralization of control over the apparatus of the state. Pay became a predetermined and recurring inducement directly linked to status and responsibility, making one a participant in an elaborate, upward-oriented system instead of a member of a primary group armed with a license to eat the people in return for maintaining a degree of order.

In 1902 the various *monthon* salary regulations of the Ministry of Interior were superseded by a comprehensive order governing the salaries of all provincial officials.[38] It was elaborate and detailed, a marriage of Western public administrative practice and Thai hierarchicalism. Within the boundaries of the salary schedule, the king himself designated the salary of the *monthon* commissioner. There were as many as three distinct pay levels for a particular functionally specialized position, such as *monthon* deputy commissioner or provincial governor. The minister allocated individual positions to the appropriate class, although some authority to classify lower-level positions was evidently delegated to the *monthon* commissioner.

Similar arrangements existed or were emerging elsewhere in the developing bureaucracy. Only ten years earlier Prince Damrong had made his celebrated inspection tour and had returned to Bangkok to begin the reorganization of the Ministry of Interior.

OTHER INDUCEMENTS

Pay Differentials and Allowances. The salary system itself included "hardship-post" differentials formalized by regulation in 1904.[39] Housing allowances were also provided for officials assigned to posts remote from their established residences. Travel and transport expense allowances were regularized by 1900, the amounts being based upon official salaries. Traditionally, an official or group of officials had traveled with a royal warrant authorizing them to claim food, shelter, bearers, guards, draft animals, and other necessities from the governors of the provinces through which they passed. Never very satisfactory, this arrangement had become totally obsolete by the time of the establishment of the *tesapiban* system.

Pensions. Creation of a retirement system in 1901 was a major step in the evolution of a modern civil service. A formula for determining pensions and pension "rights" was established, and stipends were based upon length of service, earnings, and cause of separation from the service.[40]

The 1901 pension plan assumed the payment of retirement compensation out of current revenues, and pension payments have ever since been treated as an operating expense. The Ministry of Finance was made responsible for the administration of the pension system and continues to share in that responsibility to this day. Interestingly, the Thai pension act was adopted almost two decades before a comprehensive retirement program was established for civil officials of the American national government, and the basic form of the current Thai pension system represents no great modification of the 1901 arrangement.

Decorations. Pay and pensions were supplemented by a variety of motivational devices, one of which was the conferring of decorations in recognition of distinguished contributions to the king's service. In aim—if not always in practice—decorations were rewards for effective administration.

Decorations, like the titles mentioned previously, had to be rationalized as the administrative system developed. In January, 1901, King Chulalongkorn issued a royal decree specifying the decorations which various classes of officials might receive, and setting forth the basis for granting them. "Decorations are conferred on the basis of special merit . . . , not on the basis of rank. Decorations are thus different from titles. They are based upon merit irrespective of title." [41] Royal decorations, in other words, amounted to an Oriental incentive award arrangement.

High-class decorations were not to be conferred upon low-ranking officials, and the royal decree specified the appropriate relationships between ranks and decorations in full detail, as a directive for the Department of Decorations and the Department of the Royal Secretary of the Palace Ministry in the administration of the awards program.

King Vajiravudh increased the number of decorations. He also permitted favoritism to serve as a basis for the granting of honors to an extent which was not evident during the reign of his father.

INDOCTRINATION OF CIVIL SERVANTS

Exhortation was a favored method of traditional monarchs seeking to control their subordinates; the sheer volume of reiteration in the ancient chronicles implies its limited effectiveness. The Chakkri Reformation hardly eliminated recourse to the device, which in fact persists today, but it did reject exhortation as its chief instrumentality.

Nonetheless, a code of conduct was written about 1902 by Prince Damrong, at the request of Phraya Wisutsurisak, for use in training students at the Royal Pages School, and over the years it was learned by thousands of officials.[42] Prince Damrong described the purposes of the royal service as maintaining peace, increasing prosperity, and protecting the nation's independence. To these ends, good officials must be faithful, industrious, and courteous. As royal servants they were to behave in accordance with the king's law. They were to acquire needed knowledge and skill, and should "not be easyminded and procrastinating in nature." Their courtesy was to include respect of superiors, tolerance and tact with equals, and kindliness toward subordinates, including the people. Lying, dishonesty, laziness, harshness, nepotism, disingenuousness, and overspending were prohibited absolutely.

The great problem, of course, was the enforcement of these charming values in the absence of a polity or any critical and articulate external forces, such as uninhibited newspapers or journals of opinion. The burden rested on the top of the administrative system, upon the king and the ministers.

King Chulalongkorn sought to make direct use of his charismatic power to impress officials with the importance of supporting his aims. Newly appointed judges and other officials often received their commissions from the King directly, and were given an audience at which His Majesty personally instructed them in the importance of their duties and the need for honorable conduct. During the reign of King Chulalongkorn these were memorable—and influential—experiences.[43]

Influence of this sort needed reinforcement in a continuing process of indoctrination. The ancient semiannual oath of allegiance, the "lustral water ceremony," was continued until the 1932 coup, when the idea of absolute fealty to the king was superseded by the more amorphous concept of responsibility to the constitutional regime. The inadequacies of the periodic oath taking have already been noted. Wisely, the goals of the Chakkri Reformation were generally sustained by less awesome, but perhaps more effective, devices.

POSITIVE CONTROLS OVER BEHAVIOR

The basis of increased control over bureaucratic behavior was better communications enabled by enormous developments in the technical resources. By 1907 Thailand contained more than 7,000 miles of telegraph lines linking 67 administrative and commercial centers within the nation.[44] About 550 miles of railway were in operation.[45] And several thousand miles of waterways were in use, traversed by an increasing number of steam-propelled vessels which greatly reduced travel time. Physically the nation was linked as never before.

The *tesapiban* system had meanwhile evolved into a relatively well-integrated hierarchy covering the entire national territory and furnishing effective channels for communications between center and outposts. Systematic reporting procedures were in effect, including the collection and recording of statistical data which helped provide an objective basis for the assessment of problems and performance. This was supplemented by a personnel system involving training in skills and knowledge, the maintenance of records upon the performance of officials, and the use of knowledge and experience as a basis for promotion, plus a system of surveillance through inspection and investigation.

Prince Damrong had personally inaugurated the use of periodic field inspections. He continued them throughout his career as minister, and he was emphatic in asserting that *monthon* commissioners and provincial governors must ceaselessly inspect their territories and the work performed within them.

These key officials were given assistants in order to free them from administrative detail, and they were expected to spend as much as half of their time in formal and informal inspections. As general administrators, they also directed officials of other ministries in charge of education, posts and telegraph, alcohol and opium control, land registration, and so forth. *Monthon* commissioners controlled the nomination of such officials for titles and decorations, their recommendations being transmitted through the Ministry of Interior to the ministry to which the officials under consideration were attached. The commissioners were expected to have full knowledge of the performance and behavior of these officials, and to be competent to assess their performance in terms of the previously cited code of conduct prescribed by Prince Damrong.[46]

As early as the turn of the century there was a well-established distinction between the functions of inspection and investigation, the latter being the often covert efforts to uncover instances of misfeasance and malfeasance. Within the Ministry of Interior and elsewhere the investigation function was apparently well developed, although specific information concerning its organization is not available.

Satisfactory information concerning the general quality of behavior within the civil service is also unavailable. The earliest known statistics show an average of about 150 malfeasance convictions of officials during each of the five years, 1918–1922, or about one for every 550 employees per year.[47] This rate seems rather high, suggesting the use of rather aggressive prosecution to cope with serious problems of official conduct. Yet convictions for offenses *against* royal officials were nearly six times as great during the period—almost one offense for each hundred officials per year—implying heavy reliance upon law as a means of enforcing authority in the face of a considerable reluctance to comply. Malfeasance convictions, however, amounted to less than one-third of 1 per cent of all criminal convictions during the period 1918–1922. To the extent that these data portray the character of actual crime in Thailand at the time, it would appear that officials and the royal service were not greatly involved in it.

The record says nothing about misfeasance or nonfeasance, and one has only the rather widely varying accounts of individual writers by which to judge. It is probably safe to assume that the chief determinant of the extent to which the goals and ideals of the Chakkri Reformation were carried into effect varied rather directly with the quality of ministerial and royal leadership exerted upon the system.

Conclusion

By the end of the first decade of the twentieth century the new bureaucracy was a relatively integrated assemblage of reasonably competent organizations, committed to objectives which hardly existed a generation earlier.

This bureaucracy was sustained by a set of general processes which produced a sufficient supply of suitable personnel. Arrangements for intake, for developing skills and knowledge, and for motivation appeared to be rationally related to the general goals of the system. The major operating units of the bureaucracy were organized in terms of functional objectives, and within each existed an emphatically hierarchical pattern of specialization, with jobs defined in terms of differentiated skill and experience requirements and status. The pattern of specialization, or the means for ordering personal relations, was intolerant of certain types of organizational complexity, but one could not say that it was not rational. Finally, one found in the system a set of mechanisms for motivating personnel which were logical enough, and in some cases quite advanced compared with practice in other nations. In short, the bureaucratic system was far from perfect, but it was so different from the Ayudhyan bureaucracy in its aims and its methods, and in the congruence between means and asserted ends, that we may characterize the difference as revolutionary.

All of this change had come surprisingly fast, in terms of the time it usually takes to overturn ancient and self-justifying traditions. In 1910 one might have concluded a study of this sort on a note of glowing enthusiasm. It appeared that a modern administrative system had been created in a generation or less—without violence, upheaval, or even the brutal eviction of older interests. Certainly the processes by which bureaucratic resources were procured, ordered, and energized were substantially consistent with the requirements of a rational, productive administrative system.

Chapter 6

THE ENVIRONMENT
OF THE BUREAUCRACY

WE HAVE described the development of a set of formal organizations comprising the reformed Thai bureaucracy, along with the bureaucratic processes which operated in those organizations. In all of this discussion it has been clear that the bureaucracy did not exist in a void. The organizations did not produce themselves, nor did they generate their own bureaucratic processes. The bureaucracy was built. The most immediately evident force involved in its construction was the king, assisted by his ministers and their aides. Other powerful forces were also present in the bureaucratic environment.

The interactions and the effects of these forces upon the evolution of the Thai bureaucracy are as important as they are difficult to portray with precision. The chief justification for an inevitably impressionistic, subjective treatment of bureaucracy-environment relations is simply that they are central to any analysis of bureaucratic changes in Thailand and cannot be ignored.

We use a simple image: that of a bureaucracy, consisting of a set of formal organizations and their operating processes, existing in an environment made up of certain institutionalized forces and influences. In addition to the kingship, these included traditional value orientations within the society of which the bureaucracy was so vital a part—value orientations to some extent sustained by and identified with an external religious institution, but also internalized within the bureaucracy and its participants.

Here the line between bureaucracy and environment gets thin and porous. Only by defining the bureaucracy in terms of its formal and legitimate aspects can values held by bureaucrats be regarded as environmental. However, nothing is lost by the use of this particular frame of reference.

Finally, the bureaucratic environment included certain forces that functioned as external political interests. Limited in scope and shifting over time, these, too, affected the shape and substance of the bureaucracy that developed during the Chakkri Reformation and after it.

The King and the Bureaucracy

The new bureaucracy, with all its difference from the traditional system, resembled that system in its dependence upon the king.

The bureaucracy enhanced the power of the kingship. For the first time in Thai history the king possessed a set of administrative mechanisms more or less commensurate with the principle of his encompassing authority. But, as a corollary, he was now the effective, inescapably responsible head of that bureaucracy, the legislator-manager of a complex, purposive administrative system. He was the prime source of the authority that energized the reconstructed bureaucracy by setting its purposes and sustaining its operating processes. The encompassing hierarchy, adapted from tradition to meet the needs of administrative reform, was, in principle, an instrument for the systematic devolution of royal authority to be exercised by the king's men. Of course, if this principle was to work in practice, the king had to fulfill an appropriate—and demanding—role in relation to the system.

King Chulalongkorn accepted his obligations. Using his unchallengeable authority, he demanded rational bureaucratic organizations, shaped to pursue given aims and regularized by rule and procedure. And he performed the functions necessary to give continuing meaning and effect to his demands. He chose able subordinates. He exercised his power in a legal-rational mode, in granting organizations their mandates, in controlling the allocation of resources, and in harnessing the tremendous potency of status to the performance requirements of the bureaucracy.

This, of course, did not automatically produce a legal-rational bureaucracy. In a rational-legal bureaucracy, obedience tends to be directed "to the impersonal office and not to any individual as individual." [1] In theory, and to a degree in practice, "members of the staff owe obedience only as far as their official activities are concerned, which are carefully separated from their personal affairs and acts." [2] The range of authority, in short, is limited to official matters, and the limitation is (a) sanctioned by the institutionalized legal basis of authority underlying its immediate manifestations, and (b) valued by the participants in the system to a substantial degree. In such a system there is a high degree of differentiation between the bureaucratic and the nonbureaucratic roles of participants.

Even patterns of authority in such a system are differentiated and scaled. The authority of the official is substantially (but never entirely) determined by a set of legalistic referents. The legal system, possessing its own strata of authority sources, which may range from the minutiae of administrative rules to the near-cosmic generality of a written constitution, is in turn legitimized by reference to basic philosophical-mythical sources outside itself. And the system includes effective institutionalized constraints against illegal actions.

The authority patterns produced—or adapted—in the Chakkri Reformation bore small resemblance to such a system of differentiated, rationalized authority. In the Chakkri bureaucracy, authority was essentially person-centered rather than function-centered. The authority of an official continued to be broad and diffuse (although less diffuse than before the Reformation, when the cells of the bureaucracy were hardly integrated by an effective chain of command). This inherently diffused authority was focused and channeled by commands and controls imposed from above.

During the thrust of the Reformation, the difference between limited, differentiated official authority and the diffuse pattern of Thai bureaucratic authority was splendidly irrelevant. To a substantial extent, a legal-rational pattern of bureaucratic authority was simulated under an impetus which came from the king and his ministers. But this mode of bureaucratic action rested upon a narrow foundation: the royal imperium and, of course, the tendency of large organizations toward inertia—given forms of behavior, once established, tend to persist, but not necessarily the norms underlying the forms.

Inertia is more conducive to legalism than to rationality. "Rational bureaucratic behavior" assumes a capacity to adapt means to meet changes in the relevance of ends, and to take advantage of opportunities for improving the efficacy of methods. The impetus to rationality in the reconstructed Thai bureaucracy had to come from its very top —from the king amd his ministers. Only at this level could important changes be made in the goals and processes of the bureaucracy.

Social Values and the Bureaucracy

The reformation of the bureaucracy had a ranging set of impacts upon Thai society above the level of the villages. This was inevitable in a society whose middle ranges consisted of the bureaucratic strata. The image of the king was changed. New elements of secular awareness spread. The society "opened up" as the demand for bureaucrats expanded. Bureaucratic careers became the objects of aspiration for more Thais than ever before, and the prospects for attaining relatively high status within the bureaucracy loomed large. In the last decades of the nineteenth century and the first two decades of the twentieth, a sizeable bureaucratic middle class arose in Thailand.

Society also had its impact upon the bureaucracy. The most significant aspect of this lay in the actual and potential play within the bureaucracy of certain long-standing social values.

Deeply rooted in Thai society was the value attached to hierarchical status. Comparable in importance, if less clearly manifested in formal bureaucratic arrangements, were certain powerful value orientations concerned with individualism and the appropriate character of the relationships between individuals and society. These values were embedded in the national religion. Certain other kinds of values that seem conducive to the maintenance of a rational, productive bureaucratic system, however, were not institutionalized in Thai society at the time of the Reformation.

The relevant social values, in short, were traditional values. A problem of the Reformation was to neutralize them, or to convert them to the service of bureaucratic reconstruction. The rationalization of the traditional status system, described in the previous chapter, exemplifies the latter approach. Status was linked with productivity values, and control of the terms of access to status became an important means for inducing and rewarding appropriate behavior.

Individualism was also a significant value within Thai society, and, in its fashion, it had been valued over the centuries. Individualism and elaborate, explicit hierarchical stratification seem at first glance to be inconsistent. Beyond a certain point this is undoubtedly the case. But a social system of any complexity accommodates a substantial range of values, not all of them fully consistent. It does this, in part, by regulating the way in which they come into play. Apparently contradictory values can flourish as long as they are not commonly called upon at the same time, in the same type of situation, as the criteria for inducing or assessing behavior.

Two features of Thai society contributed greatly to the accommodation of both status values and individualism: the loose structuring, or high degree of permissivity, characteristic of the social system; and the shallow paternalism that was one aspect of the appropriate reciprocal relationships among superiors and subordinates within it.[3]

Status and individualism were buffered by accepted patterns of personal interaction: [4]

Because of the looseness of the social structure, respect and deference do not necessarily imply obedience, although outward disobedience is almost unthinkable. In case of non-compliance action simply peters out. . . . The culture places great value on internal equanimity, upon being *choey* or having a "cool heart." This enables one to take life as it comes, without strain or excitement. To be *choey* is to be without anxiety, to rest at ease, survey and weigh the situation, accept cheerfully what must be, and then take advantage of the circumstances, including the stupidity of others. The maintenance of a "cool heart" is supported by an attitude epitomized in the common phrase *mai pen rai,* meaning "it's of no importance," "never mind." The expression is more than a phrase; it symbolizes a defense mechanism for minimizing events which might otherwise disturb a "cool heart."

The whole tenor of this acute statement is to suggest a detachment, a separateness between the man and the system. Identity might derive from official status; the content of one's primary role in life might be bureaucratic; and material well-being might depend directly and wholly upon one's position. But one still remained an individual apart, with an always limited commitment or sense of involvement. In short, this was not the individualism of egalitarian rights, of privileges and obligations within society and its institutions; this was the relatively anomic individualism of person vis-à-vis social institutions. Of course, the phenomenon was, and is, subtle and complex, but its existence seems verified by the observations of skilled and perceptive students of Thai society.

This ideal posture of the individual toward his environment tended to soften the potential impact of hierarchical authority. It also blunted the potential appeal of productivity as a value in itself, and the prospects for the mobilization of a zeal that finds its fulfillment in dedication to large causes. There were no Stakhanovites in the Thai bureaucracy, even during the Reformation.

In this society, one's legitimate superior stood in a broad but shallow relationship to each of those below him. His superordination was a function of status, and status was essentially personal. Hence the breadth of the diffuse relationship. The superior might issue orders, but his acknowledged status gave no automatic assurance that they would be executed. The good superior himself was *choey,* and he was also protective and permissive. Subordinates, in return, were respectful and adroit in responding to expectations and orders from above.

In short, appropriate status relations could best be described in the language of "human relations." Within the bureaucracy, the good superior was paternalistic, and the effective subordinate was one with a "good personal relationship." The depth of the appropriate bond between superior and subordinate was quite shallow, limited by the value attached to personal autonomy on both sides, but the character of the ideal relationship itself was strongly valued.

Hierarchical relationships of this sort were like buckets. They could carry a variety of loads. A superior might successfully stress productivity so long as he did not emphasize goal attainment at the expense of "human relations." He might maintain a variant set of relationships with different subordinates, for proper treatment was not necessarily equal treatment in the social system. Rather, it was effective personal treatment.

The general effect of these social characteristics was to minimize the individual's sense of involvement in the bureaucratic organization of which he was a member. His first commitment was to himself; his next concerns were with his immediate personal relationships of superordination and subordination; and these were important not merely because they were instrumentalities of effective participation in an organization; they were important in and of themselves, as expressions of both individualism and status. "The organization," in the larger sense, was a source of constraints and opportunities. In the Thai hierarchy of loyalties, organizations per se tended to rank low, in comparison with loyalty to oneself and to one's immediate subordinates and supervisor.

The reshaping of the bureaucracy had reduced the unchallenged dominance of primary group associations within it. The imposition of goals and duties from the top levels of the system—goals and duties supported by inspections, reports, and sanctions—provided a degree of integration which had never before existed. Comprehensive processes for procuring, developing, and energizing resources had also helped change the balance of relationships between primary groups and a larger formal organization system. But values within the society itself offered some overt—and more latent—resistance to the aims and processes of bureaucratic reconstruction. And the reform was limited in its scope: it did not seek to remake society, only to build a new system of bureaucratic organizations.

Buddhism and the Bureaucracy

Thai Buddhism was a potent source of the perspectives and attitudes of Thai bureaucrats. The Buddhist religion was, in a sense, a differentiated institution, offering some men an alternative to the peasant life or a bureaucratic way of life. But the line between Buddhism and bureaucracy was not a wall, and Thai society at the time of the Reformation was by no means a secularized society. There was no sharp, conscious distinction between religious premises and the premises governing behavior in the larger society, including the bureaucracy.

In attempting to portray the general character of the impact of Buddhism upon the Reformation bureaucracy, we move from impressionism toward presumption, but the only alternative is to ignore an undeniable force of great importance.[5]

Buddhism contributed to the Reformation by its tacit, passive, continuing legitimation of the social order and by providing a supply of literate manpower from the temple schools. But its impact also lay in the world view and the values which it instilled in its adherents.

The root concept of Buddhism is escape from self, from suffering and conscious existence, and Thai postures toward temporal reality have not been uninfluenced by this premise. The world is not devoid of meaning; it is the cockpit in which men as individuals strive to achieve the salvation which is nirvana, and, more immediately, a place which depends on the balance of one's past merit and demerit. The world—the immediate, sensed, differentiated and transitory aspect of existence—is essentially incidental to a more basic reality: an all-embracing indescribable immortality in which the self as a concrete, local, determinate personality ceases to exist.[6] Of course, one doesn't have to be in a hurry to escape from existence, and practical Buddhism has not ignored questions of ethical conduct in the world, but it has not been a very "worldly religion" in the Western sense of that perhaps ironic phrase. Deep beneath the common expression, *mai pen rai,* at the center of a Thai personality there may often be a religion-conduced posture of which this phrase is but one manifestation. In crude over-statement, "whatever *is* isn't likely to matter too much." As one's attention moves beyond the realms of self-interest and ego-involvement the significance attached to worldly objects drops rapidly.

In this context, an organization as something directly affecting the individual is likely to be much more important than an organization as an entity with objectives external to his own immediate concerns. Defining status, ordering personal relationships, and setting the terms of personal achievement and survival are much more meaningful than assertions about substantive output goals and abstract values such as administrative efficiency.[7]

In this Thai Buddhist setting, technical and professional competence did not acquire the appeal and the prestige which became so common in the West. At least a partial explanation of this phenomenon would seem to lie in the relative lack of high concern with worldly causality and materialism which lies at the root of Buddhism.[8]

Other salient Thai values have derived from religious sources. Tolerance and relative permissiveness are related to the Buddhist *Weltanschauung.* A man is responsible for his own fate. His present state is essentially a function of his past conduct. One is not ultimately his brother's keeper, and personal merit-making is just that— acts whose spiritual benefits are largely nontransferable. Responsibility is ultimately a personal matter, and this kind of responsibility is far more important than the detached, depersonalized responsibility required in a legal-rational administrative system.

Diffuse but limited authoritarian superior-subordinate relationships were legitimized by karma. The authoritarian aspect of the vertically oriented society was ameliorated by the need for an individual to be free to work out his salvation.

In short, Thai Buddhism nurtured important traditional values in Thai society, including values which had been reflected within the bureaucracy over the centuries. It did not resist the Reformation; but the permeating religious milieu contained no equivalent of a "Protestant ethic," and its normative and symbolic content was, at best, tolerant rather than supportive of performance-oriented public administration.

Other Environmental Forces

WESTERN POLITICAL AND ECONOMIC INTERESTS

During the Reformation, diplomatic and commercial representatives of Western nations whose opposition was to be minimized and whose support was to be sought constituted a set of articulate, powerful interest groups. They gave impetus to the Reformation effort and influenced its content.

Fiscal integrity, a system of law, order, and justice acceptable according to Western standards, a sound currency, and an orderly basis for the conduct of mining, teak cutting, and trade were among the major concerns of this "clientele" of Thai government. It was represented with singular effectiveness by diplomats, by trading concerns, and, to some extent, by British financial advisers.[9]

These forces initially pressed broadly for modernization. They did so directly and explicitly, and also by posing an implicit threat to the nation's continuance in the absence of reform. As time passed, however, external political pressures largely became focused upon commercial and economic interests. Their influence upon the relative rationality and effectiveness of the administrative system declined after the turn of the twentieth century.

In more or less parallel fashion, the role of Western officials in the Thai bureaucracy waxed and then gradually waned. These officials were not the instruments of Western political and economic interests, but they were the representatives of Western administrative values and techniques, and they were relatively free from susceptibility to the full force of traditional Thai social values. One might consider these officials, in the aggregate, akin to an "interest" which exercised a substantial influence upon the content of the reforming bureaucracy.

A DOMESTIC POLITY

One environmental force of potential significance was important for its absence: the Reformation produced no large changes in the political significance of the nonbureaucratic sectors of the society.

As already noted, the emerging middle class was a bureaucratic class, whose status and aspirations did not encourage the emergence of a sense of class identity, let alone any propensity for coherent political action. A sense of awareness of the relationships between governmental policy and group interest was only beginning to appear, one gathers. In a small and subversive fashion it found brief expression among military dissidents following the end of the Reformation period.

A sizeable Chinese commercial class was developing during the Reformation era, but it functioned as an element of a polity only to a most limited extent and in a subtle, anomic fashion.

In general, the whole force of society militated against the development of domestic, interest-asserting political forces. At best, the expanded, rationalized administrative system produced by the Chakkri Reformation received little systematic feedback or direction from the environment upon which it impacted.

Conclusion

In short and admittedly oversimple terms, the bureaucratic environment of the Reformation era was marked by a contest between royal authority and Western political pressure, on the one hand, and abiding social values, on the other.

The values had long been institutionalized within the traditional bureaucracy. Royal authority harnessed the motivating energy of one of those values—status—to the goals of bureaucratic productivity, through bureaucratic processes in which personnel were procured, ordered, and in part, motivated by appeals to the value of status. The ancient value of "personalism," or individualism, was also attacked by authority from the top: countervailing force was imposed upon the characteristics of a loosely structured social system. The short-run results were impressive.

In Thailand the first decade of the twentieth century was marked by a growing sense of achievement and by an abating of the threats and stresses of the 1890s. Relations with Western powers were rapidly approaching stability. The kingdom was on a sound financial footing, and its administrative mechanisms were growing in strength and effectiveness. Lawlessness was being curbed. Communications and transportation facilities were spreading. The nation's resources were being developed as never before.

An ageing king looked back upon a reign which had become an epoch, a period of great transition, a time of successful struggle for survival—a struggle more crucial than any of the old clashes of trumpeting elephants with ever-warring Burma, a struggle whose grimness and complexity made the moments of mastery of the ancient warrior kings seem simple.

The reconstruction of the bureaucracy had been a central element of that struggle. From the perspective of the time and place, bureaucratic reform was a substantial success. The trains—now that there were trains—ran on time; taxes were collected; and from the Mekong River to the Malay States the people felt the authority of the king's government.

But what of the future?

In 1910 the effectiveness and rationality of the Thai bureaucracy were largely dependent upon the leadership and management of the king and his chief ministers. Administrative goals and bureaucratic norms derived their effectiveness from the top of the system. Certainly, the norms which gave meaning to the processes for procuring, allocating, and energizing resources had not been internalized within the bureaucracy.

In short, the administrative system which had been built during the Reformation was a competent, responsive apparatus, but its future qualities would depend largely upon the relationships between forces in its environment. The bureaucracy could never revert to its traditional form, but it was entirely capable of responding to traditional norms, for the potency of traditional values had not been much eroded. Only in the continued presence of countervailing pressures could this be prevented.

Within the society, the only effective general source of such pressures was the king. Foreign commercial interests would protect themselves, but this would produce only small, selective forces upon the bureaucracy. Inertia would contribute considerable stability to established organizations, but rationality would not.

As an institution, the kingship had changed profoundly since 1851. But it remained the prime source of legitimate power to manage and control the bureaucracy. The resulting burden on the king was enormous.

The problem of obtaining reliable information about the efficacy of administrative activity was itself substantial. The dispersed society, the impediments to lower-level bureaucratic perception of problems of rationality and relevance, the status barriers to any easy upward flow of information, and the tinge of *mai pen rai*—all these factors impeded management's access to information.

In the golden age of reconstruction, deliberate efforts were made to cope with these problems. Thai legends include stories of King Chulalongkorn roving through the capital in disguise, seeking, like the fabled ruler of the Arabian Nights, to sense the pulse of his nation, and on one occasion being pursued to the gates of the palace by a band of nocturnal dacoits, who neither recognized nor—fortunately —apprehended His Majesty in his rickshaw.

The significance of such exploits lay in the concern they reflected rather than their usefulness for getting systematic feedback. Information was also sought through consultation (as in the *tesapiban* conferences and the consultative committees of the provincial governors) and through inspection, as well as by the covert means labeled investigation.

So long as the decision-making center of the system managed to comprehend the environment, penetrate the hierarchy, and effectively command the bureaucracy, it seemed that the rationality and relevance of administrative instrumentalities could be fairly well maintained.

Chapter 7

AFTERMATH

THE YEAR 1910 is a convenient, if arbitrary, date to mark the end of the Chakkri Reformation, although its impetus in education, public health, transportation, and some other fields continued into the middle of the 1920s.

The nation's diplomacy was never more adroit than during the era of World War I and the years following, when extraterritoriality provisions were finally eliminated from the Western treaties. In public finance, too, Thailand wrote an impressive record after 1910, maintaining a sound currency through the depression of the latter 1920s and the 1930s. From 1926 through 1940 Thailand's government ran up a deficit in only two years and in the other years of those financially difficult times public revenues exceeded expenditures by an average of about 10 per cent.[1]

But 1910 was the year in which King Chulalongkorn died, to be succeeded by his son Vajiravudh; who reigned until 1925. In 1910, too, Prince Rabi, the distinguished Minister of Justice, died. In 1910 great leaders were lost, and others were soon to follow. Prince Damrong continued in the Ministry of Interior for another five years; he resigned in 1915 "for reasons of health." The impetus of the Chakkri Reformation was felt for years after 1910, and the motive behind the Reformation—national survival—was never abandoned. But now the criteria for survival were largely effective diplomacy and financial soundness—not high competence in the domestic bureaucracy.

After 1910, a number of things that happened in Thailand—and some that did not happen—produced a significant change in the character of the Thai bureaucracy: (1) There was an abrupt decline in monarchic management and leadership. (2) The number of educated young men seeking bureaucratic careers grew rapidly. (3) Certain kinds of environmental forces failed to develop—nonbureaucratic organizations which could absorb a share of the products of the expanding educational system by offering them meaningful careers, and forces which could support rationality and productivity within the bureaucracy.

The Decline of the Monarchy

Twenty-two years after the death of King Chulalongkorn the absolute monarchy was overthrown in the coup of 1932. The all-powerful ruler, the Lord of Lives, the prime source of authority over the bureaucracy, was transformed into a passive symbol. After 1932 the importance of the king lay more in his existence than in his actions.

The immediate circumstances of this abrupt collapse included the capriciousness and imperceptiveness of King Vajiravudh, who assiduously squandered his royal patrimony. His successor, Prajadhipok, inherited the consequences, and was hampered by the financial difficulties of the latter 1920s. In 1932 he was forced to accept a constitution by a small group of military and civilian officials who seized control of the government.

Had Vajiravudh been a competent ruler, and had Prajadhipok been a bolder and more fortunate man, the monarchy might have persisted. The "revolution" which overthrew it was not the irresistible act of any broad political force clamoring for a new source of political legitimacy. It was essentially a bold stroke by a small group of dissidents. Their success was enhanced by the absence of effective leadership in the royal military forces, and the passive dissatisfaction of large sectors of the civil and military bureaucracy with the *status quo*.[2]

On the surface, the 1932 coup was a surprise. No threatening insurrectionist movements had shown themselves inside the kingdom. Only two years earlier, the adviser to the Minister of Foreign Affairs had written: "While in theory this system of organized Government . . . exists at the mere will of the King and may be abolished by him, in fact it resembles a constitution. In the future it may be modified, improved and strengthened but it is unthinkable that it will be destroyed." [3]

The statement was oracular—in its obscurity and its prescience. The system was not destroyed, but its persistence no longer required an absolute monarch.

Beneath the surface, the institutional quality of the monarchy had changed profoundly, and the nature and extent of these changes had not been appreciated. "The monarchy remained absolutist, and, with few exceptions, all the pomp and ceremony that surrounded and enhanced the royal person were maintained." [4] But the story of Thai government is much concerned with shifting relations between form and substance; and the old forms obscured the new realities of the kingship in the twentieth century.

For our purposes, these realities are two: First, the king had become the primary source of the authority upon which the bureaucracy depended for its purposive thrust. Second, the bureaucracy had acquired, in the course of the Chakkri Reformation, a structure and a set of processes which made it substantially independent of the king for its sheer continuance. The bureaucratic institutions could continue to exist and fulfill the essential needs of Thai society without royal leadership.

Fortunately for that grand and apoplectic man, King Mongkut never foresaw these shattering consequences of the reconstruction of the government. Chulalongkorn had embraced the working kingship with its complex role of potentate, legislator, diplomat, and executive. Throughout his reign he had both consciously and inadvertently diminished the mystical element of the monarchy, as he had tried to build a practical apparatus of government to support him in the performance of his worldly functions. [5]

By the time Vajiravudh ascended the throne in 1910, the new burden of royal responsibilities had been fully established—and the charismatic quality of the kingship had been undermined by the impact of the West. To villagers, the king might still be godlike, but official attitudes were more complex. The kingship commanded respect verging upon reverence, and its inherent legitimate power was certainly acknowledged; but to officials whose awareness extended to a world far more vast than Thailand, the absolutism of the monarch was no longer its own full justification.

King Vajiravudh displayed a splendid inability to understand this. Born in 1881, he was sent to England to study at about the age of twelve. He returned to Thailand in 1903, and became king seven years later at the age of thirty. Author, playwright, and "dilettante in governmental affairs," he tried to play the potentate and to ignore his obligations as ruler. [6]

. . . Wachirawut displayed a marked lack of interest in the routine administration of government affairs, with the result that, while there were some haphazard progressive developments in details, there was considerable retrogression in the over-all efficiency of government during his reign. . . . The King rarely called meetings of the Cabinet, and the other consultative councils seem never to have been utilized. He did meet individual ministers, but at these meetings he usually announced policy instead of consulting about it. . . . The King gave money, titles, and decorations away freely to those who pleased him. It has been stated that during Wachirawut's reign "appointments came largely to be controlled by patronage," that the King appointed his satellites to sinecures and, in some cases, even created offices for them.[7]

Vajiravudh became the object of the first known attempt in Thai history to assassinate a king on the basis of objection to his policies.[8] Thai history included a number of efforts at regicide; but these had been instruments of power-seeking, not of policy. In 1912, a group of officers in the Heavy Machine Gun Division of the Royal Guards Department tried to thwart Vajiravudh's military policy by killing its author.

Shortly after coming to power, Vajiravudh had created a "Wild Tiger Scout Corps," a quasi-military organization of personal favorites and "volunteers" drawn from among the civil officials. Vajiravudh thought of himself as a soldier, and his Scout Corps was something of a personal military plaything. It was bitterly resented by the regular military, and this resentment led to the unsuccessful assassination attempt.

The import of this unprecedented attack was utterly lost on Vajiravudh. Five years later, another alleged conspiracy against him was uncovered in the military. It involved German-trained officers opposed to Thailand's entry into World War I on the side of the Allies.

Oblivious of the underlying realities of his position, King Vajiravudh played soldier and dabbled in literature. He was fortunate in inheriting the able Prince Devawongse as his foreign minister, and in the fact that the Prince had trained a son to succeed to his post. Vajiravudh was also wise in supporting his foreign minister, and in generally acquiescing in the proposals of the British financial adviser, whose objective was the financial stability of the kingdom. In domestic matters, however, Vajiravudh tinkered with his ministries. He promoted the development of education, and as a result has been acclaimed in some quarters as a social progressive. He also created viceroys in the countryside to report directly to him on the work of the *monthons*. His viceregal aides were given control of the appointment and discharge of all important provincial officials, their nomination for decoration and other awards, and the preparation of annual budgets.[9] This move was made shortly after Prince Damrong's retirement from the Ministry of Interior. Vajiravudh also stripped the Ministry of many of its substantive departments, transferring its police and penitentiary functions to the Ministry of Finance.[10] In the last year of his reign, Vajiravudh's personal expenditure was nine million baht, equal to about one-fourth of the annual payroll for 87,000 civil officials.

In 1925 King Prajadhipok, another son of King Chulalongkorn, inherited the throne, plus a budget deficit and the task of acting as conservator of the national interest. Prajadhipok turned for advice to a group of the senior princes whom his predecessor had largely ignored, and also followed the counsel of his foreign and financial advisers. Prajadhipok made ruthless cuts in the civil service, reducing its numbers by 17 per cent during his reign. He slashed the military budget. He cut his own privy purse from nine to six million baht in his first year as king.[11] In 1928 he issued a Civil Service Act which established a committee of ministers to standardize disciplinary and selection procedures for the civil bureaucracy, and presumably to contribute to efficiency and economy.

Prajadhipok, the last of the absolute monarchs, was a victim of his times and, to some extent perhaps, of his policies. He sought to assert control of the goverment, and to obtain acceptance of his painful actions by the official public. He was not capricious, but he did hew grimly to a conservative fiscal policy, and he probably cut the bureaucracy more than was necessary in view of the financial record. He and the councils he created to advise him were undoubtedly concerned with protecting the international position of Thailand, and with avoiding any excuse for intervention.[12]

Fear of foreign interference may have been obsessive and unreasonable in Thailand in the 1920s. But the events of a still vivid past must have had a compelling influence upon the perspective of the king and the advisers who had lived through the struggle with France and England. An exemplary record in international economic relations, however, was achieved at the expense of painful domestic actions. The reduction of salaries, the premature pensioning of bureaucrats, and the discharge of thousands of *wisaman* employees produced uneasiness and discontent. It did not stimulate any organized efforts to challenge or resist governmental policy. Bureaucratic rebellion remained inconsistent with social reality.

On June 24, 1932, a small group of civil and military officials made a revolution—but it was not a bureaucratic revolution. There were about a hundred active participants, only twelve of whom planned the coup strategy, a take-over based upon control of a small group of military forces in the capital and of the communications system essential to any countermeasures. The revolutionaries came from two groups—junior officials, most of whom had acquired revolutionary ideas in the course of European educations, and a small number of disaffected senior military officers.

One facet of the Chakkri Reformation had been the modernization of the military, and its establishment as a professional, functionally specialized component of the new bureaucracy.[13] Modernization began with the great reorganization of 1892. Military conscription was adopted in 1905. In World War I, King Vajiravudh used the Thai Army as an instrument of Thai diplomacy. A small expeditionary force was sent to France, and Thai participation in the Allied victory facilitated the demise of extraterritoriality in the 1920s. Military officers had been sent to Europe for training from the beginning of the Chakkri Reformation, and some were "infused there with a taste for progress and modernity if not for democracy. But any sense of self-importance and expertise acquired abroad by officers was frustrated in the monopoly of top posts and decisions by high princes and their intimates."[14] This frustration, which emerged largely during Vajiravudh's reign, plus cuts in the defense budget during the reign of King Prajadhipok, produced the dissatisfaction which led to military participation in the 1932 coup.

The revolution was based more upon a simple ideal than an ideology. One of the leaders, a significant civilian figure in Thai politics for almost two decades to follow, Nai Pridi Phanomyong, has been described as the ideologist of the revolution, and Pridi's ineffective post-revolutionary efforts to build a political party and establish a coherent and acceptable economic dogma tend to support the description. But the 1932 revolution was hardly doctrinaire, and Pridi's ideological concerns were shared only by his own followers among the "civilian faction" who had come in contact with Pridi during his student days in France, or later when he served in the Ministry of Justice and taught law at Chulalongkorn University.

Other revolutionaries talked of democracy, but "they were less concerned with its political implications . . . than with the economic consequences which they believed would follow. . . . For them, democracy meant only one thing—modernization and prosperity." [15] And, no doubt, a share in the benefits. Revolution meant access to power, the elimination of a source of insecurity and inequity, and perhaps "national progress." These vague ideals were matched by no dogmatic blueprint of the future. There was bitter conflict over a socialistic economic plan drafted by Pridi after the coup, and the parliamentary pattern of governmental organization innocently envisioned by the revolutionaries quickly proved much too fragile for the Thai political milieu. Overthrow of the monarchy had produced a power vacuum, and it could not be immediately filled with a panoply of Western-style representative institutions. Power came increasingly to be wielded by those who had it; i.e., those who had access to military force. The post-revolutionary politics of Thailand became sophisticated exercises in the pragmatic wielding of power for its own sake, and for the sake of the rewards that went with it.

The civil bureaucrats—and most of the military—were distinguished by their non-involvement in the coup and its aftermath. One of the first actions of the coup group following its swift rise to power was to issue an order that civil and military officials should continue to do their work without interruption, and they complied.[16] The revolution did not touch the masses, neither did it impact deeply upon the civil bureaucracy. There were changes in organization in the post-revolutionary period. But the basic position of the administrative apparatus in the governmental structure was not much changed, nor were the prime values which governed bureaucratic behavior.

The bureaucratic response to the revolutionary change at the center of the system is symbolized by what happened to the term *kha rajakarn*. Once it had meant *"corvée* labor." The reconstruction of the bureaucracy in the course of the Chakkri Reformation gave the phrase new meaning, and there was dignity in being "the king's man." After 1932 the symbol was not changed, but only its content; *kha rajakarn* became an idiom, translated "public servant." The bureaucracy—in particular the civil bureaucracy—was as gracefully responsive to political change as the old verbal form was responsive to needs for new content.

The unmitigated acceptance of the revolution simply reflected the nature of the institution which had emerged from the Chakkri Reformation—an administrative apparatus responsive to direction from above, but also capable of existing on a basis which was not threatened by either the decline of monarchical leadership or the overthrow of the kingship.

Bureaucratic Response to the Loss of Monarchic Leadership

The reformation of the Thai bureaucracy was a dramatic and strenuous undertaking marked by ingenuity and urgency. The post-Reformation shift in the character of that bureaucracy was gradual and subtle. But it was no less real.

External authority was the key to the rationality and productivity of the bureaucracy. As authority was withdrawn, the bureaucracy did not cease to produce, but its members became relatively less concerned with productivity and it began to decline in rationality. Values which to some extent had been repressed during the height of bureaucratic reconstruction were available to give coherence to the bureaucracy and satisfactions to its participants when external leadership faded. The bureaucratic processes created in the Reformation were maintained, but the norms governing those processes shifted, becoming more consistent with traditional social values.

The agencies engaged in the production of visible goods and services—the railway, for example, and the postal service—did not stop moving passengers, freight, and mail after 1910. The Ministry of Justice did not abandon its efforts following the deaths of King Chulalongkorn and Prince Rabi. But the bureaucracy, in a sense, returned to tradition.

The return was neither simple nor complete. The Chakkri Reformation had certain irreversible features. These included the pattern of formal organizations which precluded any return to the simple unintegrated structure of traditional provincial government. They also included bureaucratic processes which could hardly be abandoned once they had been established. The same was probably true of various substantive activities within the bureaucracy, such as arrangements for regulating the mining of tin and the cutting of teak, and for operating facilities and services of various kinds. The processes, once established, tended to continue for a number of reasons, even when the norms and underlying values governing their performance shifted.

In broad and oversimple terms, the performance of activities which, on the one hand, kept the bureaucratic system going, and, on the other, kept it turning out various kinds of goods and services, became subordinate to other ends encompassed by the idea of "bureaucratic self-interest." The place of productivity was inverted—it became more of an adjunct than an end.

Certain forces continued to support productivity as one desired outcome of bureaucratic activity. Pay itself depended upon some forms of productivity—tax collection and financial administration. A host of expectations in society were also influential. People depended upon train service, for example; this tended to produce it. People used money; the mint continued to produce it. And so forth. Just as the expectations of officials at an earlier time had caused the king to issue *biawat* even when it was inconvenient, so did a variety of expectations influence bureaucratic activity to some degree. But clientele expectations were hardly a substitute for the once-effective authority of the king and his ministers.

Inertia, as noted earlier, also supported productivity to some extent. The continued doing of things long done inevitably tended to result in accomplishments.

In short, productivity was not abandoned, but the continued existence of the bureaucracy did not depend upon an abiding commitment to productivity and to the rational adjustment of administrative means to productive ends. Bureaucratic persistence was affected by a number of factors. One of them, already noted, was the differentiation of the bureaucracy and the king that had occurred as the system grew large and impersonal, necessitating a formalization, not of the status system per se (it had been formalized for centuries), but of the processes in which the status system operated. After the arrangements for ascribing and conferring status had been regularized, only nominal involvement by the king was necessary to keep them in operation. This facilitated the continuance of a system in which status was itself a vital value. As a social subsystem, whose meaning and justification to its participants were so much inherent in its sheer existence, the bureaucracy had a built-in propensity for survival, so long as status could be defined and ascribed, and so long as the necessary resources were forthcoming.

The Reformation had also included the establishment of reasonably effective arrangements for the collection and allocation of funds. These were reinforced by continuing reliance upon a financial adviser to the king whose prime concern was the fiscal integrity which would contribute to orderly commerce. Fiscal integrity required adequate financial administration, and the bureaucracy shared in the benefits of this. The size of the bureaucracy and the scope of its activities were limited by available resources. But within this boundary, funds flowed into the administrative system, usually allocated on the basis of prior appropriations, and enterprises continued.

In the course of their continuance, a significant shift occurred in the operating norms governing the processes by which the bureaucracy maintained itself. Such norms must be generally consistent with the broader values sustained by a system of organization. More precisely, if stress, and even breakdown, are to be avoided, the norms governing an organization's support processes cannot be substantially inconsistent with organizational aims and underlying values.

As noted, the personnel processes established in the course of the Chakkri Reformation were designed to contribute to productivity values. The personnel processes of the Ministry of Interior illustrate the point. Individuals were brought into the system and placed in a hierarchy within which advancement was based upon experience, training, and examinations. Training and testing were carefully and pragmatically conceived and developed. Eventually, these efforts led to the production of the *Golden Book,* a training manual for those who would advance in *tesapiban* government to district officer positions and beyond. Within the Ministry of Interior and elsewhere, intake also became linked with prior educational attainment. Thus the graduates of the law school established in 1897 were assigned to the Ministry of Justice as judges.

During the Reformation, the norms reflected in these patterns of bureaucratic action were to a substantial degree achievement norms. Ability and experience were a common basis for advancement. Hierarchical status was the prerequisite of effectiveness—the power to act was a function of rank. But access to rank was largely controlled by judgments of competence. In this way, the ancient hierarchical tradition was harnessed to the purposive commitment of the reconstructed bureaucracy. Even foreign officials were fitted into the hierarchical matrix. Their roles were defined by reference to the status system; to the extent that they could function within this system they were able to bring into play their technical and professional competence.

But the effective norms of action in the Thai bureaucracy shifted without doing much violence to the forms. After the Reformation, achievement norms more and more became "attainment norms," and access to status became less and less a function of demonstrated competence.[17] Individuals acquired the necessary certificate or diploma in order to enter the service, and served a specified period of time in order to become eligible for advancement. They studied for, and passed, the necessary examinations. Time and knowledge became requisites to bureaucratic survival and advancement—time spent in appropriate behavior within the bureaucracy, and knowledge acquired because of its utility in passing the established examination.

In short, as the years went by, training and selection processes became less and less linked to demonstrated competence. This impression stems from the record of the evolution of the Ministry of Interior to some extent; but it is overwhelmingly supported by an examination of the processes of the bureaucracy of the 1950s, which was a product of the Reformation and its aftermath.

The patterns of bureaucratic action—or, in other words, the supporting processes of the bureaucracy—which were developed during the Chakri Reformation were capable of operating in terms of more than one set of norms. With the decline of leadership and the abating of pressure to produce and to adapt means to productive ends, the means themselves became traditionalized. Both the evolution of attainment norms and the persistence of the form of bureaucratic processes that grew out of the Reformation contributed to the continuing coherence of the bureaucracy in the long aftermath of bureaucratic reconstruction.

As the educational system grew—while alternatives to bureaucratic careers for the graduates of the educational system did not grow—orderly and acceptable means for controlling access to the bureaucracy became important. In the early 1920s, for example, about 11,000 Thai students were enrolled in secondary and special schools.[18] Most of these were males, and they equalled almost 15 per cent of the total number in a bureaucracy that was about to shrink in response to the impact of depression. They presumably looked forward to bureaucratic careers, to which there were few alternatives. An examination process that did little more than regularize access to the bureaucracy—and in a way which was largely acceptable to the candidates for admission—contributed to the continuance of the bureaucracy and to the maintenance of an orderly relationship with its environment.

Aftermath: Bureaucracy and Society

At the beginning of the Reformation, the bureaucracy comprised the intermediate strata of a coherent, unself-conscious, traditional society. In the course of the Reformation, both the society and the bureaucracy were changed. The bureaucracy acquired a new dimension—a set of productive obligations which far exceeded those of the traditional administrative apparatus. The top level of the society accepted the task of leading and managing, but the functions of leadership and management were never effectively institutionalized. In the aftermath of the Reformation, the bureaucracy's significance as a productive administrative instrumentality declined relative to its importance as a self-justifying, substantially self-sustaining component of society. When it no longer had to respond to a constant flow of positive directives from above, the bureaucracy responded instead to other forces.

The post-Reformation bureaucracy was larger, more complex, and much more integrated than its traditional antecedent had ever been. It existed in a more complex and relativistic environment. It was characterized by more specific patterns of action and more limited roles. But the new and the old had more in common than appearance would suggest: the bureaucracy continued to serve as the chief source of status, security, and identity for Thais above the level of the villages.

Outside the bureaucracy there was little excepting the temple and the farm. A major aim of the developing educational system was to produce bureaucrats; and the largest part of that system was itself within the bureaucracy. A commercial sector of society evolved, but it was differentiated from the bureaucracy by an ethnic boundary:

merchants, traders, artisans, and other purveyors of economic services were Chinese or Westerners.

The bureaucracy inevitably tolerated and responded to authority from above, but it did not depend upon large, continuing infusions of positive direction in order to exist. In a sense, the bureaucracy had a life of its own. Its viability was largely a consequence of the Reformation, without which there might have been no Thai bureaucracy. Reform helped undermine the monarchic institution which had produced it; but reform also enabled the monarchy to be toppled without resulting bureaucratic chaos. In the immediate sense, the fecklessness of Vajiravudh and the fiscal policies of Prajadhipok may have enhanced the tolerance of many bureaucrats for the overthrow of the absolute monarchy. More basically, the bureaucracy as an institution had neither capacity nor effective motives in terms of which to challenge the king.

A few bureaucrats made a revolution, just as military officers had attempted regicide in 1912. The revolutionaries of 1932 were really rebelling against circumstances of the society, not merely the kingship. They succeeded in their immediate attack, but they left the social system little touched—particularly as the kingship was retained as a legitimating symbol.

The Reformation ended. The king was toppled. Control of government passed to a shifting succession of cliques, nominally operating within a constitutional framework but in reality depending upon control of military force.[19] The bureaucracy continued, the epitome of a stable, neutral administrative mechanism. But this was not the stability and neutrality of the Weberian legal-rational ideal; it was, rather, the stability of a social system whose neutrality was a function of its commitment to values not much challenged by its milieu.

Stability in the face of change implies adaptive capacity, and this, too, proved to be a quality of the bureaucracy which grew out of the Reformation and its aftermath. But adaptation in the Thai bureaucracy proved to be the shifting of operating norms to fit the implicit, residual values of the social system as the pressure for achievement abated.

In a sense, the aftermath of the Chakkri Reformation was a return to tradition—or a renaissance of traditional bureaucratic values. These were essentially the subtle, diffuse, permeating values of a social system which conferred status, sustenance, and identity upon participants in an inherently meaningful bureaucratic way of life.

This, at any rate, is the thesis of this analyis. An examination of the basic characteristics of the bureaucracy about a third of a century after the 1932 coup gives much credence to this interpretation of the evolution of the Thai bureaucracy.

Chapter 8

THE ESSENTIAL CHARACTER OF THE CONTEMPORARY BUREAUCRACY

IN THE YEARS after 1932, the civil bureaucracy resumed its growth. By 1960 it was perhaps three times as large, in terms of numbers of official personnel, as the approximately 80,000 officials who held positions at the time of the revolution.[1] By 1965 the number of regular officials was at least 250,000—and perhaps another 200,000 worked as laborers or other non-status employees in government agencies or as employees of public enterprises. No one seems to know the exact figures. Of these officials and employees, the most important for our purposes are the regular civil officials.

Part of this enlargement resulted from the incorporating of the nation's teachers within the civil service after World War II, but the bureaucracy has also reflected the persistent and inevitable growth of governmental activities. The expansion of the nation's highways—from perhaps a hundred miles of all-weather rural roads in the mid-1930s to thousands of miles today—is but one example of such growth.

Bureaucratic growth has resulted from decisions at the very top of the governmental system, by the Council of Ministers, or the prime minister himself. The bureaucrats themselves, in a few fields at least, have promoted expansion and innovation, working with the foreign advisers and the officials of foreign aid programs in which Thailand has participated extensively during the pass two decades. Within the bureaucracy, program proposals have come only from the very highest levels of the individual ministries. The contributions of subordinate officials are at best obscure; certainly specialized program planning staffs are not much in evidence within the system.

Bureaucratic growth and development have been limited by the sheer availability of resources to support expansion. In all that has happened since 1910, the tradition of protecting Thailand's fiscal integrity has not been abandoned. Domestic tax administration has not been distinguished for its effectiveness, although improvements have been made in recent years; but bold ventures have occurred in the post-World War II period in national planning, in water resources development, in electric power generation and transmission, and in communications and transportation, for example. These specialized programs have involved foreign aid in the form of loans or grants, and advice and influence from agencies such as the International Bank for Reconstruction and Development and the United States Agency for International Development.

The Thai government has also invested a substantial share of its own resources in the nation's educational system. During the years when Marshal Sarit Dhanarat directly controlled the government—1958–1964—education roughly equaled the military as prime objects of governmental spending from domestic revenue.[2]

The commitment to education seems to reflect a concern of the governmental leadership as well as the efforts of foreign advisers. It is impossible to identify precisely the bases for this posture. They undoubtedly include a recognition of the widespread desire for education that exists among the populace—a desire which is not articulate in any visible, focused fashion—and an implicit conviction that education is necessary for the continuance of the country.

The contemporary bureaucracy, in short, does have its productive aspect. Bureaucratic services provide an infrastructure for social and economic activity, and also serve as instruments of social change. The continuance of Thai society would be impossible if the services performed by the civil bureaucracy were withdrawn. Without law and order, electric power, public health services, transportation and communications facilities, and mechanisms to order and promote economic activity, life for many of Thailand's people would quickly become chaotic. Village-dwelling peasants in rice-production areas might continue to survive, but the agriculture which is the chief economic activity of more than 60 per cent of the people is no longer simple subsistence farming. Since the days of King Chulalongkorn, the Thai nation has become integrated by a complex network of functional interdependences, and the bureaucracy is a necessary—if not always seemingly sufficient—means for the maintenance of society.

This does not mean that the bureaucracy is the sensitive, discerning, responsive policy-shaping and implementing apparatus of the state. Inertia is one explanation of how the system produces results. Well-designed processes, some tracing back to the Chakkri Reformation and others as recent as the central accounting system installed by foreign consultants in the latter 1950s, tend to persist. (So do others, less well designed or suited to present conditions.) In addition, relatively small groups in continuing face-to-face relations can produce impressive results at times. Sometimes there is an *ad hoc,* hurried quality to such efforts. In other cases, a continuing activity is carried out in an impressive fashion under an effective personal leader. The work may be payroll preparation, tax collection, or the recording of statistics which will never be used. In some departments there are elaborate research laboratories with apparently competent staffs but no programs. In other offices a core of competent officials work hard while others loaf or do little work—some because they are utterly incompetent. Yet little resentment is evident in these situations where some are exploited and others are parasitic.

To a Westerner, such a system seems strange, primarily because of the obscure and inferior place of productivity values and achievement norms. Yet any earnest observer must admit that the bureaucracy has so far met the conditions of continued existence which have confronted it, and, in doing so, has also met a growing array of essential needs for the continuance of a meaningful, coherent Thai society. We shall try to explain how.

The Boundaries of the Bureaucratic System

The Thai bureaucracy is most readily and immediately perceived as a collection of administrative organizations with offices, staffs, budgets, rules, and all of the other paraphernalia of an administrative apparatus. Twelve ministries are the major units of organization. Of these, Defense, with perhaps 150,000 officers and men—the actual number is a secret—does not concern us here. The other eleven— Agriculture, Communications, Economic Affairs, Education, Finance, Foreign Affairs, Industry, Interior, Justice, National Development, and Public Health—are the primary units of the civil bureaucracy.[3]

One of the notable characteristics of this bureaucracy is its comprehensiveness. In a country with a centralized system of government, the bureaucracy is responsible for a wide array of activities; in Thailand they extend to include the institutions of public education from primary schools through universities.

Yet a number of elements of governmental apparatus are outside the bureaucracy. These include about twenty public economic enterprises, ranging from the State Railways of Thailand, which operates as an independent governmental corporation, to the diverse public enterprises attached to individual ministries. No complete description of these corporations has ever been published.[4] The National Lottery, the Tobacco Monopoly, gunny-bag plants, a plywood company, and a bevy of other public enterprises offer better pay than the bureaucracy—and less prestige—to their officials.[5] These extrabureaucratic enterprises have often served as the sources of special remuneration for high-ranking officials appointed to their boards; and some are commonly regarded as sources from which those in control of the government acquire a share of their personal wealth.

One of the most impressive governmental units outside the bureaucracy is the Bank of Thailand, an important and effective instrument for shaping and implementing the government's monetary policy. Yet it is lacking in some of the inducements of the regular civil service, despite the fact that its salary scale is much higher than that of the bureaucracy. An able graduate student in the Institute of Public Administration once observed, "In the Bank of Thailand one who receives a scholarship to study abroad must resign. In one of the ministries one can continue to draw his salary, will get salary promotions if he gets a foreign degree, and has a better chance to advance."

A small local governmental service also exists outside the national bureaucracy. It has perhaps 10,000 officials and employees. Terms and conditions of employment follow those of the national bureaucracy, but the local officials work for particular municipalities, have no opportunities for mobility beyond their particular jurisdictions, and possess little prestige. Autonomous local government is not significant in Thailand. Urban municipal government (apart from the capital area) did not even exist until passage of the Municipality Act of 1933,[6] and today more than half the nation's local officials are employed in the metropolitan cities of Bangkok and Thonburi. Outside the capital area there is one city—Chiengmai—with a population approaching 100,000; about eighty towns have average populations of 15,000.[7] These data are not necessarily adequate indices of urbanization, for city boundaries do not necessarily coincide with areas of high population density. But to this point, local government in Thailand has been more nominal than real, and this is reflected in the insignificance of the local bureaucracies.[8]

Thus the national civil bureaucracy looms large in any examination of the Thai governmental system. The broad pattern of its organization traces back to 1892, although there have been a number of changes since then. A Ministry of Economic Affairs was established. A Department of Co-operatives, created in the Ministry of Agriculture, was made a ministry following World War II, manifesting governmental intent to improve agriculture through co-operative credit, marketing, and otherwise. In 1963 the Ministry was absorbed into a new Ministry of National Development.[9] A Ministry of Culture, created in 1952 at the behest of Prime Minister Phibulsonggkram and—some say—his wife, flourished briefly to promote cultural self-consciousness and to advance the status of women in Thai society. It was not appreciated by many male officials, and was abolished after the fall of the Phibul government in 1957. The Ministry of Education, established in 1892, did not begin to grow in importance until after the Compulsory Education Act of 1921. The Defense Ministry, also a product of the 1892 reorganization, did not become large and important until World War I and after. The ministries of Education and Defense, as well as of Interior, Foreign Affairs, Agriculture, Justice, Communications, and Public Health, are substantially products of the pattern of ministry organization laid down by King Chulalongkorn. And many of their operating processes can also be traced back to the era of reform.

Today, as in the past, the civil bureaucracy exists as the intermediate strata of a stratified society. As a subsystem of the larger society, it is both part of and apart from its setting. The bureaucracy, the setting, and the relations between the two have become ever more complicated in the years since the Chakkri Reformation, but one essential characteristic of the bureaucracy consists of the arrangements by which it is bounded, or differentiated, from the larger society.

At the top, there is a line between politics and administration—an arbitrary and somewhat unreal line, perhaps, but not so unreal in Thailand as in some other places. At the bottom the demarcation is the status line between officialdom and nonofficialdom; in crude and not entirely satisfactory terms, the line between the bureaucrats and "the people." The lateral boundaries that separate the civil bureaucracy from other important social structures include the barriers between it and the world of business, between civil and military bureaucracy, between bureaucratic and nonbureaucratic governmental enterprise, and between the bureaucracy and the organized Buddhist religion. Within the bureaucracy, too, there are boundaries between ministries, and sometimes even between departments within the same ministry.

The quality of the various boundaries that delimit bureaucracy varies greatly. Often, where there are boundaries there are also bridges, and these relate the bureaucracy and its setting as well as distinguish between the two. The barrier between the bureaucratic and business worlds is partly ethnic. The Chinese control much of the nation's business activity, especially small business. Much of this enterprise is conducted on a small-group basis, familial in character. One is born, married, or adopted into the business; to participate in any other way is to have all the insecurity that goes with being a marginal participant. An exception to this statement must, however, be made to account for the high-ranking Thai officials and their associates who may own shares in, or nominally control, a Chinese-operated business.[10] Perhaps a hundred foreign business firms also operate in Thailand, employing sizeable numbers of local personnel. Ethnic distinctions do not bar Thais from employment in such organizations, but preferences do, including fear of job insecurity, dislike of the emphasis upon high productivity, and the feeling that such employment lacks prestige. Such considerations apparently cause most educated Thai males to prefer government services above business employment.[11]

Military careers were regarded with some favor by ambitious young Thais during the 1950s, partly because the military seemed to offer more rapid advancement and other better rewards than the civil bureaucracy. But there is an apparent common tendency to regard the military as somewhat inferior to the civil service as far as status is concerned. This is understandable, if hard to prove. The military services exist to fight, and to many Buddhists the function may not be attractive. The military also dominate the government, and include groups who engage in power struggles as well as corruption. The military now gives preference to those of its members who have had military rather than civilian college-level training. The military, while apparently more flexible and able to adapt to modern technology, is also more visibly and explicitly authoritarian than the civil bureaucracy. Such factors probably help sustain a preference for the civil service over the military on the part of most Thais of non-military family background.

Interestingly enough, in view of the political dominance of the military, there is little pre-emption of civil bureaucratic posts by military officials. The military hold only a small number of key posts—political and administrative—in the civilian sector.[12] In 1958, for example, when there were about 300 special-class managerial posts in the civil service, less than twenty of them were occupied by military officers.[13] Since 1958 these figures have changed, but not the general picture they portray. In 1964, in the Ministry of Interior, only two or three military officers occupied administrative posts of any consequence outside the Police Department. In 1965 the ministers of Interior, Communications, and Agriculture were high-ranking military officers. The rector of Thammasat University was then the deputy prime minister and minister of Defense. He succeeded to the prime ministership in 1964, and was replaced as rector by Prince Wan, an eminent civilian—former foreign minister and currently also a deputy prime minister. Director-generals of several departments were military officers in 1965, as was the head of the Civil Aviation Administration of the Ministry of Communications. For a time the late Prime Minister, Marshal Sarit, was also chief of the Police Department, which is one unit of the Ministry of Interior headed by General Prapat Charusathira, a powerful member of the ruling clique.

The military have usually occupied a relatively small number of sensitive posts in the civil service, but they have not treated the civil bureaucracy as a source of job patronage, nor have the nation's rulers felt it necessary to penetrate the bureaucracy extensively as a means of controlling it. There seems to be a tacit understanding that civil posts will not be used for military patronage on any sizeable scale— an understanding which the civil sector could never enforce, but which depends upon something more basic and implicit than overt rules and sanctions. This is simply the abiding acceptance of the boundary between the civil and the military services—an acceptance which is made easy by the absence of any problem of controlling the civil bureaucracy.[14]

The boundary between the official bureaucratic sector of the national civil government and the public enterprise type of organizations is largely drawn in terms of prestige and security. Public enterprise workers are not officials in the full sense of the word, and their higher pay is not sufficient to offset this fact for many Thai males. Public enterprise jobs are not as secure: lower-level workers are seldom dropped, but sometimes they are discharged for reasons other than personal misconduct. Higher-level positions in most public enterprises tend to be filled on a patronage basis.

The line between the religious and the bureaucratic ways of life is clear enough. But the separation is not total. Each male official is entitled to one leave-with-pay period of up to 120 days to allow him to serve in the priesthood. The upper levels of the Buddhist religion are themselves bureaucratized to some extent, being organized in the form of a Department of Religious Affairs within the Ministry of Education. For all practical purposes, however, the distinction between a religious career and a bureaucratic career is a sharp as any in the society. Buddhist tenets do work subtle and significant effects upon the bureaucratic social system, but to be a *bhikku,* or priest, is to exist in a sector of society highly differentiated from the bureaucracy. In discussing the relationship between religion and administration, one perceptive Thai observed, "Bureaucracy probably has more effect on Buddhism than Buddhism does on bureaucracy." He meant that the norms and the values of the bureaucratic system tend to control the behavior of officials more than Buddhist precepts—and even at the expense of the latter. The statement is gross but suggestive.

Another boundary requires comment—the line between the administrative and the political. In Thai administrative mythology, ministers are "political," and each has a small secretariat whose chief is also a political official. The undersecretary of state of a ministry, however, is "nonpolitical." In theory, politics sets goals, and administration sees to their execution. Like all such myths, this one wraps a complex set of realities in a cloak of shimmering simplicity. The myth asserts an important norm, however: it proscribes political activity within the bureaucracy, and asserts the obligation of the administrative apparatus to respond to political direction from above. In day-to-day practice, this premise reflects and sustains the ingrained practice of decision making at the top.

Like all effective norms, the axiom of political-administrative apartheid describes as well as prescribes. There is a relatively sharp cleavage between the political and the administrative along a figurative line between the minister and the undersecretary of state. In Thailand no diverse and potent political forces make claims upon government through the civil bureaucracy, except perhaps the forces of foreign aid which sometimes operate partly from a base within—or alongside—elements of the bureaucracy.

Finally, there is the boundary between the bureaucracy and the populace at large. The significance of official position as a prime source of status in Thailand hardly needs mention at this point. The bureaucracy is almost obsessively careerist; an official may not even resign without permission.[15] And the examination procedure by which entrance is gained can only be characterized as a rite of investiture. It is a symbolically significant ritual—the means to a significant alteration of status. Only to a relatively small extent are the examinations rough measures of the potential fitness of candidates.

Thus is the civil bureaucracy of contemporary Thailand bounded from its setting—by procedures, norms, and value orientations. Together, these differentiate the bureaucratic subsystem from its environment. The contemporary bureaucracy is an object of which both bureaucrats and nonbureaucrats are consistently aware. As an entity, it has meaning and qualities that are distinctively bureaucratic. One may possess expectations in relation to the bureaucracy, and one can judge or assess it in relation to other institutions on the basis of any of a number of different criteria.

Of course, the qualities which distinguish the bureaucracy from its setting, and determine the relationships between system and setting, are not limited to the factors mentioned above. The distinctive character of the bureaucracy lies largely in a small cluster of values which govern action within it. These values are also a key to relations between the bureaucratic system and its setting.

Basic Social Values in the Contemporary Bureaucracy

Thai bureaucratic agencies do produce essential goods and services, and can be regarded as productive administrative mechanisms. But such a perspective is a painful and puzzling one from which to view the Thai bureaucracy. It does not begin to explain the bureaucracy, for the dominant value orientation of the bureaucratic system is not productivity, rationality, and efficiency; and the authority which gives order and impetus to bureaucratic action is not primarily the limited legal-rational authority of the Weberian model so often applied in the study of Western systems.

It is more useful to think of the Thai bureaucracy as a social system, or at least as a major subsystem of Thai society. A social system is simply—or not so simply—a collection of basic and abiding rules and relationships which form the framework for the behavior of those within the system. This framework reflects and supports basic social values.

One may argue that at any one time the actors *are* the system. But, in a sense, the system also exists apart from its immediate participants. Individuals are born, and over time they are "socialized." They move into and out of various roles. They die. The system absorbs them and continues beyond them. The social system regulates the behavior of those within it, even outlawing some kinds of activity. Aspects of the system are always prone to change, but certain of its fundamental characteristics tend to be highly stable.

The values which are the core of any social system are basic sources of meaning and perception for those in the system. They are the standards in terms of which choices are made, and in terms of which situations are observed and interpreted as a basis for possible choice. The values need not be wholly consistent, although the system itself will be threatened, or changed, if fundamentally inconsistent values come to be held strongly by large numbers of interacting participants.

These values are not the "Codes of Good Conduct" one finds hanging upon office walls, nor was Prince Damrong's noted code of bureaucratic ethics simply a visible, explicit expression of the existing values in the bureaucracy of his time. To some extent such prescriptions are useful for socializing incoming participants—for cluing them into the ongoing value structure. But a system permeated with a coherent set of unchallenged values might have little need for such explicit, hortatory codes.

The significance of the normative motifs of a social system is matched only by their subtlety. They are more reflected in motivation than in behavior or verbal explanations of that behavior, but motivations themselves tend to be obscure as well as mixed. The motivations, behavior, and verbal testimony of individuals are not sure and certain guides to central social values. A person is not a little social system. He may be in conflict with aspects of the system; his behavior may reflect only some limited facet of the larger whole; and his perception of underlying values will probably be quite subjective.

Yet there are ways of getting at values. The technique chosen here involves a substantial element of subjectivity, and leads to statements which can only be regarded as contingent: it is based upon the premise that the central values of a social system are reflected in a network of supportive arrangements—the specific processes or patterns of action by which the system functions. These processes included norms or criteria which regulate behavior and provide a basis for judging it. In the case of a limited, specialized social subsystem such as the Thai bureaucracy, the processes and their norms are rather readily observable. From them one can infer the values or value orientations which give meaning to the system.

This strategy may be subject to challenge, and its results are certainly open to refinement; but the relevance of a concern with the discovery of central values is beyond dispute. They are the keys to understanding the intrinsic character of the bureaucratic social system.

In the past two decades a variety of attempts have been made to change the *modus operandi* of the Thai bureaucratic system. The Reformation did not succeed in infusing the bureaucracy with the values asserted by its great leaders. And efforts of the postwar period to enhance the productive effectiveness of the bureaucracy in a variety of fields have been impeded and even frustrated.[16] Much of the difficulty has resulted from trying to make elements of the system operate in ways significantly at variance with its fundamental values.

This is not to argue that these values are immutable, but only that they have impressive stability and persistence—as the record of the bureaucratic system before, during, and after the Chakkri Reformation suggests—and that the modification of immediate organizational arrangements and formal procedures is not likely to strike change into the heart of the system's values.

The evidence which follows suggests that the dominant social value orientations of the Thai bureaucracy are these:

1) *Hierarchical status,* which is inherently valued within the bureaucracy and its setting. The primacy of this value is suggested by the fact that the bureaucratic system is to a considerable degree organized and operated to give meaning and support to status.

2) *Personalism,* or the reliance upon personal relationships and

personal concerns as primary bases for behavior within the system. In a sense, this is the antithesis of the depersonalization of the idealized legal-rational bureaucratic model. Membership in the bureaucracy is viewed and valued as a way of life, and is too meaningful to be subjected to formal rules and regulations. Such rules would—if effective—reflect central sources of meaning and authority in society but beyond the bureaucracy, superior to it, and superior also to the political power center of the society.

3) *Security,* or the desire to preserve one's membership in the system is also a basic value. Security is probably a universal human value, whose significance in the Thai bureaucracy lies more in its specific content—and context—than its mere presence. In the Thai system, security is not found through compliance with explicit, universalistic productivity standards, although other clearly visible (but often particularistic) norms are guides to behavior intended to protect membership in the system. The significance of security as a value lies partly in the fact that the bureaucracy is a way of life and a source of status, and that there are few, if any, attractive alternatives to the bureaucracy within the larger society.

There are other values in the Thai bureaucratic system—social values which are widely shared, and readily sanctioned with little or no challenge to their innate legitimacy. One hesitates to say so, but one of these values might simply be *sanuk,* or "fun." The abiding enjoyment of social pleasures, the tendency to regard social and ceremonial activities as a legitimate dimension of the bureaucratic way of life, and the lack of appreciation shown to grim, earnest, manifestly serious, driving officials—these are some indications of the value which is placed upon *sanuk.*[17]

Certain other value orientations are notable for their apparent absence, or for the relatively small support they receive in the Thai bureaucracy. These include secular rationality and the related value of efficiency. Likewise, functional performance, or persistent emphasis upon productivity, is not highly valued in the system. Rationality, efficiency, and productivity tend to go together; the minimization of one usually implies the minimization of all.

Personal equality, or egalitarianism, is, of course, not a basic normative component of the bureaucratic social system, any more than of the society at large. Within the bureaucracy there is no institutionalized general concept of individual rights against the system, regularized rights protected by due process of law. Individuals are protected and authority is restrained, not in response to recognition of any principle of the political rights of individuals per se, but on the basis of religion-centered values which in subtle ways limit the scope of the social system's control over the individual.

The rule of law is no central value of the system. Rules, regulations, and routines do abound, partly because they are inevitable tools of large-scale organization. But there is little institutionalization of law per se, as a self-justifying end or value. Some rules are rather systematically supported by sanctions, especially those which directly support important values, such as status and the dignity of position which is inherent in it. Others, like rules the world over, are subject to incessant attack by those to whom they are supposed to apply. But one special feature of the Thai bureaucracy might be called the "override." A high-ranking official can often sweep aside rules which impede his immediate aims; political officials at the very top of the system can sometimes do this almost without specific limitations on their power.

At the broadest level of generalization it is not entirely incorrect to say that particularism is "valued," or at least thoroughly accepted as a normative characteristic of the system, rather than substantial reliance upon institutionalized universalistic norms. More precisely, perhaps, universalistic norms are fairly common—reflected in the personnel selection process, for example—but they are contingent upon and subject to an override under well-established circumstances, and some apparent universalistic norms are mere hortatory formalism.

Finally, innovation is not highly valued. Generally, innovation is linked with a purposive orientation, a problem-solving posture, and a concern with administrative rationality. Innovation, too, is likely to be a response to unavoidable external pressures for change and adaptation. In a bureaucratic system which tends to be valued for itself rather than as a productive, responsive instrumentality, innovation is not highly relevant, and may even be regarded as undesirably disruptive. A conscious concern about survival has persisted in Thailand for a long time, of course, and survival in a changing environment implies adaptation and thus innovation. But the sensitivity to this prime value is not so much bureaucratic as it is political.[18] The leaders of the 1932 revolution appealed to the bureaucrats and the public to remain orderly, and to the king and his supporters to come quickly and peacefully to terms, lest an excuse for foreign intervention arise out of the overthrow of the monarchy. Again, the maintenance of a sound currency and a competent diplomatic corps have reflected this concern with national survival. But the concern has dominated political rather than administrative activities; within the bureaucracy it is hard to find significant instances where the aim of contributing to national survival has been the evident basis of action.

On the other hand, it might be said that bureaucratic survival, the continuance of the established bureaucratic system, is an aim, or value, which widely influences bureaucratic behavior. Pattern-maintenance is an abiding feature of the Thai bureaucracy. But it is not the bureaucracy as a collection of formal organizations which must be guarded and protected; the previously mentioned values of the system are the real concerns. As these are guarded, the bureaucracy inevitably survives in appropriate form—at least so long as the continuation of the system is feasible.

The Pattern of Authority

Values are authoritative. The institutional values with which we are concerned tend at least to be "moral imperatives" for members of the bureaucratic society. They are internalized. The appreciation of status, for example, is learned at an early age, in the family and at the Buddhist temple. These values are the basis of limited, specific norms that are built into the processes by which the bureaucracy functions and maintains itself.

The values of the system are the basis for defining the reciprocal rights and duties of interacting participants. They also help determine the legitimacy of power in a social system, and set limits upon legitimacy. A legal-rational bureaucracy, for example, depends upon the legitimacy of legal prescriptions. The value system of the society must support the inherent authoritativeness of impersonal rules and regulations; otherwise it will be difficult or impossible to use rules and regulations as devices for controlling bureaucratic behavior. This, of course, does not mean that no norm can be inconsistent with any value, but only that effective norms must derive from effective values —values which may be quite inconsistent with other values in a given society at a given time and place, but which nonetheless possess a real potency. (Witness: law versus traditional values in the civil rights struggle in the United States in the 1960s.)

In the Thai system, legal-rational authority was not institutionalized in the course of the Chakkri Reformation, partly perhaps because of the short time available, and to a very substantial extent because the authoritative values upon which the reform was based were essentially traditional. The Chakkri Reformation extended and supplemented tradition but did not overturn it. The status system itself was depersonalized and regularized by King Chulalongkorn and by a 1911 edict of King Vajiravudh. But this hardly meant that law per se began to acquire the quality of inherent authoritativeness. Reformation edicts were the instruments of royal power. Later, regulations were also the instruments of a pattern of values and authority which was not centered in the legitimacy of law. Authority in the contemporary bureaucracy—the right to make proposals for action that are acceptable on grounds other than their evident intrinsic merit—remains essentially personal and status-derived.

In the complex reality that is the Thai bureaucracy, impersonal legal authority does have a place, but it is limited, contingent, and dependent upon outside support for its existence. Inertia supports many rules and regulations; they are accepted instrumentalities by which the system is maintained. But the override has broad play, and is not regarded as particularly illegitimate. No great stress is commonly produced in an official confronted by a conflict between an official rule and a specific order, provided the order comes from the right place.

At least three important consequences flow from the nature of authority in the Thai bureaucracy:

1) Administrative organizations are overwhelmingly "line" organizations. Within the individual agency, personnel functions are largely performed "in the line," rather than by separate technical staffs operating upon the basis of the effective rules and regulations of an authoritative personnel agency.

In effect, the quality of the authority which is dominant in the contemporary bureaucracy is reflected in the formal pattern of administrative organizations—emphatically hierarchical entities, marked by little lateral interdependence among units, and no systematic use of "staff" units. Staff functions are to some extent inevitable, but the units which perform them, such as the "technical divisions" of departments, are shown on Thai organization charts as "line" units.

2) A second manifestation of the quality of authority in the Thai bureaucracy is small reliance upon techniques of delegation. Authority being personal, one does not generally make a delegation to a subordinate of specific responsibility for some function over a period of time. One makes assignments (or gives specific orders) to subordinates. Beyond this, their broad responsibilities are already inherent in their diffuse roles. The concept of delegation is, in large part, the idea of issuing legal, impersonal, limited packages of responsibility and authority; it tends to reflect not just a legalistic style of administration, but a legal basis of authority.

"Delegation" is a popular subject of management training in Thailand these days—along with the even more attractive (and perhaps relevant) subject of "human relations." If our propositions about authority and value in the Thai bureaucratic society are reasonably sound, then no revolution in Thai administrative behavior is likely to result from talk about delegations. Social structures are not much changed by tinkering with their functional attributes. The limited relevance of delegations and the more basic limits to the potency of legal authority are illustrated by the fate of an ambitious effort, begun more than a decade ago, to publish a code of the legal responsibilities of that important Thai official, the district officer. First, it is interesting and significant that no such code initially existed. Second, the effort was pursued to the point where several volumes were published and issued to district officers. They can be seen unused in governmental offices. Third, the project was abandoned in mid-course, and with no visible consequences so far as patterns of district officer behavior are concerned. They do not operate to any great degree on the basis of continuing reference to rules and regulations resembling delegations.

3) One vital aspect of authority is the nature of the response to authoritative proposals. Western bureaucratic perspectives generally assume: (a) that the response will be in terms of the substance of the order; (b) that the informal aspects of the organizational system will usually tend to support and even supplement this response; and (c) that sometimes pathological responses will occur in the form of conflicts between "authoritative" proposals and "informal" authority, leading to sabotage, or noncompliance with legitimate—legal—proposals. The perspective, in short, is that of a

legal-rational model; and in it the true measure of the authoritative-ness of a proposal lies in the extent to which there is compliance with its substance.

In the Thai bureaucratic system, with its particular values and pattern of authority, the legal model is likely to mislead. The source of authority is personal; the response is personal; and as for the substance of a proposal—"the action often peters out," in the previously-quoted words of James Mosel. The immediate source of authority is hierarchical status; and the substantive concerns of the parties to the relationship are to some degree status-centered rather than achievement-oriented.

The action does not always peter out, of course. But authority based upon personal status is often authority frustrated by its very nature: the requisite response to a proposal for action always has a deference component; it does not always have a performance component. Furthermore, "upward authority"—the making of authoritative proposals for accomplishing results by those engaged in the work on the basis of their competence, dedication, or simply dependence upon results for rewards—does not exist in any systematic, legitimate form. There are no suggestion systems in Thai government agencies.

The "authority of competence" is not an element of a legal-rational model, for that matter. But, in practice, a limited, law-based bureaucratic system, operating in terms of a commitment to achievement, usually enables this kind of authority to operate, and even to operate in an impersonal fashion to a considerable extent. In the Thai system, "upward authority" operates only as a facet of a personalized reciprocity arrangement, involving an association of leader and immediate subordinates functioning as a team.

In this system the thrust must come from the top, but the hierarchy has an impressive absorptive capacity. Orders transmitted down through several layers are likely to lose much of their potency, if not their content. Because the number of units increases enormously as one moves down from one layer to the next, it becomes practically impossible for the men at the top of the system to keep track of the consequences of the endless flow of their orders and commands.

In recognition of this characteristic of the system, the late Marshal Sarit sought to energize and control various facets of the bureaucracy by moving units of organization into his own office.[19] In some cases the object was to enhance the authority of an agency. Thus the

Budget Office was made part of the Prime Minister's Office to give it the power of hierarchical position that it could never possess as an element of the Ministry of Finance. This hierarchical authority was reinforced by the appointment of an able and prestigious director, Dr. Puey Ungphakorn. But the result of this not illogical approach, when used in a number of instances, was to make the Prime Minister's Office a superbureaucracy in its own right. By 1960 it had a budget larger than those of the ministries of Finance, Foreign Affairs, Justice, Economic Affairs, Co-operatives (abolished in 1963), Public Health, and Industry. It included twenty-four separate units of organization, ranging from the prime minister's staffs to the nation's five universities.

Conclusion

This brief sketch of the nature of value and authority within the contemporary bureaucracy amounts to a set of assertions, supported by little evidence, about fundamental characteristics of the system. Let us now look at the available evidence.

Chapter 9

THE CONTEMPORARY BUREAUCRACY IN ACTION: MANIFESTATIONS OF BASIC CHARACTERISTICS

THE THAI bureaucracy "makes sense" when the concrete behavior that occurs within it is viewed in terms of the values discussed in the previous chapter, and the authority pattern linked with those values.

The bureaucracy does hundreds of things, from building roads to spraying mosquitoes. To examine all these efforts in terms of the values which give them meaning and order would be a large and tedious task. Fortunately, it is not necessary, for the underlying values are reflected in the processes by which the contemporary bureaucracy procures, allocates, and energizes its resources. These common denominators of bureaucratic action have already been the focus of an examination of ways in which the Chakkri Reformation changed the administrative system.

This way of looking at the contemporary bureaucracy has a significant advantage: it is not based upon the assumption that the bureaucracy's primary objective is to produce goods and services for external clienteles. The perspective merely assumes that the bureaucratic social system has certain processive or functional characteristics, and that the norms governing these will be rather direct reflections of the central values of the system. The scheme might be represented in the form of a matrix (see page 170).

In principle, the individual cells of this matrix could be filled with specific information about activities and the norms inherent in them. In practice, there is one inevitable problem: items of activity and particular norms are not susceptible of discrete, exclusive classification. A given action-plus-norm, for instance, may involve resource allocation as well as resource procurement. The same action-plus-norm may reflect both the values of hierarchical status and of personalism.

PROCESSES	VALUES		
	Hierarchical Status	Personalism	Security
Resource Procurement			
Resource Allocation			
Resource Energizing			

So long as the relevant data fit somewhere within the classification scheme, no fundamental problem results from this somewhat untidy relationship between the concrete and the analytical. But a great amount of repetition would be involved if each relevant item of data were separately listed in each appropriate cell. This would also chop the bureaucratic portrait into a set of exceedingly small pieces. To avoid these difficulties the following discussion is organized in terms of a description of bureaucratic processes. The processes themselves are discussed in two ways: first, in a series of statements concerning particular process characteristics—statements which also manifest the norms involved in action, and which can be identified with underlying value orientations; and second, in supporting examples of the processes in action. In short, the combination consists of generalizations and case-type data.

The bureaucracy portrayed here existed through the 1950s and into the early 1960s. As the latter decade has moved along, it has seemed that certain rather fundamental changes might be occurring in the normative foundations of the administrative system. It is too soon to assess their dimensions; and, in any case, they involve departures from the patterns of action described in this chapter, for these appear to be the basic operating characteristics of the bureaucracy.

Resource Procurement

In the most general terms, resource procurement in the Thai bureaucracy is to a great extent inertial: established arrangements for claiming and getting resources tend to continue with little or no effective challenge. New claims are normally made only at political levels in the bureaucracy, and systematic programing as a basis for evaluating resource use and adjusting resource claims is not commonly found within the bureaucracy.

PROGRAMING

The process of claiming and getting resources has these characteristics:

1. *Only high status persons may properly propose significant changes in, or additions to, the established pattern of resource assignment.* This is essentially a political function, and it is seldom systematically supported by empirical studies or analyses. A budget staff in the Office of the Prime Minister screens resource claims. At times a resource claim is overridden by the individual ministers who submit budget proposals.

1a. No civil bureaucratic interest groups exist to bring systematic pressure upon the political center of the governmental system for increased resources. The deliberate organization of such power centers within the bureaucracy to exert pressure upward—whether for increased salaries or for more funds for education or public health—is inconceivable. It would be a stark violation of the hierarchical status value. (An individual may properly seek to improve his own income within the system—usually by improving his status or his connections —but he may not try to form an organization to press for increases in a salary scale which was last changed in 1952.)

1b. Adjustments in the existing pattern of claims on resources tend to be made on a personal basis, as a result of face-to-face discussions at political levels. Subtle and disparate norms seem to govern such claims and the response they receive—ranging from personal favoritism to concern with national prestige and survival. Specific program goals are not compelling bases for resource claims.

2. *Little or no justification is required for the continuation of established resource allocations, so long as governmental revenues do not shrink.* The bureaucracy has customarily generated little empirical data which might be used in the continuing assessment of established claims (although the Budget Procedures Act of 1959 has established a basis for changing this, by provision for a performance

budgeting arrangement; and some shifts in the process of financial resource claim making seem to be underway). The legitimacy of established allocations helps maintain the security of participants in the
bureaucratic system.

PERSONNEL PROCUREMENT

1. *Nearly all personnel intake occurs at two entry levels at the bottom of the formal hierarchical structure, the fourth class and the third
class.* Fourth-class intake is limited to clerks, artisans, some kinds of
teachers, and others without college training. The third class is the
entry level for officials whose positions require college educations. A
few specialized types of positions requiring graduate training are filled
by intake at the second-class level.

2. *The hierarchical structure of officialdom is protected against
some of the impact of productivity requirements by the use of sizeable numbers of* wisaman, *or nonstatus employees, as determined by
the varying needs of individual organizations.* These employees can
be hired without having to be accommodated to the status system,
and they can be removed when no longer needed. In practice, most of
them tend to stay on indefinitely.

3. *The desire for bureaucratic status appears to be a powerful
motivation for seeking bureaucratic posts, just as the desire for status
improvement seems to explain the quest for advancement that one
finds within the system, particularly above the fourth-class level.*

4. *Bureaucratic intake, advancement, and removal tend to be
based upon a concern with the "whole person," and not merely job
performance in a relatively narrow sense. In principle, the service is
open, and access is not limited to those with specified ascriptive qualities.*

4a. Intake selection is competitive, although the examinations are
of little value as predictors of technical competence. Efforts are made
to determine the suitability of an individual to be a bureaucrat. The
intake procedure resembles an investiture rite: those who have shown
themselves worthy are taken into the system as vacancies occur, and
are endowed with a special status in the society.

4b. No evidence suggests that the intake examinations are "rigged"
or manipulated to assure high scores for favored candidates. Some
individuals, however, do receive preferential treatment: they are per-

mitted to work in a department on an informal basis in anticipation of an examination. When, after some months, they take the test, they are almost bound to do well. They know the answers to questions about departmental work procedures; and they usually do well on the oral examination.

4c. The examination process appears to be regarded as acceptable by most of the would-be competitors. To some extent it does provide open access to the bureaucracy.

4d. The openness of the examinations is limited by the fact that each employing agency, such as a department, announces and gives its own examinations, with nominal publicity. Finding out about entrance examinations and taking them sometimes becomes a major enterprise for would-be officials. Personnel selection is a "line" function performed by the employing agency, with a nominal degree of control exercised by the Civil Service Commission through regulations governing the preparation and conduct of examinations.

4e. Because a college education is usually needed to gain access to the third-class examinations, the desire to enter the bureaucracy is an important basis for the demand for college diplomas.

5. *The procurement of personnel for higher-level posts is almost invariably by promotion.* Lateral movement across departmental or ministerial boundaries is limited. An individual normally advances in rank and status within his own unit or organization, generally the department in which he was initially appointed.

5a. The most important promotions are "class" promotions, e.g., movement from the third class to the second class, or from the first to the special class at the very top of the hierarchy. But access to class promotions is partially determined by results of lesser promotions, "step" promotions or raises in pay within one's class.

5b. Normally, a person's pay is increased by one "step" each year. (For example, there are 12 salary steps in the second class of the civil service.) But superiors commonly use the step-promotion arrangement as a sanction: officials who please their bosses may receive a two-step raise—in some exceptional cases even more. An official who is disliked may receive no step increase. Because an official must reach a high salary level within his class to become eligible to advance to the next class, step promotions are important.

5c. The security of individual bureaucrats is to some extent protected by a requirement that failure to recommend an official for an annual step increase must be justified by a memorandum to the head of the department. But there is no effective appeal from the superior's decision, nor any formal way to dispute statements in his memorandum. Sometimes, however, personal connections can be used to prevent a decision not to grant a pay increase; an immediate superior has limited capacity to punish an official who has good personal connections at a higher level. His recommendations about pay promotions may be overridden.

5d. Class promotions are usually made on the basis of "selective" examinations when vacancies occur in a higher-ranking position. Officials who are eligible to compete, in terms of salary and length of service, must be given permission by their superiors before they can take the examination, which is prepared, administered, and graded by line officials in the department. The preference of the departmental director or his immediate subordinate will usually determine who is actually promoted. This preference may be based upon personal liking, or simply on the conviction that one of the candidates is most suitable for the vacancy for any of a number of reasons.

5e. In any case, high productivity is seldom the primary basis for advancement in rank. There is, for example, no arrangement for the "reclassification" of a job and its incumbent in recognition of the fact that the importance or the quantity of his work has increased.

5f. A protégé arrangement often influences the procurement of personnel for higher-level positions. Young and ambitious officials usually seek to establish an identification with a high-ranking patron. They support him by being helpful, informative, and deferential. He in turn is expected to obtain rewards for his followers, one of which is advancement. If the high official moves to a new organization, his protégés may also move.

5g. In the early 1960s this pattern of restricted personnel mobility appeared to be modified, as a number of new organizations appeared on the scene and others expanded rapidly. The protégé arrangement may be weakening somewhat in the face of rapid bureaucratic expansion.

5h. In general, "deviants," or individuals who are at odds with the central value orientations of the bureaucracy, do not move into high-status positions. To be critical of superiors, for example, is usually to wipe out one's chance for advancement—unless one has a highly placed patron who can provide protection, and perhaps a transfer.

6. *Separation from the system occurs only through retirement, through resignation with permission, or through serious violation of discipline.*

6a. There is no reduction-in-force procedure by which superfluous officials may be removed because they are no longer needed.

6b. One may not even resign without permission; to resign is to relinquish the status of an official, and no official is completely free to do this of his own volition.

6c. The most significant punitive sanction used in the bureaucracy is removal from the service. This is tantamount to "unfrocking" an official. Removal is almost invariably the result of violating deference norms, i.e., dignity norms, or engaging in behavior which in a sense threatens the integrity of the system—such as stealing government funds entrusted to one's care.

6d. While there is a formal procedure by which such sanctions as removal may be appealed, an appeal is a request that one's superiors be overruled, and it practically never succeeds.

In summary, hierarchical status, personalism, and security are all reflected in the arrangements by which personnel and other resources are procured for the Thai bureaucracy. Status is a potent force which makes the bureaucracy attractive in the face of more remunerative alternatives which are available outside it. Advancement in hierarchical status is usually the key to increased material rewards for members of the system. There is little or no real conflict between status norms and productivity norms in the procurement of resources, simply because authority inheres in status, and status is not determinately linked with productivity.

RESOURCE PROCUREMENT: EXAMPLES OF THE PROCESS

Budgeting and Programing. Until 1956, budget preparation and administration were the responsibilities of a division in the Comptroller-General's Department of the Ministry of Finance.[1] As part of a far-ranging technical assistance effort in the field of fiscal management, the Public Administration Service, a private, nonprofit consulting firm, assisted the Thai government in modernizing its accounting and budgeting procedures, beginning in the late 1950s. A budget office was created and, in 1959, made a bureau in the Office of the

Prime Minister, headed by a director with the status of a permanent undersecretary—the highest rank available to a civil official. By 1960 this bureau, operating under the Budget Procedures Act of 1959, had contributed an appreciable degree of order and coherence to a budgetary process which earlier had been almost chaotic—involving large-scale lending and borrowing of money among governmental organizations and a variety of *ad hoc* allocations to individual agencies at almost any time during the fiscal year.

When the Budget Bureau was created, a rule was adopted that new projects and items of expenditure must be submitted to and approved by that Office before going to the Council of Ministers for what amounts to appropriation of the requested funds. If the Bureau were actually to regulate the requests submitted by the various ministers —to reject or modify them as well as approve them—and to do so in terms of program goals or productivity criteria, the validity of previous statements about the normative foundations of the Thai bureaucracy would be open to serious challenge.

In practice, however, the Budget Bureau's control over contested resource claims has been limited—although it may be stronger now than it was in the first years of the existence of the office. In the field of economic development, for example, "it is common to have new projects and new items of expenditures introduced by the Council of Ministers after the estimated ceilings [for the next fiscal year] . . . have been approved by the Budget Bureau and the Planning office. They are introduced at this stage to avoid being screened out. . . . These projects are usually initiated by Ministers themselves or by friends of Ministers." [2]

Innovative programing is simply not a significant feature of Thai bureaucratic activity. Projects may be developed by the joint efforts of Thai bureaucrats and foreign advisers. To be of any consequence, however, these efforts must be acceptable at political levels in the system, and foreign advisers have usually sought to build and maintain political support.

Proposed foreign aid projects have been initiated in most cases by individual ministers or by aid donors. "We have come across one instance where a private foreign national initiated a project and, after receiving the approval of the Thai Government, made the initial approach to the foreign source of capital." [3]

During much of the post-World War II era, programing for the bureaucracy has been done largely by foreign advisers and foreign aid officials, planning and working in such fields as transportation, statistics, fiscal management, highway engineering and construction, mining, agricultural education and development, community development, the development of the educational system, and fisheries improvement. Planning assistance has often been linked with economic aid, and the program proposals of American foreign aid advisers have often generated pressure from Thai political sources to get the United States to undertake the recommended programs.[4] As a result, early in the 1960s the United States Operations Mission in Thailand began to reduce its advisory efforts, particularly in the field of economics.

In 1959 the National Economic Development Board (NEDB) was created as a national planning agency. In 1963 a Ministry of National Development was also established to implement various developmental projects. It is possible that a new commitment to programing—and to the values inherent in it—may be emerging within the NEDB and the Ministry, but one cannot yet assess the norms which actually govern the resource claims of the Ministry or the allocation power of the Board.

In this context, a prime contribution of the Budget Bureau has been to bring order and regularity into what might be termed the inertial aspect of financial resource procurement. This is a matter of no small importance to the continuing operations of a bureaucracy that grows ever larger and more complex. The Budget Bureau now appears to have substantial authority to regulate resource claims and allocations which do not bring into play the power of influential ministers. Thus the establishment of new positions becomes largely a matter of getting Budget Bureau approval, and Budget Bureau operating norms seem to be productivity-centered. The Bureau can assert the inherent power of the prime minister, unless this involves conflicts with his ministers which the premier wishes to avoid.

Personnel Procurement. The procedures by which personnel are procured for the civil bureaucracy support the inferences which have been made concerning resource procurement in the Thai bureaucracy and the values they reflect.

Several thousand persons are taken into the civil service in a typical year as replacements and additions.[5] Several hundred more are promoted in rank and thus "procured" for new posts.

The major facts of intake selection are these: [6]

a. The entire process is geared to prior education and training.

b. Eligibility is established by passing either a "competitive" or a "selective" examination.

c. The examination is announced, prepared, administered, and graded by the ministry, department, or province in which positions are open; job eligibility is established in a given examination only within the administering agency. The examination procedure is subject to regulation and a limited review by the Civil Service Commission.

d. Appointments are made in order of examination scores, from highest to lowest on the register of eligibles. A register is effective for up to two years.

e. Appointees must be free from certain personal blemishes and must attest that they subscribe to certain stipulated values. Job candidates must be Thai nationals, at least eighteen years of age, "sincerely believing in the constitutional form of government" (*Civil Service Act,* Section 44, Clause 3), physically and mentally sound, moral, financially solvent, free from past conviction of a serious crime or any major violation of civil service discipline in any prior employment.[7]

f. They must serve in probational status for six to twelve months before they are instated as full-fledged officials.

g. Women can compete equally with men for appointment, except when the minister in charge arrives at an understanding with the Civil Service Commission that they shall be barred from appointment to a particular post.

The Civil Service Commission has the authority to determine educational standards which must be met by applicants. Would-be fourth-class civil servants must generally have the certificate of secondary education (i.e., have completed *Matayom* 6, or the tenth year of common schooling) or a specified equivalent, with a lowering of this standard authorized in some regions where educational facilities have been limited.[8] Candidates in third-class examinations must be graduates of a college or university granting a bachelor's degree or diploma, or the equivalent, or they must have five years' service at the fourth class, or certain comparable experience.[9] Third-class eligibility requirements have remained substantially unchanged since 1933, and those of the fourth class have undergone no profound modification.

And the practice of linking educational background and eligibility for appointment to a certain rank in the bureaucracy is older than the civil service system itself.

1. Competitive Intake Examination. The central feature of the intake selection procedure is the examination. There is a touch of quaint charm in the Thai civil service examinations, although this quality affords small solace to those subjected to them.

The fourth-class competitive examination is the most commonly used selection instrument. Between 1954 and 1958 as many as 20,000 Thais participated in about 650 of these, with slightly more than one in three individuals passing.[10]

This examination is conducted in accordance with the "syllabus" of the Civil Service Commission, a detailed guide—in effect a regulation—which requires applicants to be examined in writing concerning "theory" and "practice," and then orally concerning their intelligence, knowledge, and personalities.[11]

An examination typically requires three or four days' time, although in cases involving large numbers of candidates as many as six have been required. The written parts of the examination are entirely subjective, and no specific key or set of approved answers is prepared beforehand.

The "theory" portion of the examination, in accordance with the Civil Service Commission's rules, covers these subjects: (1) the Civil Service Act, (2) the Thai constitution, (3) history and geography of Thailand and neighboring countries, (4) the Act Reorganizing Ministries, Departments, and Public Bodies, (5) the Administration of the Kingdom Act, (6) the four kinds of "culture," and moral, legal, social, and official behavior (in effect, official ethics), and (7) Thai and English languages.

The "practical" portion of the examination varies, insofar as specific permission has been granted by the Civil Service Commission to incorporate specialized material. For clerical workers generally, the practical section of the examination covers correspondence work —writing letters and reports, and filing, typing, and handwriting. In some instances it may deal with knowledge of particular laws and work procedures. The stated aim, in any case, is to determine in a rather loose fashion the applicant's ability to do certain kinds of work. About 15 per cent of the written examination time is allotted to practical subjects. Then comes the oral interview, perhaps ten to fifteen minutes before the examination committee whose individual members score the applicant's personality, general knowledge, and intelligence.

Under the Commission's rules, applicants, in order to pass, must make a mark of at least 60 per cent of the Thai language portion of the test, at least 50 per cent on the cultural (or ethical) part, and a net grade of not less than 60 per cent. The total examination is usually worth a possible 950 points, of which the interview counts for 100. The practical part of the examination is worth 200, or about 20 per cent. The results of the examination are posted, showing the names and scores of those successful.

The Civil Service Commission (CSC) is nominally responsible in law for the selection of officials, but responsibility for examinations is delegated to "Civil Service Subcommissions" (CSSC) which exist in each ministry, in each department of any size, and in each province. The CSSC is an ex-officio body consisting of top-ranking line administrators. It formally determines that an examination is needed (in response to an assertion to this effect from the ranking line official); it appoints an examination committee of lesser line administrators, or it may appoint two committees, one to prepare and evaluate questions and one to supervise the examination. The rank of members of these committees is higher than that of the posts for which the examination is to be given. In the Bangkok-Dhonburi area a member of the Civil Service Commission staff is normally appointed to the examination committee.

The examination is announced about two weeks before the end of the application period, by bulletin-board notices in the examining agency and, usually, by one announcement on the Official Notice program of the National Broadcasting Station. Knowledge of the forthcoming examination circulates chiefly by word of mouth. An applicant obtains an application form and submits it with an official certificate of education, a birth certificate, and a reference letter from an official of suitable rank. He pays an examination fee (20 baht for a fourth-class and 40 baht for a third-class examination), which goes to the Civil Service Commission, and presents himself to be examined on the appointed day. Signature comparisons are used to prevent falsification of identity.

Commission regulations specify the subjects and the number of questions, as well as the points allotted for each section of the examination. A member of the CSC staff, Nai Praween Na Nakorn, Chief of the Division of Discipline and Appeals, is probably known throughout Thailand for his book on the Civil Service law. It is used both by examinees in preparing for tests and by examination committees in drafting questions.[12] But the final determination of the questions to be asked rests with the committee, as does the assessment of the answers.

Examination papers are identified by number rather than name, and each paper is graded by every member of the examining committee. In one presumably typical instance "each examiner judged the quality of the paper from his own knowledge and experience," without co-ordination of the ratings. Thus the same answer may receive a different number of points from different examiners.

The secretary of the examination committee totals the points earned on the examinations and indicates who has passed, being guided by CSC rules. The scoring is not complex—the "raw scores" are also the final scores. Results are announced by the chairman of the CSSC, who posts them for the information of the examinees and also submits the following information to the Civil Service Commission: (1) a list of the names of the candidates who passed, (2) a form recording the grades for each section of each examination, (3) three copies of the examination questions, (4) the answer papers of the top-, bottom-, and middle-ranking examinees, (5) a list of the names of applicants, and (6) a copy of the announcement of examination results.

The report to the Civil Service Commission is made at leisure. It may be sent months after the examination has been given, and its receipt by the CSC is usually not acknowledged. Meanwhile, a number of examinees will have started their service as probationers, at salaries of 450 baht (about $22.50 per month).

The third-class competitive examination taken annually by a thousand or more would-be officials is not fundamentally different, nor has it changed much since 1933. It includes: general knowledge (100 points, 3 hours, 10 questions); cultural subjects (200 points, 4 hours, 10 questions); Thai language essay (100 points, 3 hours); English language (100 points, 3 hours); civil service law and regulations (100 points, 3 hours); "practical subjects"—not more than three, related to the particular work (100 points, 3 hours); general administrative practice (100 points, 3 hours); oral examination (100 points, 15 minutes per candidate).

A Representative Fourth-Class Competitive Examination

Examination schedule:

First day:	9:30–11:30—General knowledge
	1:30– 3:30— " "
Second day:	9:00–12:00—Culture
	1:30– 3:30—Thai language
Third day:	9:30–11:30—English language
	11:30–12:00—Handwriting
	1:30– 3:30—Correspondence and filing
Fourth day:	9:30–11:30—Typing
	1:00– 4:00—Interviews

Examination content:

General Knowledge—Part 1. Answer the following 10 questions:
1. What is the meaning of the words "civil servant?"
2. What are the classes and positions of civil servants?
3. List the kinds of civil service discipline.
4. List the penalties provided for breaches of discipline.
5. Indicate the punishment appropriate for the following breaches: (a) dishonesty in performance of duty; (b) contempt of the public; (c) divulging official secrets.
6. State the organization and functions of the Civil Service Commission and the Civil Service Subcommission.
7. What are the component parts of the sovereignty?
8. What are the duties of the Constituent Assembly?
9. What are the duties of the Thai people according to the Constitution?
10. Why was the Constituent Assembly established?

General Knowledge—Part 2. Ten questions.

A somewhat similar pattern, but with questions on history and geography as well as government organization and administration.

Culture. Ten questions:

1. What does "culture" mean?
2. What are the sources of culture?
3. What is the importance of culture to the individual and to the nation?
4. What is meant by the "sense of duty and responsibility" of the public official?
5. Explain: "The civil official is the public servant and not the public master." Is this right or wrong?
6. What is a "good citizen?"
7. What are the disadvantages of taking drugs and liquors? Should officials indulge in these?
8. What are the "four factors for success" (*itti-pat-see*)?
9. If a citizen criticizes an order of the government, what would you tell him?
10. What type of person would you make friends with?

Thai Language.

Write an essay of at least 25 lines on the topic, "Life as a woman is difficult, but life as a man is more difficult."

English Language.

1. Translation of a simple paragraph into Thai. (One I have seen contained references to "snow" and "snow bank.")
2. Translation of several short statements from Thai into English.

Correspondence.

1. Write a letter conveying certain specified information.
2. Indicate the abbreviations commonly used for certain government organizations.
3. Indicate the proper headings and closes for certain specified types of official letters.
4. State how long official documents must be kept, and which kind may not be destroyed.

Handwriting.

Write 200 words on a subject (such as "devotion to one's duty").

Typing.

Type a copy of an official letter.

The third- and fourth-class examinations are only incidentally concerned with the assessment of functional competence. As predictive instruments they probably screen out some unsuitables—inarticulate individuals, and those unable or unwilling to subject themselves to the grinding effort of preparing for the examinations by the study of the printed commentaries and other available information. Thus the examinations are subtly and obliquely valid to some extent. They "measure" verbal proficiency. They force the learning of a glut of knowledge, much of it extraneous to the work of the bureaucracy, but not quite all. Knowledge of rules, regulations, procedures, prescribed behavior, manners and poise—all these are examined to some extent, in one relatively unstandardized way or another. The typical candidate who has passed the examination probably has the capacity to fit the mold of the civil bureaucracy, including the willingness to do things because their doing is beyond thought or question, and the ability to say things because it is proper to say them, and to say them with a touch of finesse. The examinations have a certain intrinsic and unpremeditated consistency with the underlying values of the bureaucratic system.

And, of course, they perform another function, serving as a barrier and a bridge between the bureaucracy and the rest of society. Some device is inevitably necessary to control access to the system, and merely by existing the Thai examinations serve this purpose. Linked with educational levels, they are not really very much correlated with the substance of education beyond the relatively rudimentary business of knowing how to read, write, absorb, and regurgitate information.

As one graduate student put it, "These subjects on the third class competitive examination were very hard for me, for I had never studied any of them before. I must look for documents, books, acts, rules and orders dealing with the Civil Service Act and the particular functions of the department offering the examination. It is very difficult to understand . . . , as there are many technical terms. . . . About five hundred candidates passed, and those with the highest points ranging from the first to the ninetieth were appointed. A large number had been fourth class officials in the Department. Their ability to answer the questions was better than the outsiders. For instance, I cannot answer any of the questions for I have never known the technical terms of this department, and hence cannot translate them into Thai, or from Thai into English. People who studied in the university have much theory, but often they have never known the present practice or the rules and procedures. . . ."

With a persistent and widespread surplus of job candidates, except in a few sectors of the bureaucracy, individuals not uncommonly seek "employment" as nonofficial workers in a ministry or department for small pay from non-salary funds, in order to acquire knowledge for the examinations after they have finished their college work. Or they may obtain appointments at the fourth class in order to establish a basis for qualifying for the third class, for which their educational level makes them eligible provided they can pass the examination. The object is to attain a position in the service and with it the security and dignity afforded by a bureaucratic career.

The examinations are thoroughly unattractive but not necessarily unsuitable tools. They may seem to be otiose, and from the perspective of a concern with productivity they are—but this viewpoint does not take account of the values of the bureaucratic social system in which attainment is sanctioned far more than achievement.

2. *Selective Intake Examinations.* A portrayal of the competitive examinations must be qualified by notice of an adaptation which is significant at least in its portent—the selective examinations. Under present civil service legislation, a particular department or ministry may substitute for a part of the regular competitive examination a specialized test in which somewhat greater stress is placed upon specific qualifications required for technical or professional posts. Quite a few agencies have taken advantage of this arrangement.

To substitute such examinations, the agency submits a proposal to the Civil Service Commission for preliminary approval, and then to the Council of Ministers. This leads to promulgation of a royal decree authorizing a variation from the competitive examination.[13] There is significance in the fact that a royal decree must be issued to authorize a variation from established procedure for the selection of fourth-class officials in a particular department of the government: the formalism and traditionalism of the Thai bureaucracy are clearly manifested in its examination process, with its great concern for the manner of action.

To take an example: the Department of Central Information, or Central Intelligence, has special selection requirements for its personnel, in view of the confidential character of its work. To permit selection of suitable fourth-class officials, a royal decree was obtained in 1957 authorizing a selective examination. Candidates in this examination were required to have the qualifications and educational backgrounds applying to competitive selection, plus not less than six months of "indoctrination training" in the Department and clearance by top-level officials of the agency. A similar arrangement was also adopted for the selection of third-class officials. All the usual examination procedures were followed, and the general format of the competitive examination was used, with these exceptions: the special subjects required in both third- and fourth-class examinations dealt with the work of the Department, and part of the examination consisted of an assessment of performance during the trial period. The real substance of selection was, beyond all doubt, based upon judgments of the performance and demeanor of the official during his trial period. But this examination, like all the others, was essentially a symbolically significant ritual, the means to an important alteration of status—and this is what really counted about it.

In many cases the selective examinations involve only a small departure from the competitive pattern. Even the specialized aspects of such examinations may have little relevance to the duties to which a successful candidate is appointed. One such examination stressed statistics. The successful examinee notes: "After I was appointed I worked in the statistics section, but for six months I did no statistical work; I read departmental circulars and was the secretary of some temporary departmental committees. . . . For four years my work went on in this way. Then the director-general ordered me to be trained in statistics. This study duplicated my university work, but an order is an order. The director-general did not know about statistics, and I cannot tell him, [although] I know well that it is a waste of time to repeat the studies. At any rate, I thought for a long time to try to do my best in the civil service but I failed. . . . Although I desire to do my job, to do my duty honestly, the superior never used his order to me to do more work. This circumstance has . . . created the habit of idleness among the officials. I think that the causes come from the top down."

This statement is not unrepresentative of commonplace reality. The increasing use of selective examinations throughout the bureaucracy is not by any means a simple indication of the renaissance of functionalism; selective examinations themselves are not necessarily evidence of more basic systemic change.

Yet in some areas within the bureaucracy selective examinations are more closely linked with functional effectiveness. In these instances the examinations have lost their discriminatory, but not their symbolic, significance. Everybody—or nearly everybody—with the appropriate specialized qualifications passes. Thus in five recent years, ninety-two selective examinations were held in a department of the Ministry of Public Health. Of the 1,294 candidates who took the tests, 1,294 passed, and 1,294 were appointed. Nearly half were medical technicians, nurses, or doctors; the others were nonmedical personnel.[14] With relatively small variations, this seems to be the pattern of selection in the Ministry, which makes little use of competitive examinations. The symbolic significance of the examinations is evidenced by their retention in the Ministry, even though they are of no discriminatory value whatever.

3. *Promotion.* One interesting reflection of the reformistic zeal which appeared briefly after the 1932 coup was the adoption of the principle of promotion upon the basis of competitive examination, which was applied to all but the highest administrative positions of director-general and undersecretary.[15] For promotion purposes, officials were classified as clerical, third, second, and first class. For each class there was a competitive examination. Clerical and third classes were intake levels. Access to the second class and first class required, in addition to success on the examination, appropriate combinations of education and experience. The promotional examinations were to be given annually by the Civil Service Commission. But this awkward and idealistic arrangement lasted only briefly. It existed during a time when, because of fiscal conditions, there was little intake or promotion within the bureaucracy. In 1936 the arrangement was abandoned, and the amount of competition involved in promotion was greatly reduced. Promotion methods have not changed greatly since 1936.

An examination is normally required; but competition is limited to a particular jurisdiction, typically a department. Seniority is an important factor, and the examination is "selective" rather than competitive.[16] However, a fourth-class official with at least fifteen years of service, who has been at the top salary grade of the class for at least four years and who has been working as an "official of section" rather than in a more menial capacity, may upon recommendation of his superiors be promoted to the third class without examination.

Promotion from third to second class involves passing a qualifying examination. But one must also have a bachelor's degree and one year of service or no degree and three years of service, *and* be recommended for promotion by his director-general or undersecretary. Promotion to the first class is again based on a qualifying examination, seniority (at least three years at the second class), and, of course, the approval of superiors. According to Nai Gaewchaiyo, "Generally speaking, [such] promotion . . . is usually a matter of selection within a department" (p. 78). But in both cases the examination ritual is required.

Promotion to the special class, the top level of the bureaucracy, is without competition. This exalted level requires a special method of selection to emphasize with suitable symbolism the distinction between it and all other classes. At least three years of first class are required, and the first-class civil servant must be at least at the seventh pay step of his class. The proposed promotion must be approved by the Civil Service Commission for the Council of Ministers, and then formalized by a royal command.

Other requirements preclude casual advancement to the special class. The Civil Service Commission first considers the justification for establishing the proposed special-class position if a new one is to be created. The minister in charge submits a detailed work plan for the post and a statement describing the proposed incumbent's prospective contribution to the service.

Promotion from one class to another in the bureaucracy is no easy matter. To move from one class to another one must, among other things, be at or near the top pay rate for one's class and there must be a vacant post at the next higher class. Class promotion is the ultimate form of advancement, lesser promotions consisting of advancement in salary "step" or "grade." Step promotions are increases of one or more salary steps within a grade, usually granted at the beginning of each year, with anything more than a two-step increase subject to approval by both the minister in charge and the Civil Service Commission. Grade promotion, or promotion from one salary grade to another within a class, *may* involve a nominal job transfer; the top pay rate for a particular job may be less than the top pay rate of the class. In such a case a person at the top pay rate of his particular position must move to another with a higher ceiling, to advance in pay. The new job may be only nominally different.

By behaving oneself, one can achieve annual "step promotions," which in turn can lead to "grade promotions" in due time. These may eventually lead to "class promotions," the most difficult of all. Yet neither time-serving nor eager devotion to duty are in themselves likely to lead to class promotions. The selective forces which produce the upper-class bureaucratic elite are subtle and highly informal, but they are also very real. A true competence is involved in advancement, but it is "functionally diffuse," and it is also variable and unstandardized. Promotional examinations are almost utterly irrelevant to the assessment of such competence. They ratify and legitimize decisions to promote.

In some cases, at least, intermediate status may be attained by acquiring degrees from abroad which can put one high in the third-class pay range—or even make one eligible for direct appointment to the second class. In other cases, social connections extending beyond the immediate organization appear to be important. Perhaps the nearest thing to a generalized characterization of the selective forces which facilitate advancement to the upper levels of the system includes (a) possession of the necessary formalized requisites, including time-in-class, and (b) "talented stewardship." These requirements call for the deft fulfillment of the desires and expectations of one's superior, or key superiors.[17]

A tradition far more ancient than the Chakkri Reformation lies behind the intense personalness of vertical relations in the Thai system that vitally affect advancement in it. But a much more immediate factor also helps explain the circumstances of advancement in rank and status within the bureaucracy: lateral movement across the formal boundaries of departments (excepting only the smallest) is quite limited. One usually moves upward in one's own organization, if one moves at all, barring the most exceptional of circumstances, which are usually indicative of good personal connections at a high level. Thus, if one wishes to advance one pleases his supervisors.

This, of course, is entirely consistent with the central values of the bureaucratic social system. A strong and widespread dedication to productivity might encourage emphasis upon other criteria of advancement and thus "open up the system," but productivity is not a powerful bureaucratic value.

Intake selection enforces the boundary between the system and the public at large, and it tends to screen out gross misfits—functionally and, of perhaps more importance, socially—from the system. Promotional selection in its lesser form—pay promotions—is an acknowledgement of suitability, and step promotions are normally expected by officials who have not fallen afoul of "the discipline." Class promotions are likewise a function of suitability, but of a somewhat different sort. In this case, a sufficiency of talent and years of service are involved, plus a strong and evident ability to conform to norms which are far more diffuse than functionally specific, and far more social than job-oriented, including of course the evident capability of fulfilling supervisory role requirements.

The process of promotional selection helps the system to maintain itself. It persistently upholds fundamental values which it has manifested since its inception in the Chakkri Reformation. They were transposed into it then, and were regarded as desirable because they manifested the traditional order of things and because they readily enabled the governmental center to energize the system by its instrumental use of hierarchism.

Personnel procurement is strongly influenced by the value placed upon hierarchical status by the members and would-be members of the bureaucratic system. But personalism is also a value of the system; for some it ameliorates the formal rules governing access to the bureaucracy and advancement within it. In any case, advancement is highly contingent upon successful personal relations with superiors. Finally, the system protects its members. "Once a bureaucrat always a bureaucrat." The system is saturated with tolerance; only through death, decrepitude, or a grave violation of discipline is an official likely to be removed.

The Allocation of Resources

The arbitrary line between resource procurement and resource allocation has already been breached at a number of points, for in the real bureaucratic world there is no sharp distinction between these two facets of a system which is impressive for its coherence. Yet the conceptual difference is worth asserting. Allocation of resources involves a pattern or set of patterns for arranging resources. Such patterning inevitably reflects some underlying ordering principles, although these are never fully specified (or even wholly consistent).

Patterning may be considered as the static aspect of organizations —the aspect partially sketched in organization charts. But patterns may be properly regarded as static only for certain purposes of analysis and understanding. The nature of the patterns affects the dynamic characteristics of organizations—and reflects them as well. For that matter, some patterns can only be inferred from the observation of behavior. The behavioral importance of the patterns in which the resources of an organization are arranged is evidenced by the extent of the literature on the planning and design of organizations, as well as by the widespread existence of organization and methods staffs in organizations with substantial commitments to productivity.

One such pattern, a feature of all large, purposive organizations, is hierarchy. Hierarchical patterns of resource allocation are probably inherent in all complex, purposive arrangements of human beings. But the hierarchical theme has many variations, and hierarchy itself may not be the sole—or even the dominant—basis for administrative resource allocation. Among small groups within organizations, for example, relationships are often much too complicated to be comprehended in terms of a hierarchical perspective.

Both the formal and the implicit patterns of organization that one finds in an administrative system are, to a considerable degree, particular to that system; these patterns reflect and support underlying values. In the Thai bureaucracy, the dominant pattern is hierarchical. The formal, official, legitimate, Procrustean framework into which resources are allocated is a framework of hierarchical levels. The informal patterns of behavior which take place within the formal framework are also to a large extent hierarchical. And where they are not, the deviations do not challenge the basic formal pattern; at the least they accept it, and perhaps more commonly they sustain it by compensating for some of its limitations.

1. *A basic characteristic of the hierarchical pattern of the Thai bureaucracy is its importance as a means of expressing status.* Hierarchical differentiations inevitably reflect differences in responsibilities, serve as the markers of paths for the flow of communications, and are an accepted, elemental means of relating organizational components. But in the Thai bureaucracy, hierarchical differentiations are also the primary status differentiations in the system. Their importance as means of defining and expressing status is suggested by the absence of other means of comparable importance—such as recognized technical or professional competence—by which status can generally be acquired. The abiding significance of hierarchical status is reflected, too, in elaborate arrangements for regulating access to

various hierarchical levels within the system—arrangements which are not based in any determinate general way upon productivity norms. Finally, the importance of hierarchical status is shown by the pervasive concern with it found among officials, and by the fact that hierarchical status differences are primary guides to interpersonal behavior.

In short, the dominant feature of the framework of the Thai bureaucracy is an elaborate, largely explicit structure of hierarchical statuses.

1a. The hierarchical structure has two facets: an encompassing framework of hierarchical levels which controls the organizational structure of all components of the bureaucracy, and a personal ranking of individual bureaucrats which defines the status of each individual in the system. Thus a bureaucrat has his personal rank, and his position has an explicit rank, and the two almost invariably coincide. (It is hard for a bureaucrat to function "outside of his rank." In a higher-level job he will not readily command respect; a lower-level post is unworthy of him.)

2. *Hierarchical status norms govern all allocations of resources into the system.* Other considerations also apply, of course, but never at the expense of status norms.

2a. Authority is defined in terms of hierarchical status, as noted.

2b. The ability to claim resources and to make decisions regarding their allocation is a function of the authority which goes with high status. Operating units at low hierarchical levels are normally unable to exercise much influence over the process of resource allocation.

2c. Hierarchical status considerations are of prime importance in changing established resource allocations.

(1) Important decisions can only be made at the very top levels of the government, by political officials possessing higher status than bureaucrats.

(2) Within the bureaucracy, adjustments in particular organizational arrangements are made in ways which always reflect the value of hierarchical status. A person is not promoted if his work grows in importance. A new higher-ranking post may be created; if it is, it will be filled in accordance with norms governing access to higher hierarchical status.

3. *Hierarchical status is the prime yardstick for determining the significance of practically everything within the bureaucracy.*

3a. The importance of an activity is usually determined by the hierarchical level at which it is performed. The importance of the work of a section—the major subunit of a division—is more or less equal to the work of any other section, although in one case the duties may be clerical, and in another they may be regulatory, or creative. All particular organizations are composed of a limited series of layers—ministries, departments, occasionally bureaus, divisions, sections, and sometimes subsections. A political decision to emphasize some activity will usually result in its being assigned to a high-level organization (thus, a ministry was created to promote co-operatives in rural areas instead of this work being assigned to the existing Ministry of Agriculture). But it is most common to add or expand activities by creating new sections or divisions within existing organizations.

3b. The rank of an individual position is usually determined by its hierarchical level. Section chiefs are generally second-class officials; division chiefs are first-class officials; division directors—where these exist—are special class officials. Some adjustments of positional rank in terms of functional considerations are found, but these are relatively uncommon exceptions to the pattern.

3c. Skill and responsibility inherent in particular work are not the prime determinants of hierarchical status. Medical doctors enter the bureaucracy as second-class officials. Most elementary teachers, not having college degrees, are fourth-class officials, at the very bottom of the hierarchy of the Ministry of Education. Artists and artisans in the Fine Arts Department, some extraordinarily skilled, are usually fourth-class officials. Work at the bottom levels of the hierarchy often requires some degree of specialized competence, but the performers of it must be fitted into the structure below the upper levels of the hierarchy.

3d. The functional content of the bureaucratic role of an individual is less emphasized than its status content. Job descriptions are not used in the Thai bureaucracy. Formal statements are often made about specific functional responsibilities, as a basis for determining the salary range of a position, but these are usually formalistic as well. Performance requirements do exist in many positions, of course, but they vary greatly from job to job, and effective performance is not necessarily the key to advances in one's status. Performance norms within the system are variable and particularistic; status norms are not.

3e. Except in a few fields, such as medicine, education, and engineering, positions above the third class in the hierarchy are usually supervisory posts, in which advanced status is combined with authority over subordinates. Advancement in status is thus usually advancement into administrative, as distinguished from technical, positions.

3f. Resources are generally allocated in a manner suggestive of the "trickle down" theory of the distribution of wealth. The lower the hierarchical level, the less the likelihood of a plentiful supply of resources.

4. *The pattern of organization has a strongly autarkic character. The general hierarchical arrangement is given particular expression in organization units in which the predominant relationships are vertical, except where persons work in lateral face-to-face relationships.*

4a. The system has limited capacity for the establishment of lateral working relationships among officials who do not have immediate personal contact. Work-flows tend to be hierarchical; where possible, a particular functional responsibility is allocated entirely to a particular organization unit. If the work is too large for one unit such as a section, it may be divided into two discrete parts, each of which will be assigned to a substantially self-contained section. Sections may be co-ordinated by a division; but as the compass of an activity grows larger the co-ordination of units involved in it grows more difficult. Departments tend to resemble enclaves in most cases.

4b. This aspect of resource allocation reflects the facts that legitimate authority in the system is hierarchical, that hierarchy and status go together, and that both are in a sense personal.

4c. Administrative staff units to aid higher-level managers are not fully acceptable; to create such units would be to authorize lower-ranking staff officials to pass on the work of proposals of line officials who outrank the staff.

4d. The line official is expected to be in full charge of his organization. Complex patterns of organization, in which overhead agencies issue rules binding upon line officials, or in which parallel line agencies issue rules binding outside their immediate jurisdiction, are not common. "Outside" rules are not as authoritative as the orders of the line official, generally speaking. A complex pattern of allocation in which authority is exercised in an impersonal manner at many points in the system is substantially inconsistent with the values governing action in the Thai bureaucracy. Thus, for example, high-ranking line officials are responsible for preparing, administering, and evaluating personnel examinations, and for making appointments. They are guided by rules of the Civil Service Commission, but they are subject to small control over their application of those rules.

4e. This autarkic pattern of allocating responsibilities minimizes needs for continuing co-ordination of the work of separate units of organization, or for frequently adjusting complex allocations. It thereby reduces the managerial needs of the bureaucracy, or at least reflects the minimization of the management function within the bureaucracy. Managerial roles in the bureaucracy are usually played as "trouble-shooting" jobs, and reflect a high concern with the maintenance of the established pattern. The rewards of management are largely increased status and the accompanying access to perquisites of various kinds, not increased power to determine and direct programmatic action.

4f. The share of resources allocated to managerial functions within the bureaucracy is impressively small. There are perhaps 1,000 officials, on the average, in the four lesser bureaucratic classes for each special-class managerial official in a department or ministry.

5. *The elaborate hierarchical pattern contributes substantially to personal security based upon knowledge of where one stands.*

6. *Personalism also plays an important part in resource allocations, and the formal hierarchical structure is supplemented and sometimes short-circuited by complex, subtle personal relationships.*

6a. The system is permeated with personal associations that exist on the basis of extraorganizational relationships, including family connections and school associations.

6b. The hierarchical structure forms a background for a host of personal relationships, but hierarchical status, and the quest for it, is an important factor in these nonhierarchical patterns.

6c. Within the bureaucracy, the previously mentioned reciprocal relationship between patron and protégé is one significant supplement to the formal hierarchical pattern.

6d. High-ranking officials generally take pains to create personal communications networks within their organizations, relying upon informants for information about activities within the organization.

6e. As noted in the previous section, personal considerations much affect access to higher status. The promotion of officials is always influenced by—if not based upon—the personal preferences of superiors. Personal considerations play a considerable part in determining other kinds of assignments as well.

To summarize, the dominant pattern which governs the allocation of resources within the contemporary Thai bureaucracy is a sweeping manifestation of the value placed upon hierarchical status. This pattern is also the backdrop for a rich set of personal relationships. These in turn derive much of their meaning from a concern with the hierarchical status conferred upon its members by the bureaucracy. Finally, the pattern which governs resource allocation is so visible and in a sense so simple that the security of a participant in the system tends to be assured. He is not constantly faced with the need for discovering, assessing, and responding to subtle and conflicting sources of authority. His own standing and prospects for movement in the system are usually well demarcated. True, at higher levels in this intensely personalized as well as hierarchical system, officials feel compelled to guard against "surprises" in the form of unanticipated actions (or inactions) at lower levels. Through their own personal networks of informants they keep track of what is going on.

RESOURCE ALLOCATION: EXAMPLES OF THE PROCESS

The Hierarchy. Civil service is divided—vertically—into five levels. These are the five basic bureaucratic strata called classes.[18] Every civil official in the kingdom, except for a small number of special officials, special foreign service officials, and political officials, has a personal rank pegged at one of these class levels; and each regular position in the civil service is also assigned to an appropriate class. The class (or rank) of a civil servant is conceptually distinguished from the class of his position. There are several levels of positions, but the relation of personal rank and positional rank is always precise:

CLASS OF CIVIL SERVANT	CIVIL SERVICE POSTS
fourth class	clerk
third class	official of section
second class	chief of section
first class	chief of division
special class	director of division, deputy director-general of department, director-general, deputy undersecretary, undersecretary

Other posts in the civil service "shall be equated to the above [list of posts] by Civil Service Commission regulations." [19]

The first comprehensive civil service law, enacted in 1928, classified officials into a series of categories: the *sanyabat,* or royally commissioned class, and the *rajaburut,* or noncommissioned class. The *sanyabat* class was divided into three major grades, and each of these was in turn divided into three subgrades. The general pattern was to parallel in the civil service the rank pattern of the military hierarchy, a practice tracing back to the Chakkri Reformation and earlier. This first civil service act contained at least ten clearly differentiated rank levels. The shallower structure of five basic ranks was established in the Civil Service Act of 1933.[20] No significant change in this pattern of stratification occurred in the decades following.[21]

The person-position classification scheme is reflected in the salary schedule of the civil bureaucracy, as the following table shows.

General Salary and Classification Plan

Class	Salary Grade	Pay (baht * per month), showing Salary Steps
Fourth	1	450– 475– 500– 525
	2	550– 575– 600– 625
	3	650– 675– 700– 725
	Special	750– 800– 850– 900
Third	1	750– 800– 850– 900
	2	1000–1050–1100–1200
Second	1	1200–1300–1400–1500
	2	1600–1750–1900–2050
	3	2200–2350–2500–2650
First	1	2650–2800–3000–3200
	2	3600–3800–4000–4300
Special	1	4300–4600–4900–5200
	2	5700–6200–6700–7200
	3	7650–8000

* One baht equals about U.S. $0.05.
SOURCE: *Civil Service Act B.E. 2497,* Schedule 1; and *Regulation Specifying Temporary Extra Salary Increment No. 2, B.E. 2495,* as combined in B.E. 2502.

This schedule, with its fourteen salary grades and fifty-four specific rates, enables the classification of both officials and positions with more discrimination than by merely allocating them to one of the five available classes. For example, distinctions are made among special-class positions: the top salary step which can be paid to a deputy director-general is lower than that available to a director-general. Similar differentiations are made at lower levels, and there seems to be an increasing tendency to classify positions functionally, from the third-class level upward, in terms of some nominal assessment of duties and responsibilities. But the latitude for differentiation within this hierarchical matrix is indeed limited. The fourteen salary grades are of some importance in differentiating positions, but specific assignments to posts are sometimes juggled so that acceptable officials continue to be eligible for salary increases as the length of their service grows. The real differentiation of persons and positions is based on the class structure, for class distinctions are the most important status differentiations. An official's class or rank means much more than the salary ceiling of his particular position at a given moment.

From one viewpoint, the shallowness of the civil service hierarchy is a matter of small concern—an overwhelming proportion of the civil servants are in the bottom class, and subtle or sophisticated differentiation of officials and positions at intermediate levels does not affect them. A tabulation of civil officials by class for a relatively recent year showed: [22]

Special class	0.35 per cent
First class	0.87 per cent
Second class	3.74 per cent
Third class	8.10 per cent
Fourth class	82.20 per cent
Wisaman	4.70 per cent *

The vast fourth class is a thoroughly diverse group. It includes great numbers of clerks, the noncommissioned members of the police, some janitorial workers, and more than 80,000 local teachers. According to the Ministry of Finance payroll records for 1957, 98.4 per cent of all local teachers were fourth-class officials in that year, and the percentage remained about the same in the following year.[23]

The diversity of the fourth class of the civil service is illustrated by the following tabulation.

* 97 per cent of these *wisaman* (extraordinary or nonstatus officials) receive salaries in the fourth-class pay range. A portion of them, perhaps 10 per cent, are actually probationers, awaiting appointment to regular (*saman*) positions at the end of a specified trial period.

Fourth-Class Officials, Department of Fine Arts, 1958

Musicians	250	Teachers (including one teacher of English)	14
Dramatic Artists	183	Draftsmen	7
Clerks	53	Photographers	6
Librarians (including at least 7 specified as competent in an ancient Oriental language)	50	Messengers	5
		Chauffeurs	4
		Gardeners	4
Curators	39	Instrument Keepers	4
Janitors and Custodians	36	Stagehands	4
Craftsmen	34	Workmen	4
Watchmen and Guards	26	Labor Supervisors	2
		Models	2

SOURCE: "Position Classification of the Department of Fine Arts," unpublished paper, Institute of the Public Administration, Bangkok, by Miss Kulasap Chuenroongroj and Miss Em-On Bookabandhu, January 15,1958.

Fourth-class officials are generally those whose education has stopped short of a college certificate or degree. They may compete in examinations for promotion to third-class positions after five years of service, and they may be promoted to the third class without examination after fifteen years of service. The fact that promotions are relatively few is suggested by the existence of a special salary grade for fourth-class officials with many years of service.

From the third class upward, officials are usually college graduates; the upper strata of the bureaucratic system are sharply differentiated from the fourth class. Here one finds a sizeable and undoubtedly growing amount of functional specialization reflected in the titles and to some extent the classifications of jobs. Nonsupervisory positions involving identified technical or professional competence are relatively common in the third class, and are found even higher, at the second and sometimes at the first and special classes.[24] In a more-or-less random sample of 1,960 civil positions of all classes, Chap Tharamathaj noted that 46 per cent were "essentially nonadministrative, technically or professionally specialized jobs, involving some special skill or knowledge and duties which have been recognized in the establishment of the positions according to their titles." [25] A high proportion of these positions, however, were in the third and fourth classes. In general, personal status and authority derive from hierarchical rank, and only indirectly from functional specialization, and even less from technical or professional competence. Positions at and above the second class are usually supervisory posts. Only to a limited extent can middle and upper hierarchical levels be achieved by demonstrated specialized nonadministrative competence; access depends much more upon prior education, time serving (seniority), and deft fulfillment of the "nontechnically specialized" component of role obligations which will enable a person to be promoted to a supervisory position. In short, the stratification of the bureaucracy is a prime manifestation of one basic value of the system—hierarchical status. The arrangement also provides a foundation for the play of the other values of the system.

Administrative Organization. The shallow pattern of hierarchical levels is one dimension of a set of administrative organizations that are highly standardized and largely self-contained. Each ministry is divided into departments. Each department is divided into divisions. Each division is divided into sections. There are a few variations: the Department of Interior has a "Bureau of Provincial Administration," intermediate in level between department and division, and similar intermediate elements are found also in the Land Department of the Interior Ministry, and in a few other places.

The beginnings of this pattern trace back to the Chakkri Reformation, and it was well established by 1929.[26] Each unit of organization at a given hierarchical level was—and is—generally regarded as "equal," regardless of differences in functions performed. A section is a section, and this fact is usually more significant than substantial differences among sections in the level of skill or knowledge necessary to work performance and supervision. The college-graduate officials who work in a section are generally third-class officials, and the chief of the section is almost invariably a second-class official, reporting to a division chief (first class), assistant division director (first class), or division director (special class).

To cite an example: the Civil Service Commission contains five divisions, and a Secretary's Office equivalent to a division in hierarchical status. Subordinate to these divisions are nineteen sections, each headed by a chief, who is a second-class official. [In the Secretary's Office there are correspondence, budget and finance, stores and accounts, and statistics and library sections.] The correspondence section receives, records, reviews, refers, and files the Commission's correspondence, performs routine personnel functions for the staff of the Commission, and serves as a public relations unit. The public relations function, admittedly a matter of small concern, is more or less tacked on to the agency's central clerical unit.

Budgeting, accounting, and the control of cash and stores are divided among two sections within the Commission. An accounts and stores section keeps the books and supplies. A budget and finance (cash) section prepares the Commission's budget, keeps track of and disburses the agency's money. The two sections are sharply separated. If functional rationality were an important norm controlling the pattern of organization, budgeting and accounting would certainly be more closely linked. But budgeting came along as a function long after accounting and stores work were well established in a section. That section would have been overloaded if budgeting responsibilities had also been added; so they were placed elsewhere—in the unit which actually pays out the money.

The bureaucracy is replete with examples of the division of work on the basis of norms that make small sense in terms of the logic of productivity. In the Civil Service Commission one finds several sections engaged in filing, while others are charged with drafting civil service regulations, examining requests for special salary promotions, evaluating agency proposals for specialized selection examinations, and representing the Civil Service Commission in competitive examinations conducted in the Bangkok area. Nominally in some instances, and more than nominally in others, these latter functions call for skills and abilities far in excess of those needed to maintain records on civil servants. Yet all are organized in parallel, equivalent sections, in the agency responsible for what centralized personnel administration exists within the bureaucracy. Clearly, status in the system is not in any general way determined by duties and responsibilities; it is determined by the hierarchical level of one's position within an organization in which work is allocated in a highly traditional manner, in order to maintain a proper hierarchical structure.[27]

Autarky. One feature of the arrangement for allocating work is a high degree of self-containment within units of organization. This is a practical consequence of the basic values of the bureaucratic social system.

At the very top of the governmental edifice, a degree of co-ordination is produced by the prime minister and the Council of Ministers, where all decisions of any importance are made, along with

numerous others. The balancing of claims of various ministers is a
subtle and complicated business, beyond the scope of our concerns.
The ministries themselves are essentially autonomous, with only a
few exceptions. The Budget Bureau has already been mentioned; in
addition, the Ministry of Finance functions to some extent as an
overhead agency, operating a centralized accounting system and administering payrolls, pensions, and other disbursements. It applies a
set of technical norms which govern pay, promotion, and fiscal
accountability, thus contributing to the coherence of the system.

The Ministry of National Development and the National Economic
Development Board seek to operate in a much different sphere—to
provide an integrated approach to national economic development. It
is too early to assess the success of this effort, but it is not too early to
assert that the co-ordination of these two agencies must depend to a
large extent upon the personal power of the prime minister.

The provincial governors of the Ministry of Interior also have certain responsibilities for co-ordination and integration within their
jurisdictions. They are "in control of all provincial administrative officials in the *changwad* [province] and . . . responsible for the government service of the *changwad* and *amphurs* [districts]." [28] This
pattern dates back to the 1890s, but the control powers of the provincial governor are no longer as strong as they once were. They are sustained by the governor's status and prestige and a fair amount of
"whiskey-soda co-ordination." [29] The governor, however, does not
control the major share of the resources available to field officials of
various ministries and departments, nor can he determine the substance of their work. His power over the police is particularly limited,
and he has small positive authority over organizations such as the
Department of Irrigation whose field areas do not necessarily coincide with provincial boundaries. As the specialized program content
of the Thai bureaucracy increases, substantive control by generalist
administrators inevitably tends to shrink.

The major units of each ministry are its departments. Departments
are headed by director-generals who report on most matters to the
top-ranking administrative official of their particular ministry, the
undersecretary. "The director-generals and the under-secretaries are a
kind of elite group in the bureaucracy. But because their lines of loyalty run up to the minister and down to their subordinates, there is no
more than a minimum of cooperation among them as a group." [30] It

should be added that undersecretaries often function "like post offices," in the words of one observer. They have little supporting staff, and they involve a hierarchical position immediately above director-generals, who are also special-class officials. One is tempted to characterize undersecretaries in general as high-status officials with limited managerial power. Departments usually preside over divisions, each of these responsible for a discrete and well-bounded sphere of activity. Interaction among divisions is again limited. The pattern of work specialization does not require it, and the orientation of the division head, like that of his director-general, is vertical. The tendency toward self-containment is carried down to the section level, as the case of the Civil Service Commission suggests.

The logic governing the allocation of resources and responsibilities in the Thai bureaucratic system almost inevitably calls for adding units when functions are added or expanded.[31] To cite one small example, as the record-keeping work load of the Civil Service Commission has grown, new sections have been created. This is more appropriate, given the values and characteristics of the system, than any other conceivable change in organizational pattern (such as enlarging the compass of the established records section).

Sections can, of course, be upgraded to division status, and sometimes are. But this is a fairly complex change, involving the selection of a new division chief on the basis of a selective examination and, therefore, the assessment of qualifications of a group of eligible officials which may not even include the original section chief. The establishment of one or more new sections will also be involved, in all probability, should a new division be created. Hence, lateral expansion is often the simplest response to functional growth.

The Procrustean character of the bureaucratic pattern which governs allocations reduces its capacity for response to changes in its milieu. One of the most obvious and elemental of these has been the emergence of trained stenographers and secretaries as administrative functionaries. Such skills are practically inaccessible to the bureaucracy. Stenographers are clerks; clerks are fourth-class officials; fourth-class officials have an absolute top pay of 900 baht (about $45.00) per month, and this only after extensive service. Third-class officials, almost invariably college graduates, begin at as little as $37.50 to $45.00 per month. Section chiefs earn from $60.00 to $132.50 per month, and the middle ranges of this pay level are roughly equal to the salary available to a competent stenographer in nonbureaucratic employment.

The dominant premise in the logic of Thai bureaucratic organization is this: Fit the function to the structure; and in doing so, be guided by traditional norms which reflect the hierarchicalism that is a central value of the system.

Over the years, however, the scope and quantity of bureaucratic activity has grown. Jurisdictions that were once discrete or nonexistent now impinge increasingly and inexorably upon each other. The growth has been a political response to forces largely external to the bureaucracy itself, but the consequences are increased needs for the co-ordination of separate programs.

The allocation pattern of the bureaucracy militates against such co-ordination. In one unnamed office, in the 1960s, three adjacent sections shared responsibility for the collection and preparation of statistics whose utility lay in their integration for use in development planning. Much of the work was performed in the same room, but by separate sections. The hierarchical distinction between the three units, plus the personal connections of at least one of the section chiefs, plus the absence of any compelling demand for the statistics at high levels, were sufficient to block efforts at co-ordinated statistical analysis. Utilitarian considerations were simply of no practical relevance in nurturing co-operative arrangements among the three sections, and in this case as in many others, hierarchical authority was not brought to bear to foster meaningful productive effort.

When interdepartmental and interministerial co-operation is required, the problem is, of course, even greater. For example, irrigation works must be protected against damage, and the wastage of irrigation water must be checked. These enforcement functions were assigned to the police. The results were so inadequate that the World Bank mission to Thailand recommended that the responsibility be handed over to the Irrigation Department.[32] Self-containment was the only feasible solution to the problem.

In another instance, the Irrigation Department constructed water storage tanks in the northeast. Under a decision of the Council of Ministers, the Ministry of Co-operatives was ordered to construct canals to get the water from the tanks to the fields. The work was not completed until canal construction was also assigned to Irrigation in response to pressures generated upon the top level of the government.

The Ministry of Co-operatives lacked the engineering competence to do the job—a fact which did not preclude the original assignment of responsibility to it.[33]

But there are more complex problems to be faced as the significance of irrigation grows. Timber cutting and slash-and-burn agriculture in the north of Thailand have created flood and erosion problems in watersheds which feed what is now Thailand's most important irrigation system. The policies and practices of the Department of Forestry, which regulates timber cutting and the regeneration of forest and ground cover, have a direct effect upon the preservation of irrigation resources, and it is not conceivable that this agency be incorporated within the Irrigation Department. Even if it were, the work of the ministries of Interior and Justice in policing and enforcing the Forestry Department's regulations would continue to affect the interests of irrigation. Self-containment has its limits as a feasible solution for such problems—to the extent that they are regarded as problems —and autarky does not minimize them. But autarky is consistent with the basic values of the system. Sometimes personal actions can overcome the impediments to co-ordination that result from autarky, provided the individuals involved have high status, knowledge of the problem at hand, and concern with solving it.

Management Organization. In considering such characteristics of the system as autarky, one comes to the matter of management. If specific, immediate problems of co-ordination are perceived and resolved, this will be done by management.

Management is commonly regarded as a process—a pattern of action for procuring, allocating, and energizing resources, for setting goals, determining methods, and assessing outcomes. But one aspect of management is its sheer presence. What resources are allocated to management within the Thai bureaucracy? How does the pattern of allocation reflect the central values of the system?

The answering of such questions inevitably intrudes to some extent upon another topic of concern—the energizing of resources. Yet the structure of management organization in the bureaucracy is impressive evidence of the system's underlying normative characteristics. First of all, the sheer quantity of resources allocated to the performance of management functions is impressively small. Second, the most significant part of management's decision making normally occurs outside the bureaucracy, at the political level of the government. Finally, the management pattern is impressively simple, and to some extent variable in accordance with the tradition-sanctioned practices of different ministries.

As noted earlier, the number of Thai civil officials who might be roughly regarded as occupying positions in the top managerial level of the bureaucracy is small—something of the magnitude of one special-class managerial official per thousand officials.[34] In 1958, when there were considerably more than 200,000 civil officials, only 290 special-class officials were clearly engaged in line administration at or above the level of a province or a division. (Another 395 special-class officials were judges, educators, diplomats, and prosecutors.)

Not only were the sheer numbers seemingly small—they overstate the resources available for directing the work of divisions, departments, and ministries. Full-time, or substantially full-time, assignments at the level of the special class are uncommon. An official at this level spends much of his time on other duties, from which he derives much of his income. These include: committees whose members are remunerated (one official to my knowledge was at a given time a member of 47 committees, not all of them active); boards of public enterprises which pay stipends to their members; representational assignments involving foreign travel; private entrepreneurial activities, in some cases; and even multiple managerial posts. Thai bureaucratic managers are often able, experienced, and impressively diligent. Their services are in wide demand, and their monetary needs and expectations usually far outrun their salaries. The managers are often exploited by the political leadership whom they serve in an endless array of *ad hoc* assignments, and the managers in turn exploit their own status in a quest for material rewards, and in carrying out their own assignments from above.

Both practices are consistent with the central character of the system. Bureaucratic managers are managers more in name than reality. Decisions of any importance are generally reserved to the prime minister and his Council of Ministers. "In its day-to-day operations the cabinet is essentially an administrative committee to which many decisions must legally be submitted." [35]

Bureaucratic management is more a matter of system maintenance than the pursuit of programmatic goals. This is evidenced by the paucity of resources allocated to management support. As noted, there is no well-developed concept of management staff in the bureaucracy; staff functions consist largely of the work performed in the office of the secretary of a department or ministry, much of it concerned with housekeeping and technical services. Planning and analysis are usually organized in an *ad hoc* fashion on the basis of personal confidence. The extent to which such units as the "technical divisions" of departments function as staff aids to director-generals varies considerably, depending upon ministerial traditions and the personalities of department heads and the subordinates involved. As in the days of the Chakkri Reformation much staff work antecedent to decision making is performed by foreign advisers who draw plans, make surveys, and nurture political proposals. Such efforts, when reinforced by resources, have been relatively influential.

In essence, management within the Thai bureaucratic system "copes." It does not initiate or make powerful claims upon the political sector. The rewards of a management position are status, access to perquisites, and a great deal of work. In the event of a significant failure in a politically meaningful program, managers may suffer. In response to political desires, managers may propose and espouse. But most of all, they keep the system going.

Bureaucratic management is not generally sustained by systematic, analytical reporting arrangements. Performance reporting, some of which traces back to the Chakkri Reformation, is not regarded as reliable. The use of empirical information as a foundation for analysis and decision making is minimized. In a division which is supposed to produce commercial statistics for economic planning and regulation, the endless work of collecting and tabulating data goes forward. But financial shortages in the late 1950s made it impossible to man all the posts; so the analysis jobs were left unfilled. The department would not be acting on the basis of the analyses in any case—nor would anyone else, it appears. A long list of instances of this sort might be cited to indicate the minimal importance of "hard data" to decision making in the system, above the bureaucracy as well as within it. Much more reliance is placed upon personal communications than upon impersonal reports.

This characteristic is part of a system in which line officials are impressively authoritative in relation to their subordinates. The emphasis upon personal decision making on the basis of hierarchical authority militates against any flow of relevant decisional premises from a wide variety of points in the system. The important premises come from above. They may be transmitted personally. The terrain of authority is not divided into a multiplicity of specialized, laterally related, interacting jurisdictions, each generating more or less impersonal flows of premises which are highly authoritative in the decision-making activities of the others.

Part of the price of simple hierarchicalism and autarky is limited capacity for integrated approaches to complex problems and goals. Such a price is high only if the achievement of the goals is valued. Generally speaking, in Thailand achievement is not valued more than the continuance of the system of hierarchical status and authority and the personal basis for transactions. The functions of the bureaucracy are rather sharply distinguished from the functions of the political sphere, but some of the values are shared—particularly the values of hierarchical status and personal transactions. As a result, the managerial arrangements of the bureaucracy are reasonably stable and acceptable.

Resource Allocation—The Case of the Malaria Control Program. The 1963 survey of the Thai national malaria control program is a vivid portrait of the complex pattern of resource allocation within the bureaucracy, and of the mixture of values underlying the allocation pattern.[36]

Started in 1951, the government's malaria control program has in some ways been a distinguished success; "only 10–15% of the original reservoir of cases now remains."[37] Ten years later, in 1961, the focus of the program was switched from control to the more ambitious goal of malaria eradication, and the project, earlier operated as a division in the Department of Health of the Ministry of Public Health, was elevated to a project in the Office of the Undersecretary of State for Public Health. The deputy undersecretary was placed in charge, although he also continued to have substantial additional duties. In 1963, he had no full-time deputy to help him direct the program.

The results obtained in the malaria control effort over slightly more than a decade are particularly impressive in view of the context of their achievement. During the entire period, no manuals of operation were developed to cover such major areas of effort as spraying procedures, surveillance of the treated population, laboratory procedure, and equipment maintenance. Training manuals were prepared but not necessarily used. Not even scale maps were systematically used in plotting program operations, to determine such things as the proximity of vector sources to areas of population settlements. And as late as 1963 the entomological work conducted as part of the project was both limited and uneven, and much of it was practical rather than systematic.

> While scattered efforts have been made in past years to determine vector species susceptibility to DDT, no records of such work or results are available. Expression is made of the difficulty of obtaining adequate numbers of specimens with which to carry out scientific susceptibility tests. The Project operates on the assumption that no DDT resistance exists in Thailand. . . . Some of the zone chiefs and assistant zone chiefs have acquired considerable competence in mosquito identification and interpretation of vector density.[38]

In short, the project was characterized by minimal reliance upon systematic management, and by a thin supporting structure. The headquarters units showed little sign of integration. Entomological studies were the responsibility of a section in the Surveillance and Evaluation Division. Between this section and two others (Statistics and Epidemiology) in the division no clear-cut definition of working relations existed, nor was there any "defined written understanding" of the relationship of the sections to the regional offices of the project.[39]

Field operations were conducted by sector offices, reporting to zones which in turn were responsible to regional offices. At the sector level, malaria either is or is not controlled, for here is where spraying operations and other control activities are performed. The sectors were headed by chiefs, either fourth-class officials or temporary non-status employees. To achieve official status, sector chiefs had to complete a two-year training course for malaria technicians, which made them eligible for appointment to official posts with starting salaries of about $27.50 per month, plus per diem, housing allowances, and other fringes. The two-year training requirement, which is quite unrealistic in terms of the time required to acquire the necessary skills, was established by the Civil Service Commission in the early years of the program.

In practice, quite a few sector chiefs were "acting chiefs," and had received only brief training. In some cases these chiefs had no offices out of which to work. At the sector level, one found cases in which "Sector Chiefs, Squad Chiefs, Spraymen, House Visitors and even Porters receive the same pay—B450 month. The only incentive appears to be that the Sector Chief is paid throughout the year (like the Squad Chiefs and House Visitors) and does have some hope for future advancement." [40]

Sectors reported to zone offices, headed by second-class officers. The zone offices were presumably responsible for the effectiveness of the work of the sectors. In practice, the zone chief and his assistant appeared to spend most of their time keeping track of finances, reports, and supplies. "All spraying personnel, squad chiefs as well as spraymen, are paid twice monthly in the field. . . . Where there are very few Sector Chiefs with Ministry status, then the Zone Chief himself will pay all temporary employees. The Zone Chief of one such area reported that it took approximately 10 days of his time to complete payment of 160 temporary seasonal personnel." [41]

The survey team which studied the malaria program recommended that an administrative officer be assigned to zone offices, along with a typist and typewriter, to provide administrative support. Such a change would leave zone management free to focus upon the substance of the program, provided the traditional responsibilities of the supervisors could be delegated to a subordinate.

The allocation of resources to the zones tends to support generalizations made about the process of resource allocation in the bureaucracy. A "great discrepancy" was noted in the assignment of vehicles to the zones. "One zone had 22 four-wheeled vehicles and 7 motorcycles while others are assigned anywhere from 3–14 vehicles. In general, those zones closest to Central Headquarters and the individual Regional Headquarters are observed to have a greater number and variety of vehicles than those more distant. This is significant with respect to the degree motorized vehicles can facilitate operations throughout the entire Nation." [42]

Zones report to regional offices, and again the survey team found the regional malariologist spending a major share of his time serving as "the approving officer for practically all administrative activities that take place in the region." [43] He signed every financial document generated within the region, for example.

After its study, the survey team came to the conclusion that the program was not yet ready to move into an eradication phase, and indicated that "a gradual transition from control to more administratively difficult eradication" would be appropriate. The survey team also observed that "inadequate budget is the most important deterrent to the establishment of a personnel system which would ensure adequate field supervision." [44]

Budgetary considerations are real and tangible, but underlying them is a set of forces which deter a more "rational" allocation of resources to the sector level and to the management aspect of the program. These same forces help to explain a noted tendency in the program for administrative operations to be conducted on a face-to-face basis, rather than through manuals, memoranda, and other impersonal means. Also, line supervisors sign all the papers and disburse funds in keeping with a concept of their role, not simply because of a shortage of subordinate administrative personnel. Further, the limited amount of integration of laterally related units is not explainable upon the basis of budgetary considerations, any more than is the absence of a "desirable" emphasis upon entomological studies. These characteristics of the program do make sense when viewed from a perspective which imputes certain thematic values to the bureaucratic system. Given such a perspective, one of the most impressive features of the malaria control program is its substantial achievement of programmatic results.

The Civil Service Commission as an Allocative Mechanism. The foreign experts who studied the malaria control program found that it was impeded by a civil service rule that required two years of training as a prerequisite to appointment to a fourth-class post as malaria technician—a post often filled adequately enough by nonstatus personnel with some experience but little formal training. The CSC rule had been effective for about ten years at the time of the survey. The incident illustrates a primary function of the Thai Civil Service Commission, which is to help maintain the established bureaucratic system by continuing to interpret and apply norms sustaining the fundamental values which give essential meaning to it. Through its rules and procedures, as well as through the civil service law, an orderly, continuing process of personnel resource allocation occurs that is consistent with the fundamental values of the bureaucracy.

On the auspicious day of April 1, 1928, the first comprehensive Thai civil service legislation became effective, laying down a series of rules for the organization and governance of the civil service, and creating a committee responsible to His Majesty for the administration of the law.[45] The act itself was significant for two reasons: it explicated and it extended the patterns of structure and process that had developed during the Chakkri Reformation, patterns which have been distinguished by their persistence. It is not difficult to see the relationship between the major premises of the 1928 act and central features of today's bureaucratic structure.[46]

The 1928 act spelled out a formal hierarchical structure for the civil bureaucracy as a whole. It specified intake levels for the system, and linked opportunities for access to the system to levels of educational attainment. It prescribed open competitive examinations as a basis for appointment as ordinary civil officials, with appointments to be made in an order determined by scores on the selection tests. Appointees were to serve probationary periods of six to twelve months before being formally instated. Finally, a number of interesting and significant disciplinary provisions were incorporated in the law: The official was to devote his full time to his work; he was not to exploit his position for his personal interest. He was forbidden to "go around" his supervisor without permission; any objection to an order was to be submitted to his superior immediately, in writing, and if the order was not then withdrawn, the official was to execute it. And the official was to maintain an impeccable reputation and at all times preserve the dignity of his position.

This rather idealized piece of legislation was intended to contribute to the efficiency of the government at a time of financial difficulty, to proscribe the favoritism and opportunism which had become endemic under King Vajiravudh, to contribute to the morale of the civil officials who had recently had their salaries reduced and had been subjected to new taxes, and to set out in unequivocal terms some of the central norms of the established system, including, of course, hierarchism and the premise that the official *as a person,* being the king's man, must in his total behavior avoid any unfavorable reflections upon the system and thus upon the monarch himself.

The systematizing effort that produced the 1928 civil service legislation was supplemented by a standard salary schedule for all ordinary civil officials.[47] Existing pension legislation was also modified somewhat, with the same general aim of increased uniformity. Together, these measures somewhat tardily completed the work of constructing a uniform, centralized bureaucracy, more than a third of a century after the radical reorganization of 1892, and almost two decades after the death of King Chulalongkorn.

The structural aspect of the 1928 legislation essentially standardized a pattern which had already emerged. The selection process was far more of an innovation, an effort to apply, on a system-wide basis, the "merit principles" that had evolved in British and American practice but also in some sectors of the Thai administrative system—notably those developed under the aegis of the Ministry of Interior in Prince Damrong's time. This process was put to the test of utility in the years 1928–1932, but only in a small way. From 1928 through 1931 the civil service grew slightly—from about 77,200 to 78,500 officials. But the number of regular or ordinary (*saman*) personnel covered by the selection and promotion provisions of the act showed a net decline of about 2,000. There were few new appointments and many retirements. Then, with the budget deficit of 1931 came drastic cuts: in 1932 the number of *saman* officials was down almost 3,000 below the figure for twelve months earlier, and 3,500 *wisaman* officials were also chopped from the governmental payroll.[48]

In 1933 the Civil Service Commission was made part of the Office of the Prime Minister and was given added authority over appointment, promotion, transfer, removal, and some aspects of pay and discipline.[49] It was also made responsible for the selection and supervision of scholars to be sent overseas. During the following years a number of changes were made. Selection procedures were modified. Some relatively minor changes were made in the classification structure, and provisions governing appointments to "technical positions," or those classified on the basis of special competence requirements instead of hierarchical rank, were developed. Regulations governing various aspects of discipline emerged in seemingly endless number. In 1948, teachers were brought into the civil service. The Commission staff grew from 34 officials in 1936 to 169 in 1959.[50] (The current ratio of Civil Service Commission staff to total national civil officials is about 1 to 1,200, suggesting that the relative quantity of Commission activity—somewhat like the quantity of managerial activity —is quite small.)

From 1933 to the present, only two really great changes occurred in the pattern of civil service law and procedure: selection provisions, particularly those governing promotion, were amended to reduce the amount of competition involved after a few years' experience with the

1933 act, and the line agencies of the government acquired responsibility for the actual administration of civil service regulations and procedures. The Commission itself became a regulatory and record-keeping agency, not very extensively engaged in direct operations.

Since 1928 the central personnel agency of the Thai government has been headed by a committee or commission. Section 6 of the current Civil Service Act provides that this body shall consist "of the President of the Council of Ministers as Chairman, the Deputy President of the Council of Ministers as Vice Chairman and not less than five but not more than seven other members experienced in the principles of the service and holding or having held a rank not lower than Director-General or its equivalent." Members are appointed to two-year terms.

The background of most Commission members is political or military, or both. This might imply that the Commission is a means by which powerful political control is exercised over the civil bureaucracy, an implication which is somewhat erroneous. The composition of the Commission does preclude the likelihood of its serving as representative and advocate of bureaucratic self-interest; the civil bureaucrats are practically unrepresented. And the Commission membership does insure that the personnel system will not be unresponsive to political control. But the work of the Commission per se consists largely of passing upon proposed regulations and making group judgments about a variety of individual issues presented to it, ranging from review of specific disciplinary actions to recommendations for promotions to the special class. The Commission, in short, ratifies proposed (or accomplished) technical actions, and by its nature and presence exercises a relatively passive control over the interpretation and enforcement of civil service law and regulations. It is an agent of stability rather than of change.

Its character is reflected in that of the Commission staff, largely concerned with routine personnel housekeeping and regulatory activities within the boundaries set by the Civil Service Act and the values it reflects. The staff maintains personnel records and serves as a limited proprietary partner in the regulation and conduct of selection examinations. This examination system, previously discussed in detail, has a strongly ritualistic aspect, and the Commission staff is responsible for the general enforcement of the proprieties although the actual examinations are conducted by the ministries or departments in need of personnel.

The staff drafts myriad rules and regulations concerned with selection, promotion, discipline, and the salary value of particular foreign academic degrees. It supervises Thai students studying abroad. It publishes the monthly *Civil Officials' Magazine,* a useful and informative gazette of text and commentary on rules and regulations, information concerning discipline and disciplinary action, and other material of value to those who would compete in civil service examinations. This journal, widely read among civil bureaucrats and would-be bureaucrats, probably exerts a significant influence upon the "socialization" of officials and prospective officials, and upon the maintenance of some coherence in disciplinary practices within the bureaucracy.

The character of the Civil Service Commission and its staff is perhaps as evident in what it does *not* do as in what it does. It participates in the administration of civil service examinations only in the smallest way—by prescribing the general regulations which apply over time, by modifying these in some specific cases in response to agency requests, by nominally reviewing examinations after they have been given, and by sending staff members to participate in selection activities in the Bangkok area. It has done little or no systematic research in the design of selection instruments or in the assessment of those now in use.

The Commission and its staff do "classify" positions, fitting them into the fabric of hierarchical and salary levels. In doing this, it follows the hierarchical principle spelled out in the civil service law, except when special concessions are made in response to personal influence from high in the governmental system.

The Commission does not investigate applicants or appointees. It engages in no training activities. It sponsors no "employee relations" programs—or even service evaluation procedures. It does control promotions by regulation, which means that it assures an orderly process consistent with basic values. It must also approve each proposed promotion to the special class. And it does evaluate the salary value of advanced education in each new case in which an official requests such as assessment. It is not active in shaping or reshaping major personnel policy. Through the years since 1928 and 1933 it has "operated" the system set forth in the law without making any extensive efforts to examine and assess that system generally, or to adapt it—other than in detail—to changing needs and circumstances. It has, in short, evinced an unswerving responsive dedication to the system and its underlying values.

A recent paper has suggested the need for stronger leadership by the Thai Civil Service Commission, to "police the personnel programs of operating agencies and sometimes deny the requests of powerful officials . . . to publicize civil service activities and accomplishments . . . [to foster] the recognition and advancement of the personnel profession . . . [and] actively champion the expansion and improvement of efficiency and integrity in the civil service." [51]

From a Western bureaucratic viewpoint these aims are certainly sensible. But the Thai Civil Service Commission exists to help maintain a system in which productivity values are not prime criteria. The CSC is admittedly not much of a source of leadership; it spells out the technical rules needed in the endless work of procuring and allocating personnel, and responds to pressures from high officials. It champions nothing. But the Commission does protect the viability of the value of hierarchical status as a criterion governing resource allocation. It adapts this central premise to the specific, immediate needs of bureaucratic agencies. It also contributes to security, by the stability and predictability of the process of allocation which it helps control. Further, it does not intrude too much upon the hierarchical authority of line administrators. They conduct the examinations and apply the selection rules. Certainly the Commission does not challenge the authority of political-level officials. Its secretary-general looks after the relatively routine matters. Any issue of consequence must be decided by the Commission itself, headed by the prime minister, with the deputy prime ministers acting as vice-chairmen. The arrangement contributes to the coherence of the bureaucratic system.

Other exemplary data might be cited to illustrate ways in which the basic values of the bureaucratic system influence and control the allocation of resources. They would strongly support the contention made earlier—that hierarchical status is a prime value governing allocation, and that the actual allocative process is conducted upon the basis of hierarchical authority exercised personally, to a great degree, but in such a way that the security accorded members of the system is not jeopardized by great caprice.

Energizing the System's Resources

In practice, the energizing of resources is essentially a matter of shaping and directing the behavior of persons. The full range of ways by which a social system influences and controls the behavior of its members defies delineation. But some specific arrangements inevitably exist to elicit behaviors consistent with system values and goals. In the case of a bureaucracy, these arrangements are to some extent distinguishable from other bureaucratic processes, although the distinction is not complete.

Authority, of course, is a key to the control of administrative behavior. But authority must have its basis and its inducements. Authority is grounded in some source of legitimacy; in its specific manifestations it is both bounded and sustained by the range of what is proper and acceptable. To understand behavior in a system it is necessary to know about these things.

1. *Hierarchical authority and status are a primary basis for controlling and influencing behavior in the Thai bureaucracy.*

1a. This is reflected in a rather common recourse to hortatory rules and orders, regarded as self-fulfilling and often not reinforced by efforts to determine compliance.

1b. The nature of the response to such rules and orders is variable. Written rules tend to be acceptable as conveniences in the absence of any particular challenge to them, or to be used in support of sought-after advantages. Orders are most likely to be carried out when they call for immediate, specific action. "Standing orders" quickly tend to lose their force. Deference is habitually an element of the immediate response to an order; sometimes it is practically the entire response.

1c. Much of the action of individual members of the system is conditioned by the aims of asserting, protecting, or improving personal status, and acknowledging the status of superiors.

2. *Exploitation is a common type of action in the system; it has many forms and degrees.* It is often part of a reciprocal relationship which cannot be explained entirely in terms of hierarchical authority, as it involves personal relationships and subtle sanctions.

2a. Segments of the public—the Chinese engaged in commercial enterprise, and almost anyone seeking some right or privilege from the bureaucracy, for that matter—are likely to be exploited, in the sense of being expected to reward or at least gratify the official to whom they make their claims or requests. This is a simple overstatement of a complex reality, in which a host of particular norms apply. Merchants seeking licenses or other necessary documents will often be given preferential treatment in return for gifts. Common people with personal requests must at least be polite and respectful. In no case is a demand for one's rights likely to produce the desired response from an official.

2b. The vertical relationships, such as deference obligations, in the rules of officials are well defined. The functional content of rules is less well defined. In a sense, the role of a Thai official at any level below the very top of the system may be regarded as having a clear-cut top and bottom, but very vague lateral boundaries. Obligations of a subordinate toward a superior are broad and diffuse, and by no means limited to what might be called official business. Hierarchical authority helps energize the system, but the action it produces is not sharply focused upon productivity.

3. *Disciplinary norms and practices reflect the importance of hierarchical authority as an energizing force, and the importance of status as a basis of action.*

3a. Offenses against the dignity of an official—such as financial embarrassment, conviction of a criminal offense in no way related to one's position, even the loss of a civil suit in some cases, and other forms of behavior not regarded as consistent with the dignity of a bureaucrat—are bases for punitive sanctions.

3b. Other "offenses against the system" also tend to be regarded as serious. Stealing small sums of government money entrusted to one can lead to summary dismissal; the gentle extraction of sums from the public—so long as this is done discretely and not by overt coercion —is likely to be tolerated.

3c. Superiors may, in practice, exercise considerable personal discretion in applying disciplinary norms. There is little or no effective right of appeal against punitive sanctions. (Extra-legal restraints do, however, apply.)

4. *Performance or productivity values are not a dominant incentive energizing the system or eliciting action*

4a. Where achievement is rewarded, the most important reward is an improvement in one's status.

4b. Achievement norms are not widespread features of the system. Performance standards, for example, are usually lacking. Punitive sanctions are seldom imposed for performance failures, unless these represent some particular disaster for which an individual can be found responsible—such as failure to preserve government property in one's control, or failure which embarrasses one's superiors.

4c. Status is always thoroughly visible, but responsibility for performance is often blurred by the use of committees—even networks of committees—for the conduct of particular operations.

4d. Limited emphasis is placed upon what is often called "administrative rationality." The system does not foster innovation, or a continuing concern with the efficacy of means. One finds neither suggestion systems nor incentive awards in the Thai bureaucracy. In general, arrangements for nurturing and stimulating initiative are lacking.

4e. The general orientation of the system militates against systematic management and operation on the basis of objective information. Officials will seldom place full trust in impersonal official reports of remote subordinates, for these may not be very reliable. Reporters tend to treat report writing rather casually, but they are careful to avoid implicit criticisms of superiors, or to generate pressure on superiors via reports.

5. *Behavior within the bureaucracy is saturated with norms reflecting a high value placed upon personalism.* The personalism of the bureaucracy has at least three facets: the personalism of status; personalism which either checks or supplements hierarchical status as a basis of action; and the personalism of the individual vis-à-vis the system from which he seeks rewards.

5a. Status within the bureaucracy is personal at the same time that it is hierarchical. There is no sharp distinction between official status and personal status in a broader sense. Relations based upon official status are at the same time personal relations. Duties and responsibilities of subordinates are not fixed and legitimized by an impersonal system of performance-based rules. In practice, one's work may be substantially standardized as a result of sheer exigency. But subordinates are often expected to serve their superiors in a wide and varying range of activities—and may seek to do so, in order to protect or enhance their positions.

5b. Overt expressions of disrespect toward a superior as a person are flagrantly improper. Even an incompetent superior cannot be attacked openly. Superiors and subordinates tend to develop personal reciprocal relationships which are broad but seldom deep. A superior will depend upon personal informants, and at times upon the unstinting efforts of his staff in coping with some crisis or in carrying out some urgent activity. The response to such claims by subordinates will be based at least in part upon attitudes toward the superior shaped by his ability and willingness to look after his loyal subjects. Such superior-subordinate relationships are likely to be thoroughly particularistic. Equal treatment of subordinates is not a common norm. The able ones may be overloaded with work while the ineffectuals are kept on and given little to do. Formal rules governing such matters as leave, step increase in pay, and discipline may also be applied in a personal fashion—usually to reward the loyal, but not necessarily to punish the incompetent. The good boss is paternal and his subordinates are loyal. Much of this is a matter of style and manners rather than a manifestation of deep feelings.

5c. The behavior of a superior is not constrained by such formal, regularized devices as employee representation or grievance procedures. But certain implicit norms—perhaps related to a Buddhist ethic to some extent—do tend to limit the power of a superior to take advantage of subordinates. Thus he may not take their money or force them to act in ways generally regarded in the society as immoral. The personal support of a high-status official may also be used to protect one against his immediate superiors. Finally, the system condones the use of anonymous letters directed against a superior as a means by which to sabotage a boss (except at the highest levels) who behaves improperly, and this device tends to act as a determent to flagrant coercive exploitation of subordinates. The anonymous letter, of course, is the personal instrument of an individual seeking to protect his official way of life—or perhaps to destroy another official.

5d. Socialization rather than training is the key to effective bureaucratic behavior. This begins at an early age, in the temples and in the schools, where the forms of deference and manifest respect are taught.

6. *The personalism of the bureaucracy is a reflection of the fact that to be an official is to have a way of life.* With all of its implicitness the system is relatively secure.

6a. As noted, the absence of multiple sources of official status and authority greatly simplifies behavior. There is not much chance of conflict among different bureaucratic criteria upon which a particular behavior might be based. The specific criteria do, of course, vary greatly from place to place; but in a given context the effective guides to behavior are likely to be clear, and no great conflict between the formal and informal aspects of the organization is likely to exist. Of course, the requisite behavior may not be attractive to the individual, and may subject him to considerable stress.

6b. But cautious, deferential time serving assures at least some rewards. Inertia governs much of the work. The effective disciplinary rules are clear, even when they are at variance with formalistic official regulations. And one is not caught up in deep intra- or inter-organizational struggles.

6c. In a subtle sense, an implicit "right" of security tends to protect most officials against the loss of their bureaucratic identities. Perhaps this is better expressed by saying that a substantial amount of tolerance for the behavior of subordinates characterizes the system. An annual pay increase of one step is practically habitual; withholding it from an individual is a fairly serious punishment, although it is within the purview of one's superior (subject to approval by his boss). To get thrown out, one must commit a flagrant violation. For most of its members the bureaucratic way of life is a secure way of life. Its material rewards are poor except at higher levels, but the status it confers is meaningful, easy to keep, sometimes capable of being enhanced, and almost always hard to lose.

ENERGIZING RESOURCES—EXAMPLES OF THE PROCESS

Supervision, discipline, and remuneration are three facets of the system which bear directly upon behavior within it. The communications patterns of the bureaucratic system are also pertinent, as well as the characteristic patterns of small-group behavior. In the latter, a particular quality of personalism flourishes, sometimes in ways at variance from the formal hierarchical structure. Finally, there is the social posture of individual participants. While this differs from person to person, certain common patterns greatly affect the quality of behavior within the bureaucracy.

Supervision. If there were an ideal type by which to assess Thai supervisors, it would be a wise, just, paternal, authoritarian official who does not lose his temper, who is at least as clever as any of his subordinates, who regards and understands them as individuals, and whose concern with productivity never overrides his concern with the well-being of his subordinates.

In common practice, the typical supervisor is authoritarian. The full force of superior hierarchical status supports his position. It is backed by the availability of sanctions as well as by its inherent legitimacy. "Walk behind the supervisor and the dog will not bite you," and "Don't spit upwards," are two administrative proverbs known to all Thai bureaucrats.

There are no effective formal means by which subordinates can check the power of the superior—as through a grievance procedure —but potential upward sanctions do exist. The supervisor who is a fool—who is patently not clever—and the supervisor who grievously oppresses his subordinates may be punished. The foolish supervisor will be deceived by his subordinates and may get into trouble as a result of their mistakes. The oppressive supervisor may be attacked by anonymous letters, or passively tolerated in hope of an eventual better day.

The norms which define oppression are particularly Thai. A supervisor who drives certain subordinates hard while letting others go about their ordinary business, or even loaf, is not necessarily being oppressive. Presumably, rewards will be forthcoming to match the demands. The oppressive supervisor is one who violates reciprocity in one way or another. To take advantage of unwilling female subordinates is wrong; to squeeze money from subordinates is unheard of. But to maintain a disparate set of relationships with individual subordinates may be quite acceptable. Again, to call on them for various personal services not directly related to the work of the office is acceptable, within broad limits. To reward them for manifestations of deference and respect is commonplace. To be relatively permissive is also expected. In a loose way, the supervisor resembles "the father." His status derives from hierarchical position, but his role is not limited to bureaucratic actions.

Productivity as a basis of action is not irrelevant in this setting, but it is usually subordinate to other concerns. As individuals, subordinates may seek to exploit their positions in ways ranging from flattery to diligence—but such diligence had better be consistent with a supervisor's desires. Individual subordinates may bring to bear the protective influence of a high-ranking patron. They may *not* unite forces to form a formal group for purposes of dealing with superior authority.

In Western-style supervisory training programs in the Institute of Public Administration at Bangkok, instructors have consistently encountered an impressive interest on the part of Thai supervisors in discussions of employee counseling and "human relations" approaches to management and motivation. The explanation of this interesting phenomenon seems to lie in the intensely social character of supervision in the Thai system, rather than in any widespread concern with such techniques as means to increased productivity.

Thai supervision seeks to maintain the system, to solve immediate problems, to cope with immediate demands, and to keep the routines working. Supervision is the primary means for linking components of the organization system, and for providing continuity and coherence in the activities of the system's units. It is not consciously adaptive, nor are supervisors systematically involved in setting productivity goals in a "rational" manner.

They inevitably do become involved in goal setting, if only by default at higher levels in the bureaucracy. Such goal setting, particularly at low levels in the hierarchy, produces a great deal of variation in the substance of a given activity from place to place. Thus, in the malaria control program some sectors did "mop-up" spraying to cover areas missed in the original effort, but others did not. And the field workers were found commonly making unavoidable decisions to alter prescribed procedures and practices when supplies and funds available at zone and sector levels were insufficient for the formally specified work.

At lower levels in the hierarchy, the ability to cope with circumstances of this kind is an important quality of any supervisor. The prime measure of his effectiveness will be the judgment of his own superior, for Thai supervisors are also subordinates with obligations not unlike the ones they enforce upon their own staffs. Viewed from above, the good supervisor is one who can fulfill the expectations of his superiors with a minimum of trouble for them, and in a manner suitably expressive of his broad responsibility for deference and assistance.

Discipline. By "discipline" is meant a set of norms specifying behavior, and the sanctions which are intended to enforce those rules. The effective norms and sanctions may vary considerably from the formal rules and regulations but are to a substantial extent selected from among them.

More than one-fourth of the current civil service statute consists of disciplinary provisions, a collection of edicts and exhortations which would provoke the envy of an Ayudhyan monarch. A civil official is required to support the "constitutional form of government," to conduct himself properly and to give due respect to his superior (and not to by-pass that superior without his permission), to perform his work diligently and with alertness, to get permission from his ministry before engaging in commercial activity, to avoid using his office for personal gain, to be just and honest, and to preserve his good reputation. He is not to be contemptuous of or disrespectful to subordinates or the public, and he is not to disclose official secrets. The civil official, in short, is to be a paragon of virtue and diligence.

In practice, (a) certain formal norms tend to be enforced but not others; (b) the enforcement process is based upon the exercise of hierarchical authority and there is no effective right of appeal; (c) the sanctions tend to be severe; and (d) the entire process tends to be conducted on a highly personalized basis.

The norms which are most commonly enforced are those prohibiting dishonesty, "meaning the abuse of official authority for personal gain, such as demands for money in return for the official service and misuse of government funds." [52] In the three years from 1956 through 1958, almost 40 per cent of the disciplinary charges and allegations made against officials of the Department of Interior (now the Department of Local Administration) involved dishonesty. Dishonesty is regarded as a serious disciplinary violation, punished by expulsion, dismissal, or discharge. A categorical breakdown of other allegations of disciplinary infractions is not possible from the available data. In general terms, it includes misconduct, inefficiency, and improper performance of duties. The absence of detailed, systematic information on the formal working of disciplinary arrangements is in itself interesting. It suggests that such information is neither important nor meaningful. Discipline is an implicit facet of the system, not something to be analyzed and assessed.

One cannot even judge the meaning of the heavy emphasis placed upon the rule of honesty. Fragmentary evidence suggests that dishonesty really means two things: stealing government funds or property, or exploiting members of the public in circumstances where the relationship was not regarded as reciprocal. In the Department of Interior, from 1956 to 1958, 36 per cent of the complaints were brought by anonymous letters written by other officials or members of the public, but only about 6 per cent of these complaints led to punishment. About one-fourth of the charges were filed by immediate superiors—and half of these led to formal sanctions. An immediate superior may charge a subordinate with violating discipline; his superiors must judge the complaint. Interestingly, in only about half the cases did the allegation lead to punishment. What informal considerations came into play is not known.

The general impression fostered by this one limited study of disciplinary practices is that norms governing honesty receive more official support than any others. Certainly, there is no clear evidence that inefficiency or inattention to duty are common reasons for invoking punishment.

In the system of discipline there is great discrepancy between the formal and the actual, and considerable selectivity appears to be involved in the application of punitive sanctions. "The flexibility of Thai moral standards not only condones, but may elicit sympathy for, the underpaid civil servant who accepts bribes to supplement his meager income." [53] (One might add: provided he gives something in return, does not force the bribe, and is otherwise discrete.) But 4,602 civil officials, exclusive of teachers, were discharged, dismissed, or expelled from the civil service between 1954 and 1959, almost 1 per cent per year, for dishonesty and other offenses. The system admits of appeals, but of the 4,602 persons discharged only 263 appealed—9 of them successfully.[54] In the Interior Department, from 1956 to 1958, of 614 punishment orders, 10 were appealed, and 1 sentence was reduced.[55]

A complex system of inquiries and adjudications is prescribed in cases involving possible infractions of discipline, but this is largely formalistic.[56] It provides a pattern of action to be followed when serious disciplinary action has been decided upon. The pattern is known by all, and when activated it grinds inexorably on its way to some largely predetermined outcome—expulsion, dismissal, discharge, demotion in salary step, reduction in salary grade, or reprimand, the six formal sanctions of the system.[57]

Expulsion, the strongest formal sanction makes an official outcast of one subjected to it; he loses his pension rights, seniority, status

—everything. Only after a lapse of three years may the Civil Service Commission even consider the possibility that the former official has reformed and may once again be eligible for examination or reappointment.[58] The official who has been dismissed is in almost as bad a condition, except that he can appeal to the Commission for the right to become eligible for re-entry after only two years. A discharged person at least retains something—his retirement. Discharge applies in the case of officials who have become incompetent, careless, or otherwise unfit, or cases in which the offense is serious but the proof of guilt is not clear; the official is regarded as "blemished" and no longer acceptable as an active member of the bureaucracy. Therefore he is retired, i.e., "discharged." [59] The lesser and much more common penalties, demotion within class, reduction in salary step, and reprimand, are, like the more serious penalties, thoroughly formalized and the circumstances of their application are spelled out at great length and with exquisite precision. A reprimanded official may, for example, be required to submit a written statement to the effect that he will amend his behavior.

Under the aegis of the Civil Service Commission's Division of Discipline and Appeals, a voluminous collection of case materials has been produced to detail with vivid example the nuance of the various disciplinary regulations. For example, a district clerk misappropriated public money with no extenuating circumstances, i.e., he took money for gambling or other evils. He was caught. The penalty: expulsion. Another case involved a clerk who confessed that he was severely ill and needed money for medicine—which was why he stole fee payments and speculated with them. "Therefore he was adjudged with great mercy to be dismissed." [60] An official who leaked information to the press was expelled. Another who took advantage of his departmental position to obtain information for his own sideline newspaper work was discharged. A police officer disguised himself to trap some criminals, carelessly let a friend know what he was up to, and the outlaws disappeared. "But his confession and the fact that this was a first offense caused him to be reduced in salary by the maximum possible amount." [61]

Theft of public money, disclosure of official secrets, and grossly improper conduct toward superiors—these seem to be the most serious offenses. Culpable negligence in the performance of work is also officially regarded as serious, and is punishable by removal from the service if the results are serious. "Yet any man is likely to be negligent some time. . . . [But] the frequent offender must be denounced as an unfit person whose behavior is thoroughly detrimental to the official service. . . . Eventually, if the offender is truly culpable, he must be punished severely and without mercy. If this does not succeed, he must be expelled." [62]

Culpable negligence is distinguished from a lesser offense—carelessness or casual neglect of duty, which is generally punished by a salary cut or reprimand. Lack of industriousness is another category of offense. A section chief who was dilatory in disbursing officials' salaries in his department was dismissed. A *changwad* health officer who failed to take any action during an epidemic was expelled. A telegrapher who was slow in sending out urgent messages was reduced in salary, and a talkative typist who did not finish his work within the assigned time was reprimanded. All this, of course, in the implicitly horatory illustrations of the *Civil Officials' Magazine*.

The catalogue of offenses and penalties is extensive; the available materials provide guides to handling nearly every conceivable disciplinary case which might arise, and contribute some coherence to disciplinary practices. One effect is to sustain an awareness that there *are* penalties and they may be applied. More basically, the Thai literature of bureaucratic discipline spells out a hierarchy of norms indicating patterns of proscribed and undesirable behavior. The sheer scope of the disciplinary provisions tends to blur the outline somewhat, but certain themes remain quite clear: some types of offenses are more serious than others. Also, as the literature suggests, the quality of mercy is not strained in the Thai bureaucracy, and under identifiable conditions appeals to mercy are likely to produce certain kinds of results.

In practice, these formal statements of norms are interpreted by informally transmitted premises which may be highly particular in their application. Formal statements about offenses "against proper application of official working time" will often be taken for what they usually are—hortatory devices. In a few places, supervisors may apply them, or some of them, but this is not common.

The norms emphasize the hierarchical character of the system and the encompassing obligations one has toward his superior. Some of this is explicitly indicated in specific norms. More is implied by the obvious relationship which the subordinate can see between all these

rules and the actual norms of conduct stipulated by his own supervisor, who more than anyone or anything else gives immediate meaning to the legion of disciplinary provisions which are part of the
system.

A superior officer has full discretion in deciding whether to take
action on a complaint against one of his subordinates; no rule or law
specifically requires him to do so. In view of the fairly common
tendency to use anonymous letters to harass officials, there is some
merit in this; but the authority of the superior also reflects the
emphatic hierarchical approach to discipline, as well as the latitude
for personalism in its application. "Personalities seem to figure more
prominently in the disciplinary process than does the law itself." [63]

Pay. The pay system of the bureaucracy is intimately linked with the
hierarchical classification system, as noted. The general level of pay
in the system is not high, from any of a number of points of reference. Fourth-class salaries start at about a dollar a day and rise to a
maximum of roughly $45.00 per month. A single man might live
within such an income range in Bangkok or a provincial city, but the
raising of a family in Bangkok on a fourth-class salary is difficult to
conceive. Unlike the pay at higher-class levels, however, fourth-class
pay rates have increased more nearly in accordance with the great
war and postwar inflation in Thailand. The inflationary trend diminished during the early 1950s, but it has been estimated that living costs
have risen as much as 30 per cent between 1952 and 1964.[64] Living
standards have also continued to rise, and at the bottom level of the
bureaucracy the only things that can be done to accommodate rising
desires and expectations is to enhance one's income from nonofficial
sources, or to be a member of a multiple-worker family.[65] Yet at the
fourth-class level pay is relatively good compared with the middle
levels of the system. Manual and semiskilled labor in the Bangkok
area works longer—and infinitely harder in most cases—for wages in
the 500–750 baht category, and has neither a 35-hour work week nor
any of the bureaucratic fringes.

Third-class pay is not very generous. "A third class civil official
. . . , holding a bachelor's degree and a certificate equivalent to a
master's degree, having received total salary at 1,100 baht per month,
had to live with priests in a monastery, ate cheap food at a street-side
stall three meals a day or sometimes (nearly the end of the month)
only two, dressed with only plain or sometimes a worn-out shirt and

trousers, had no hope of having a family, and seldom had a chance for recreation. He was lucky that he was never sick." [66] The pay at this class level ranges from about $37.50 per month to a top of $60.00.

Second-class officials, including chiefs of section and a number of types of professional officials including medical doctors with little or no seniority, receive pay within a range of $60.00 to $132.00 per month. The doctors, however, may practice privately on a part-time basis.

At the top two levels of the service the spread between minimum and maximum pay is greater. First-class officials—division chiefs, for example, or district officers—are paid from $132 to $215 per month, and in the special class pay ranges from $215 to $400. But in the special class, pay is often only one source of income. Pay for individual committee meetings, for instance, ranges from 20 to more than 1,000 baht. And there are other fringe benefits.

At all levels the real incomes of officials have declined in the past quarter-century, and they have declined more than proportionately in middle ranks, where the pay increases adopted at intervals since 1943 have been on a percentage basis less than at the bottom of the system, and where fringe benefits are less than at the top.[67]

For technicians and skilled office workers pay rates are relatively low in comparison with going rates outside the bureaucracy—including government enterprises.[68] In private enterprises and in such organizations as the Thai Cement Company, a quasi-public business, skilled clerks and typists earn from about $40.00 to $62.00 a month, and the earnings of stenographers can readily match the middle of the second-class pay range. Also, nonbureaucratic employment usually involves bonuses, which may equal 10 per cent of one's annual salary.

It is openly recognized by top-ranking officials that present salaries of middle-rank officials—particularly well-trained ones—are "incomparably" lower than going rates outside the government.[69] The feeling is shared by great numbers of officials at all ranks.

Yet nothing has been done about this and the demand for bureaucratic employment continues strong. In the Thai system it would be inconceivable that civil officials would "organize" to seek wage improvements. The stratification within the system, the autarchy, and the power of tradition—such forces are enough to eliminate the prospect for organized bureaucratic self-seeking. The conditions of pay and the degree to which they are tolerated are stark evidence of the social characteristics imputed to the bureaucracy. Given these characteristics and the absence of alternative employment for many officials, pay does not serve as a motivational force in a manner similar to more emphatically performance-and-reward oriented Western administrative systems.

Pay nonetheless *does* motivate. Perhaps the most powerful practical sanction available to a supervisor is his ability to withhold a step increase in salary. The desire for increased income—and status— encourages conformity with the values of the system. "Getting ahead," and particularly advancing into the second or first class, also has a monetary significance as well as certain attractive fringe benefits that are part of one's remuneration. Given the shape of the bureaucratic pyramid, with its impressively small proportion of upper-class jobs, and given the manner of promotional selection, advancement inevitably requires conformity to system values, and this in turn sustains them.

The broad outlines of the pay pattern are clear enough; the precise details of its operation are as intricate as anything in the bureaucracy. Much of this complexity stems from the arrangements for the "classification" of positions in terms of their "technical" qualifications.

"Technical positions" are those whose incumbents are required to have special technical qualifications. The allowances are actually salary rates within the regular pay system. The monetary increment attached to a technical position depends largely upon the specialized educational qualifications of the incumbent, for it is these which are assessed by the Civil Service Commission in determining the pay rate for the post. The assessment of the monetary values of education— particularly foreign degrees and multiple degrees—has become as precise and formalized as could happen only in the Thai bureaucracy. A standardized set of values has been compiled for various kinds of degrees and academic certificates, and these are set out in neat tabular form. When these cannot be applied, specific rulings are made.

A simple example: the starting pay for a third-class position filled by someone with a college diploma is 750 baht; but the base pay for an individual with a four-year degree from a Thai university— assuming, as one safely may, that he is assigned to a "technical" position—is 900 baht. If a position "requires" the holder to possess an M.A. degree from England, the United States, or the Thai Institute of Public Administration, the beginning salary will be 1,900 baht, and the post will be placed in the second class of the civil service. The pay goes with the position—but the amount will depend upon the educational qualifications of the individual.

In practice, but not in formal specification, there are really two kinds of "technical positions." A technical position may be a class of jobs all of whose incumbents, selected by a "selective" rather than "competitive" examination, are required to have a particular background of educational training, or training and experience.[70] Thus, for example, the former Ministry of Co-operatives requested that the post of second-class district co-operative officer be recognized as a technical position. In supporting this request to the CSC a four-page specification of the "quantity and quality" of the work and the background required was prepared, and a special salary rate was approved.

Another situation arises when a third-class official at the basic pay rate of 750 baht goes abroad, acquires an M.A. in two years, and returns with the degree. He will usually be placed in a "technical position," in response to a specific request that such a position be established, following the same formal pattern of request as in the case of a class of positions. If the CSC follows its usual practice, the individual will receive a salary of 1,900 baht. "It seems to be common practice in the civil service to establish technical positions for most—if not nearly all—officials whose educational qualifications would make them eligible for the salary benefits accruing to such positions. In fact, requests for such establishment of such positions are usually initiated (informally, at least) by the individuals possessing the appropriate qualifications within the civil service." [71]

Between 1954 and 1959 the Civil Service Commission issued 20 regulations governing "technical positions," or the specific pay rates to be applied to more than 50 different sets of specific educational qualifications, ranging from one-year courses beyond the minimum educational qualifications required at the fourth class to doctor's degrees.[72] In addition, the commission has made numerous allocations through official precedent-setting letters to agencies.

Basic factors involved in determining the pay value of education beyond the minimum required for appointment to a specific class appear to be: (1) the nation where the person studied—British and American degrees currently having top monetary value; (2) the educational institution at which the work was done; (3) the courses taken, number and kinds of degrees or certificates received, and length of time required to complete the work; (4) the difficulty of the course, as determined by the Civil Service Commission; (5) the nature and extent of practical training, if any, received following the completion of academic work, or in some cases in lieu thereof.[73]

The technical-position pay policy of the Thai government "motivates." It has given much impetus to degree-oriented study, at home and abroad. In Thailand the bachelor's degree has become the lowest cut-off point for college educations, and the bottom grade of the third class has been replaced with a higher level applying to the "technical positions" thus resulting. Practically all third-class appointments now are to technical positions, so far as pay is concerned.

The desire of young Thai officials to go abroad to study has never been stronger. Officials are particularly benefited. They usually continue to draw their salaries while they are on student leave, and their time in residence as students counts as service for retirement purposes. However, they cannot receive step promotions while they are on such leave, to the chagrin of some.

According to the records of the Civil Service Commission, between 1936 and 1959 a total of 1,391 government officials studied at academic institutions in the United States, England, and France, or were otherwise trained there, and subsequently requested that their credentials be evaluated by the CSC for salary purposes.[74] Of these officials, 927 studied in the United States, and 330 in England. Nearly a thousand (968) were foreign graduate students, and over 60 per cent of the total group studied education, medicine, engineering, science, and business. This group, equal to about one-half of 1 per cent of the present civil service, comprises an impressive collection of technicians and professional specialists. It is reinforced by hundreds of domestic graduates, some of them exceptionally well educated, and several hundred Thais currently studying abroad, or returned since 1959.

One value attached to such education and training is monetary, given the terms and conditions of Thai bureaucratic pay policy. Another, of course, is access to opportunities for advancement in rank. This is fostered in a number of ways by advanced education, which gives an official a running start, leaving him with fewer pay steps to work through before he can reach the top pay levels in his class and thus become eligible for possible promotion to the next higher one.

The relationship between education and pay in the Thai bureaucracy is substantial evidence of the effective attainment (as distinguished from achievement) norms mentioned elsewhere in this study. Education has acquired a tremendous capital value, and substantial investments are made in education by Thais seeking bureaucratic careers. The resulting pressures upon the Thai educational system have been great, and the foreign aid programs of the postwar era have both reflected the widespread desire for education and stimulated it. Nothing in the Thai social system is likely to elicit any more effort and sacrifice than an opportunity for a young ambitious man to acquire a foreign degree.

Fringe Benefits. A basic benefit of the bureaucracy is best expressed as an abstraction—"security." This is manifest in a variety of specific arrangements, some of which have been mentioned. Another is the retirement or pension, benefits governed by the Pension Act of 1901 as amended. The basic retirement benefit is determined by taking an official's salary during his last month of service, multiplying by his years of service and then dividing by 50 if his service is 25 years or more, or by 55 if it is less than 25.

Pension provisions are inevitably complex, and the Thai system is no less elaborate than most. The Ministry of Finance administers the pension law and regulations, pension being financed on a current appropriation basis. About 35,000 retired officials and dependents of deceased officials are being supported under one or another aspects of the pension system. Dependent survivors—spouse, parents, or children—are entitled to half the amount of the pension that the deceased official received.

Leaves are an important fringe benefit in the bureaucracy. There are thirteen holidays a year, and all government offices are closed when these occur on days of the 5-day, 35-hour work week. There are also sick leave, "business" leave, military leave, maternity leave, study leave, leave for temporary entry into the Buddhist priesthood, and "informal leave." [75]

An official is legally permitted a maximum of 120 days of sick leave, but in practice the amount which may be taken is usually quite a bit less. An official who becomes ill is obliged to submit an excuse letter on an official form. A doctor's certificate may be required by individual agencies for illness of less than 30 days, but general regulations require such evidence when illness extends over a month or more. An individual who is injured while on duty may have 120 days' leave; if he acquires a serious infectious disease as a result of his duties he may be placed on leave with full pay for up to 270 days. Maternity leave is treated as a subtype of sick leave, and a maximum of 60 days is allowed but departments heads are often unwilling to grant more than 45. Officials who have been on leave more than 45 days may not receive salary promotions at the end of the year in which the leave was taken, except in cases of priesthood or maternity leave.

"Business leave"—actually business or vacation leave—is an interesting although relatively uncommon arrangement. An official who has personal affairs to attend to, or is in serious need of a rest, may request leave by letter to his supervisor. If circumstances merit, he can receive up to 45 days' leave—or as much as 75 days if he goes abroad to nearby countries, and 165 days if he travels to Europe or America. This provision sounds most generous, but practice is less liberal and such leave for purposes utterly unrelated to one's official position is not very common. Eligible officials must usually have at least five years' service, and frequent grants of such leave are not made. In practice, "when one takes leave on business for one day or a few days, usually he will say that he is sick."

Any male civil official who wishes to enter the priesthood may be granted leave for 120 days at one time in his official career. Officials mobilized into the military service in time of crisis are automatically granted leave. They continue to draw their civilian salaries in addition to their military pay, under the premise that they are still civil officials. This generous provision does not, however, apply to officials who are drafted.

Foreign study leave is granted whether the official goes abroad to study under governmental auspices or his own. Each ministry has a "quota," specifying the number of its officials who may be on leave for foreign study. Any person going abroad under this quota continues to receive his salary.

With all these leave provisions, there is in the Thai bureaucracy no general regulation prescribing for ordinary annual vacations. The Council of Ministers or its president issues orders from time to time granting such leave. Thus, the prime minister stated in a recent year that "government officials will be given ten days' holiday each during the hot season. They will go off on a vacation on a rotation basis."

In view of the permissiveness which characterizes Thai society and the great variation in emphasis upon work performance within the bureaucracy, it is not uncommon to find a substantial amount of "informal" leave-taking. Common practice calls for each official—at least at lower classes—to "sign the book," or sign in when he reports for work in the morning. The signature is *prima facie* evidence of his attendance for that day. But not infrequently, with—and sometimes without—permission of his supervisor, an official will disappear shortly after signing in, on some errand of his own. Practice varies according to supervisors and work situations. In some sections or divisions there is very little such leave-taking. In others it is rather common among fourth-class menial officials. A casual attitude toward working hours in many units, and the array of leave provisions in the system generally, reflect a limited stress upon productivity and imply that being an official is as much a way of life as a way of working.

Other fringe benefits available to officials include medical care at public hospitals for themselves and their families at half rates; equal matching by the government of the forced savings contributions of about 3 per cent of the pay of each official; government "payment" of the income tax which would otherwise be levied upon official salaries; and preferential access to low-cost public housing if it is available, and particularly if officials are assigned to work at posts away from their place of initial appointment.

At the upper levels of the service there are special fringes: second- and first-class officials are likely to get preferential access to public housing. Most first-class and special-class administrative officials are assigned government automobiles, in some cases with drivers, which they may use freely. And at the top, particularly in the special class, officials may receive supplemental incomes from service on government committees for which allowances are granted, the amounts varying from committee to committee. They also have considerable opportunity for extensive travel. And in some cases they may be inclined and enabled to leap from the bureaucratic to the political milieu, or at least to partake of some of the rewards of the latter as members of the coterie of an important political official.

Communications. Quite a bit has been said at one place or another about the generation, transmission, and interpretation of premises which underlie decisions and actions in the bureaucratic system. Communications is in a sense a part of all that we have considered. Yet a few explicit observations are pertinent, for communications is a source of premises which are the immediate bases of behavior, and the particular characteristics of the process manifest the normative foundations of the bureaucratic social system.

The Thai bureaucracy, like all large administrative systems, uses vast quantities of paper in its work. Part of this consists of documents which are instruments of action—licenses, permits, vouchers, receipts, and similar items. A considerable amount of the paper also consists of records made in order to evidence (or minimize) responsibility for particular occurrences and events. The ubiquitous police kiosk would be fundamentally unfurnished without its large journal into which someone is usually scribbling entries, and it exemplifies the fact that written records are made about practically everything recordable that concerns the operations of the bureaucracy. But such records do not serve as a basis for the systematic analysis of activities and the programing of work. The data of decision making are to an impressive degree personal rather than objective, and their significance tends to lie in their source more than their content.

Administrative reports abound. But reporting does not have its primary pay-off in managerial decision making. For example, in the previously mentioned malaria control program, the zone chief and his assistant spend as much as 20 per cent of their time in preparing reports. These are concerned with spray inspection, finances, the pay, travel, and per diem of each employee in the zone, supplies on hand and disbursed, monthly progress, a quarterly narrative of activities, a monthly report on each vehicle operated within the zone, and three or four others. These reports are made by either the zone chief—a second-class officer equivalent in rank to section chief—or his assistant, who is usually a third-class officer. The papers flow from the zone to the region to Bangkok, along with additional sector reports. But what happens to all the data?

To cite one suggestive example: The National Malaria Eradication Project headquarters has formulated work standards: ten houses to be sprayed per sprayman day and five house visits per house-visitor work day. Data generated in sector reports indicated that these general standards were quite inadequate. In densely populated areas workers met the standards in a few hours and quit. In other areas only about 50 per cent of the quotas could be met because of the time required to get from one house to another. But personnel and other resources continued to be allocated to sectors on the basis of the headquarters standard, and not on the basis of any analysis of data generated from reports on field operations. There is nothing stark or dramatic in this small incident, but it does seem to be a rather typical illustration of one aspect of the communications processes of the Thai bureaucracy. Significant communications come down from the top and not up from lower levels. And objective data are not used to challenge the soundness of orders issued by high-ranking officials.

Perhaps because of its limited relevance, much of the "hard data" generated in the system tends to be unreliable anyhow, so that the personalized, subjective approach to decision making is supported by the dubiousness of the available alternatives.

Personal inspections are a means by which higher-ranking officials seek information on the state of affairs within their jurisdictions. With all its utility, inspection has its limitations as a source of reliable knowledge of what is going on. In the Thai bureaucracy these limitations are enhanced by the effects of status. On inspections, one commonly sees the inspectors talking instead of listening; the posture of subordinates is usually deferential and protective. A truly masterful Thai administrator I have known made a success of his field visits by convincing most of his subordinates of his paternal pride and interest in their work and their particular problems, and by loosening their tongues with liquor. The dinners that went with his inspections became lively and uninhibited discussions. He stayed sober, listened, and always acted judiciously. But he was an uncommon leader. More often, inspection tends to be a formalism, unless some particular trouble has already occurred and needs to be set right

Inspection is supplemented by a gentle sort of espionage. Any special-class administrative official will have one or more trusted minions within his organization to keep tabs on matters. They report to him personally, often at his home in the evenings, bringing the gossip, the confidences, and the suspicions which will help protect the administrator against painful surprises. The identity of such reporters is seldom secret and the fact of their existence offers occasional opportunities for intrigue reminiscent of an earlier era in Thai government. Granting all the subtlety and caprice involved in such an arrangement, espionage does tend to reflect and sustain the system's values, and to provide some of the information on which administrative action is based. Misfeasance and malfeasance are sometimes exposed, and loose, disrespectful talk about superiors is discouraged. A variety of problems of concern to superiors may be uncovered, and informants contribute to the effectiveness of the trouble shooting which is a prime concern of Thai bureaucratic managers.

Committees are also much-used communications devices in the Thai bureaucracy. They are well suited to an administrative style that is emphatically personal, but the ways in which committees function is also conditioned by the hierarchical status value which permeates the system. Committee deliberation tends to be inhibited and committee decisions usually reflect the opinion of the highest-status participant. To some extent, of course, premises are brought into consideration by lower-status personnel, but the significance of statements made in committee deliberations is largely a function of the status of the speaker.

Committees are also used to blur responsibility for particular decisions and actions. Thus, examinations are administered by committees; bid requests are prepared by committees, received by committees, opened and evaluated by either the receiving committee or another, and accepted by a committee. The committees usually consist of line officials, but they as individuals are relieved of decisional responsibility by the committee device.

It has been said that if committees did not exist, the Thais would have invented them. But committees in the Thai civil bureaucracy appear to be most effective as devices for obtaining shared responsibility, and much less as deliberative devices leading to widely assessed decisions. Deliberative committees are seldom supported by systematic staff work; and for a junior member to make or criticize proposals in a committee is a delicate matter.

The importance of status as a factor influencing all personal communications is illustrated by the careful attention which is given to manners. Language in Thailand has an "instrumental" quality distinct from its use as a means of conveying impersonal messages. This is perhaps most commonly manifested in the extreme reluctance of anyone to say "No," even to another person not of superior status— and one simply does not give an explicitly negative response to a request from a superior. Disagreeable messages are often conveyed through intermediaries, while the principles involved maintain a pose of politeness and even affability.

Rules and regulations are commonplace instruments of communication within the bureaucracy, the inevitable concomitants of large-scale organization. But they "work" in complex ways. On the one hand, many rules and regulations tend to be effective without question. For example, the retirement system and personnel selection arrangements are both rooted in elaborate collections of rules. Once established, the rules tend to be sustained by inertia unimpeded by any continuing assessment of their effect upon the system. On the other hand, specific rules and regulations can be, and occasionally are, ignored or modified in particular actions by officials with high status. Or, if it might not be considered good form to violate a tradition-sanctioned rule about some important matter such as re-source procurement, an additional rule may be adopted. The new rule then becomes a convenient justification for future action at variance from the older norm. Rules are the instruments of an authority which is essentially nonlegal, and which resembles legal authority chiefly be-cause any large administrative system must have a fairly sizeable number of available premises in order to continue to exist and oper-ate in a coherent manner.

Underlying the place of rules and regulations in the system is the absence of systematic and comprehensive requirements of legal man-dates for major units of organization within the bureaucracy. The organization structure is, of course, the product of specific edicts of the Council of Ministers or the king (pre-1932). But agencies do not operate upon the basis of "rule of law"; they do not have to assert the legitimacy of their particular activities or claims for resources by reference to enabling legislation. In some cases there is no such legis-lation; in other cases it does exist but the potency of claims and ac-tions does not lie in legal legitimacy to any great extent, as the previ-ous reference to the budget process shows.

When challenged, an individual may have recourse to rules to justify his behavior; when technical questions arise—e.g., the amount of a retirement stipend—it will be answered by reference to the rules. But in the Thai bureaucracy, rules and regulations are not so exten-sively called into play as "instant premises" for decision making as they are in systems centered in the legitimacy of law. In the Thai communications process one must often look outside the rules and regulations for information about their meaning—often to personal sources with status commensurate with the importance of the question at hand.

One qualification is in order in this sweeping discussion of communications. Some kinds of quantitative data are relatively important bases for decisions and actions. Revenue statistics, data on the balance of payments, and information concerning the international position of the baht—such matters as these are watched rather carefully, as a basis for a financial policy which has been rather adroit over the years. The Bank of Thailand, rather than a regular bureaucratic agency, has been the instrument of monetary policy. It has generally performed well the functions of protecting Thailand's international fiscal position.

One common dimension of communications has not been mentioned up to this point—communications linking the bureaucracy with its setting. The volume of bureaucratic communications into the environment is substantial. It moves by radio, television, newspaper, and word of mouth. Much mass-media communications is hortatory and of little potence as a basis for action in the environment. Word-of-mouth communication tends to be specific, and is normally loaded with the authority inherent in official status.

The most interesting aspect of bureaucracy-environment relationships involves feedback, or the flow of premises into the bureaucracy as a basis for action. There is little systematic communication into the bureaucracy from organized interests or clients of the bureaucracy. Some is directed to the top levels of the bureaucracy and, above it, to the political sector from a few representatives of economic interest, such as the Chinese Chamber of Commerce, the American Chamber of Commerce, diplomatic and foreign aid representatives, and important foreign firms. But economic activity is to a large extent in Chinese hands, and systematic claim making by such interests is not generally acceptable.

The transactional relations between the bureaucracy and its environment tend to be particular and personal, and to depend upon subtle and informal (and, sometimes, illicit) arrangements between individuals or firms and the bureaucratic agencies with which they are involved. Thus in the case of the small business—most firms in Thailand are small and are conducted on a highly personal basis—the formal rules and regulations, such as the schedule of customs duties, may become the point of departure for a set of transactions which may not follow the official norms. At the least, an import transaction will probably involve a certain amount of expediting through small gifts to clerks in accordance with a set of customary norms. In some instances much more may be involved. Needless to say, data about bureaucratic-business relationships are hard to come by, and generalizations from particular cases are especially treacherous, for these relationships are highly particularistic. However, the amount of "arm's length" dealing between bureaucratic organizations and economic concerns is relatively small, and the existing relationships do not elicit a substantial flow of significant and reliable data from the economic sector of society into the bureaucracy.

The quality of bureaucracy-environmental communication seems to be fraught with significance for the future. The spread of governmental activities is inseparably linked with a spreading sense of the impingement of bureaucratic activities upon a variety of people and groups. And the growing array of governmental objectives (economic development, for example) increases the significance of bureaucratic action or inaction. The cost of errors and miscalculations is likely to rise as the government pushes its bureaucratic apparatus further beyond law-order and the maintenance of a simple infrastructure into the realms of a managed society.

Reliable feedback from the environment concerning the actual effect of bureaucratic activities grows more important. But status barriers and the absence of any meaningful and widespread mechanisms for articulating—let alone aggregating—interests are serious barriers to such feedback. For example, in the community development program to which the contemporary government appears to have made a serious commitment, the bureaucratic culture must be modified in some respects if village development officials are to stimulate and encourage nonofficial leadership, and not merely engage in ineffectual exercises of authority.

If community development succeeds in fostering village initiative, manages to build a promotional rather than an authoritative bureaucratic apparatus, and creates useful flows of information into the program agency from its clients, this will be tantamount to a small revolution, involving a variation from persisting bureaucratic values. Those values are clearly reflected in the existing communications patterns of the Thai bureaucracy.

Other Factors. The above-mentioned arrangements which influence and control bureaucratic behavior are parts of the visible, deliberate devices for "energizing" the administrative system. Along with the pattern of authority discussed earlier, they direct and produce certain kinds of behavior.

These arrangements reflect more subtle, underlying cultural influences—influences more fundamental than the immediate bureaucratic arrangements. Systematic studies of these cultural characteristics and the ways in which they affect bureaucratic behavior remain to be made, but some relevant evidence is available, and a certain amount of speculation is not without its merit.

Buddhism, the benign, apolitical Theravada Buddhism of Thailand, is beyond all doubt a potent acculturating and socializing force. The norms that a man should keep his temper under control, that he should be benevolent, that he should be tolerant of the behavior of other individuals—these find their sources in Buddhism. The limited intensity of most personal relations, and an apathetic posture toward secondary associations generally, also seem related to Buddhist tenets.

Buddhism subordinates the affairs of the world generally to a concern with escaping from it. It offers a variety of sources of protection against anxiety for the individual, but it is not social-action oriented. It ascribes no particular merit to purposive, impersonal administrative organizations. At best, productive bureaucratic behavior is Buddhistically neutral, and not highly meaningful. The personal relationships of members of the bureaucratic system are something else; Buddhist tenets afford a plentiful set of guides and norms for interpersonal relationships.

Limited studies of the Thai personality, reported and analyzed by Professor James N. Mosel, provide a picture of a man who is relatively self-satisfied, who views his world in terms of personal status and the differential status of those with whom he has meaningful relationships, and whose concern in this world is self-protection and the achievement of his own status desires.[76]

Judging from limited data, Thais tend to regard the proper person as "carefree," "generous," and "gentle," and to be relatively well pleased with their self-perceptions in relation to this model. Their political posture is largely apathetic and beyond that, spectatorial, and their posture toward administrative organizations per se seems to parallel it. Looking out on the world, the individual tends to regard the information that comes to him in terms of its social utility in the manipulation of the behavior of others and in the maintenance of status relationships. The meaning and utility of knowledge seems to depend "upon the craftsman who made it, or more specifically, the social status of the information's source." [77] This suggests an intensely personalistic perspective, and one with little bias in favor of impersonal empirical data as a basis for perception and action.

The typical Thai seems to show great "flexibility in slipping from one role to another—as long as the roles are of the same status level." [78] Diffuse bureaucratic roles, whose most explicit components are status definitions, are thoroughly compatible with such personality characteristics. The reciprocity which is a pervasive, if not officially mandated, element of bureaucratic relationships is also thoroughly consistent with the loose social structure, the benevolent tolerance sanctioned within it, and the personalistic Thai *Weltanschauung*.

In short, the Thai culture appears to be marked by the persistence of the traditional, and not by any marked tendency to break with it. So, too, has the bureaucracy been distinguished by the persistence within it of values whose antecedents lie far back in the society's history, values which remain substantially compatible with its broader cultural context.

Fortunately, that culture has been marked by impressive capacities for adaptation. But the changes which have taken place within it have not represented a profound break with tradition so much as the changing expression of persistent tradition to meet new needs. The techniques by which the contemporary bureaucracy is energized do differ greatly from those which were commonplace before the Chakkri Reformation; but the central premises upon which those techniques are based are hardly new.

Chapter 10

STABILITY, CHANGE, AND THE THAI BUREAUCRACY

The Bureaucracy and its Contemporary Setting

THE MOST impressive feature of the Thai bureaucracy is the stability it has shown since its reconstruction more than half a century ago. By and large, the bureaucratic environment has also been marked by substantial stability. On the surface there have, of course, been changes. Regimes have come and gone. A shifting group of actors have played their political roles in different ways. The roles themselves have not changed much.

Today, new forces for change seem to be gathering beneath the surface of Thai society. The foundations of a new political awareness may be emerging in an increasingly educated populace. Certainly, new material desires and expectations are spreading. The terms of existence available to people within Thailand are themselves shifting with population growth and urbanization.

To this point in time, social and political change in Thailand is more latent than overt. To this point in time, the bureaucracy has fulfilled the nation's requirements. But some changes in the relationship between the bureaucracy and its environment are evident. And some new problems of bureaucratic adequacy are emerging.

GROSS CHANGES IN THE BUREAUCRATIC ENVIRONMENT

The Thai society is rapidly expanding in numbers. From about 25,000,000 persons in 1960, population is expected to rise to 40,000,000 or more by 1980. The rate of urban growth is even greater, although this growth proceeds from a small base. Greatest, perhaps, is the growth in the proportion of literate and educated persons.

Between 1916 and 1922, for example, the average annual number of domestic civilian and military college graduates in Thailand was

70 or less. Between 1949 and 1958 the average number of degrees and diplomas issued by only three schools—Chulalongkorn and Thammasat universities and the College of Agriculture—was more than 1,100 per year. In 1957 alone, 1,905 persons graduated from five Thai colleges and universities.[1] (And during the five years 1954–1958, an average of fewer than 380 college graduates per year were appointed to third-class civil service posts.) [2]

In the early 1920s about 11,000 Thai students were enrolled in secondary schools above the primary level.[3] Between 1953 and 1957, average annual enrollments in secondary and pre-university classes were more than 313,000 students.[4] (And more than 10 per cent of these were at educational levels which would qualify for admission to the bottom level of the bureaucracy—*Matayom* 6 or preuniversity grades 1 and 2.) [5]

The Thai military has helped absorb part of the "surplus" products of the educational system in recent years. Now, however, it limits its intake of commissioned officers to graduates of its own educational facilities.

The growing flood of college and secondary school graduates presages a possible shift in long-established social patterns. One alternative to bureaucratic absorption of the burgeoning numbers of school graduates is nonbureaucratic employment. Another would be massive bureaucratic expansion.

To this point, however, there is little evidence of a basic modification in the traditionally bureaucratic career objectives of sizeable numbers of Thai students. A 1958 survey showed that most of a sample of 292 students at seven Thai colleges and universities desired to become bureaucrats.[6] A later survey of a larger sample of students at Chulalongkorn University and nine teacher training colleges give no clear indication of any shift in student expectations away from a preference for bureaucratic careers.[7]

Before any quick conclusions are drawn from the evidence of the large gap between bureaucratic career expectations and opportunities for fulfilling them, it should be recalled that this is not an entirely new situation in Thailand. The 1930s were also marked by a significant discrepancy between the supply of prospective bureaucrats and the demand for their services. Yet an undeniable potential for a shift in the relationship between bureaucracy and society is inherent in the relation between college and secondary school graduates and bureaucratic career opportunities.

To this point, however, the bureaucracy continues to exist as the major component of the intermediate levels of the Thai social pyramid whose base consists of more than 20,000,000 villagers. Between the bottom and the top of Thai society, the social strata are largely bureaucratic strata, and bureaucratic rank remains a critical index of social status.

Social status, of course, is hardly the only human motive, but once a person need no longer be concerned with sheer survival he becomes increasingly interested in status. The Thai social system, with its emphatically and traditionally hierarchical character, may be more prone to the production of status sensitivity than some other social systems. Be that as it may, in the Thai society status is to a great extent expressed in terms of bureaucratic referents.

In general terms, wealth is no full substitute for rank in Thailand. For some, wealth is a function of status and the perquisites that go with it. But wealth alone does not seem commonly preferable to high status. Thais who are shrewd and discerning in business affairs devote substantial amounts of time to bureaucratic careers, partly to protect or advance business interests, but also to try to reach the top class of civil service. And money alone does not necessarily provide easy access to this class.

Such premises suggest at least that an abandonment of bureaucratic preferences will not come easily and automatically in Thailand. Yet the desire for access to the bureaucracy is not likely to lead to militant demands for bureaucratic expansion in order to create more posts—not at least in the short run. The bureaucracy itself has never functioned systematically as a self-conscious pressure group or political interest, and empire building within it commonly—though not always—has been linked with external advice and aid. Bureaucratic expansion has generally been restrained by the abiding goal of fiscal soundness.

As for the would-be bureaucrats, they have so far engaged in no systematic or persistent attempts at political organization in order to press their claims. Secondary associational activity—political or otherwise, but especially political—is not sanctioned in Thai society. The above-cited Schuler-Thamavit survey indicated that only 30 per cent of the students interviewed at seven colleges and universities claimed membership in any kind of secondary association whatsoever. Of these, half were members of either an English language club or similar organization, or of a "career club" directly related to ongoing studies.

As for the larger social environment, no effective domestic political forces exist outside the government to press for services and standards of performance. Desires and needs exist; to some extent they are made known by spokesmen for towns and villages, by foreign advisers, and by economic interests. But in the language of Gabriel Almond, the "political input functions" in the Thai system are weak and unstructured at best.[8] This is hardly surprising in a society with a large, atomistic, village-centered populace; a traditional emphasis upon the unchallenged legitimacy of a hierarchical order; and a lack of sanction for secondary associational activity.

Whatever pressures may be growing within Thai society have as yet little opportunity for finding effective, focused political expression. Yet a tutelary government often manages to discover or acknowledge needs, and to produce bureaucratic instrumentalities by which to try to meet them. One consequence of this awareness and response, notable during the Sarit regime, was an expansion in the scope of bureaucratic activity.

CHANGES IN BUREAUCRATIC PERFORMANCE REQUIREMENTS

The Thai bureaucracy is not fundamentally resistant to innovation, provided the impetus comes from outside and the approval from above; yet two important problems are emerging in the course of current bureaucratic growth:

The first problem concerns the expansion of the scope of activity and the increasing interdependence among the actors. Mention has already been made of problems of co-ordinating watershed development and protecting irrigation facilities. The success of the Thai bureaucracy to this point has resulted from its ability to fulfill whatever expectations have been imposed upon it. These demands have not exceeded the system's capacity for co-ordination. As the substance of bureaucratic activity grows still more, however, problems of co-ordination will grow at least apace. To some extent they are being met through the development of integrative agencies—the Budget Bureau, the National Economic Development Board, the Ministry of National Development, and the various units of the Prime Minister's

Office. But there is in the bureaucracy an inherent resistance to co-ordination through impersonal mechanisms, and through nonhier-archical authority. In the future it may become increasingly difficult to achieve needed co-ordination, given the normative characteristics of the system.

Why? In part, because of the established relationship between authority and traditional values in the bureaucracy. The Budget Bureau and the National Economic Development Board, for example, are essentially instruments of authority. They are adjuncts of the power at the top. To the extent that they are supported by those who control the government they can inject rationalizing premises into the bureau-cratic system.

The history of the Thai bureaucracy is, in a sense, the study of a continuing, shifting struggle between external authority and internal values. External authority counters the intrinsic normative character-istics of the bureaucracy. Now, as in the past, there are legitimate and effective sources of such authority, which in recent years have been used to foster bureaucratic productivity and, with it, better co-ordination of an expanding bureaucratic apparatus.

In part, the authority of this leadership stems from the king, whose major function is to legitimize the political system. Entwined with this is the legitimizing effect of hierarchical status itself. In reality, the two—kingship and hierarchical status—cannot be separated. Nor can it be said that the political leadership depends entirely upon legiti-mate authority as the basis for its existence and actions.

This authority to impose control upon the bureaucracy derives in part from the value imputed to hierarchical status. From this premise certain other interesting, if highly speculative, premises seem to fol-low:

First, the wry observation that the status value which contributes so much to the stability of the bureaucracy and to its tendencies to-ward self-serving behavior can also help mitigate the deterrent effect of bureaucratic status concerns upon productivity. Authority can be used to promote productivity and the co-ordination of bureaucratic activity.

Second, in the event of the withdrawal of authority from without, so long as status is meaningful within the bureaucracy, it facilitates bureaucratic survival and the continued performance of useful func-tions as an incident to the service of bureaucratic self-interest. In

view of the fact that the imposition of authority in the service of productivity goals is more personalized than institutionalized, this capacity for bureaucratic continuance remains important.

Third, if the potency of hierarchical status within the bureaucracy
were weakened by the development of a multiplicity of nonbureaucratic institutions in the middle ranges of Thai society, one of
the sources of authority now available for control over the bureaucracy would also be weakened. Quite possibly, the very processes of
constitutional change in society would involve the development of
new sources of political power—but one hesitates even to speculate
about the ways in which this might happen.

Meanwhile, the problems of bureaucratic co-ordination, bound up
as they are with the characteristics of authority and value found in
the Thai system, may grow greater in the near future, although they
have so far been met by new administrative instrumentalities.

A second problem that is emerging in the course of current
bureaucratic growth also threatens bureaucratic efficacy now and in
the short-run future. This is the problem of agency-clientele relationships in a bureaucracy moving into fields which require co-
operation and consent from the clients, rather than responses to
hierarchical authority.

The bureaucracy has functioned largely in an authoritarian manner
in its relationships with external clientele groups. This authoritarianism has been much ameliorated by reciprocity arrangements, of
course. Now the government embarks upon a growing array of activities intended to support and to promote nonbureaucratic developmental activity within the society. The community development program
has already been mentioned; it is a prime example of an effort which
relies not upon enforcement but rather upon education and the
mobilization of consent and support.

Few of the bureaucracy's clients have any conception of such a
pattern of bureaucratic action (except perhaps in some sectors such
as education where teachers may be supportive, not just authoritarian). The bureaucrats themselves are abidingly conditioned to rely
upon authority as the basis of action, or at least to rely upon superior
status as the justification for the assertion of an authoritative posture
toward subordinates. Nonbureaucratic clients are, generally speaking,
subordinates. The normative foundations of the bureaucratic system
militate against the extensive and effective use of techniques by which

to mobilize consent and co-operation. A commitment to efforts which inherently require such techniques may pose one of the greatest challenges to the continued efficacy of the bureaucracy in the years ahead; a shift of basic bureaucratic values is involved in the use of consensual rather than authoritarian tactics.

Yet it cannot be said today that the bureaucracy has grown obsolete, or that it has failed to meet the nation's needs. The bureaucracy has demonstrated an enormous adaptive capacity in the years since 1892. It has shown an impressive ability to persist and to function in the absence of effective, continuing, productivity-oriented external authority. It has also been able to respond to such authority when it has been exerted, expanding the scope of its functions to meet new demands, and performing those functions in a fashion adequate to the society as well as satisfactory to the bureaucrats themselves.

Now, however, the scope and tempo of change in Thailand seem to grow relentlessly, and the problems of the past will not necessarily be those of the future. The problems of bureaucratic growth may themselves be growing. The requirements of effective bureaucratic action are changing in some sectors of the administrative system. The bureaucratic environment itself is being transformed. Past and present capabilities may not suffice for future needs.

Lessons from the Case

The Thai case offers a few lessons for the student of modernization and development. They are not novel; they tend to support an existing body of knowledge and suppositions. But they are worth some consideration, if only because in Thailand it is possible to examine the aftermath of a unique effort at administrative transformation, and to consider the consequences as well as the effort.

1) Administrative reform does not necessarily lead to the internalization of the values imposed upon the bureaucracy by the reformers.

In the Thai case, an effort was made to recast the bureaucracy into a relatively rational, productive collection of administrative agencies. Both traditional values and traditional authority were brought into play in this effort. The authority produced a significant set of changes; and traditional values were the source of inducements which enabled the changes to serve their intended purposes. In response to

STABILITY, CHANGE, AND THAI BUREAUCRACY 251

effective tradition-sanctioned demands, the bureaucracy behaved for a time in a manner thoroughly consistent with the requirements of high productivity. In fact, it acquired enough of a productivity posture to continue serving the society after the authority imposed upon it had withered.

The withdrawal of the transforming authority—the decline of the monarchy—did not threaten the integrity of the system. It did result in a shift in the substance of behavior within the bureaucracy—a declining concern with productivity. But the integrity of the bureaucracy depended upon its central values, and these had been neither changed nor attacked in the course of the Chakkri Reformation. The elaboration and differentiation of the bureaucracy that took place in the nineteenth century enabled its survival without the king, for the reconstructed apparatus was furnished with a series of bureaucratic processes by which it could maintain itself with only minimal needs for outside intervention and support.

Had the time dimensions of the Chakkri Reformation been different, and had some institutional development occurred outside the bureaucracy, a greater change might have occurred in the normative foundations of the administrative system. But the traditional authority of the king was not shifted to institutions which could persistently press the bureaucracy to adhere to the value of productivity. What happened to the Thai bureaucracy after the Chakkri Reformation was hardly surprising: in broad and simple terms, it merely continued to respond to the effective forces which impinged upon it. To assume that anything else might have happened is to assume very much indeed.

2) The abiding impact of the central values of the bureaucracy offers its lessons, too. One of them is simply the tremendous vitality of the values of an established social system. Another is their impressive capacity for accommodating change by adjustments in the expression of the values themselves.

One might argue that if the values are so flexible, or capable of expression in a rich variety of ways—ways which are responses to forces impinging upon the system—then why not forget about the values and get on with the business of increasing the productive capacities of administrative systems in developing nations? In other words, why not manipulate the "functional" aspect of an administrative system and not bother too much with its "structural" aspect? This, of course, was the unconscious and inevitable strategy of the Chakkri Reformation.

This may be a thoroughly suitable approach to the solution of pressing and immediate problems—given the presence of sufficient, and sufficiently able and dedicated political authority. But the basic lesson of the Thai case is perhaps this: great adjustments in the functional component of a social system do not necessarily result in comparable changes in its normative foundations. And if those normative foundations are in some ways fundamentally inconsistent with some stipulated or visualized developmental needs, then tinkering will not produce development.

The Thai case raises, but hardly answers, the question: What is the nature and magnitude of force which must be brought to bear in order to change a bureaucratic social system? Actually, there may be a new Thai case in the making, as such forces as professionalism begin to permeate various sectors of the system—a professionalism characterized by dedication to specific purposive aims and a rationale for pursuing them. Possibly evolutionary changes in the thematic value orientations of the system are occurring, but no one knows at present.

3) The values of the Thai bureaucracy are also the values of its setting; the coherence of system and setting is a key to the persisting stability of the bureaucratic system. One lesson of the Thai case is simply that administrative change cannot take place only within a bureaucratic system; it must be matched by environmental changes, and these changes must be relatively basic: they must include the effective manifestation of fundamental values that will challenge the continuing relevance of the bureaucratic *status quo*.

One special case of this general postulate is that bureaucratic modernization depends upon political modernization; and political modernization involves extensive changes in social structure. In the Thai case, the Reformation was not tantamount to political modernization, nor in reality was the coup that overthrew the monarchy. The overthrow of the monarchy may have produced some of the prerequisites or preliminaries to political modernization, in the form of a formalistic commitment to constitutionalism and representation which might over time accrete substance. To this point, post-monarchical government in Thailand has varied from authoritarian to tutelary. Today it remains substantially devoid of mechanisms for mobilizing elements of a domestic polity and responding authoritatively to claims from within the society. To say this is not to criticize that government, for there is no polity to mobilize in a coherent way, and to respond to meaningfully. If anything, one of the critical immediate problems looming before the Thai government in 1966 is the possibly premature establishment of would-be democratic representative institutions. Such institutions require normative underpinnings and social relevance fully as much as do bureaucracies. Such underpinnings may be evolving within the society, and over the longer run the greatest challenge ever faced in Thailand may be the reasonably orderly conversion of the present political system into one meeting the common criteria of "modernity"—the ability to mobilize a polity, to resolve interest conflicts on a consensual, relativistic basis, and to cope with the political problems which must be faced if the society is to survive

Fortunately, it is not our task here to blueprint such developments, or even to assess their probability. But one thing seems relatively sure: the quality of the Thai bureaucracy will continue in the future to be shaped to a great extent by the nature of the effective environmental forces that impinge upon it. To the extent that such forces persistently make greater claims for rational and efficient action, to that extent the bureaucracy will probably respond within the limits of its capacity. This capacity, however, will be limited by the basic values inherent in the bureaucratic motivations. Efforts to push, prod, preach, and train elements of the bureaucracy into changing their patterns of action because this is regarded as good and desirable by persons and groups with little or no political potency are not likely to have any fundamental effect. They may, of course, politicize the bureaucracy, or elements of it, but experience elsewhere does not give much encouragement to the idea that a politically effective bureaucracy would be more altruistic or service-oriented than the Thai bureaucracy is at present.

In conclusion, if "development" is viewed as an expansion of capacity as well as scope, and if administrative development is prescribed to be increasing commitment to the rational pursuit of an expanding array of purposive goals, then not much development has taken place in Thailand since the Chakkri Reformation. But this is no indictment. After all, development itself is a value of varying relevance. In terms of another criterion—survival—the Thai system has sufficed. The bureaucracy may not produce in the idealized bureaucratic fashion, but it has not been guilty of failures in the form of inadequacies contributing to social collapse.

As for the future, it is difficult to say. What has been sufficient until now may not continue to be sufficient in the future. The long-continued predominance of the bureaucracy as the strata of society above the level of the villages seems improbable. But there is little immediate evidence of great stress within the society, and it is entirely possible that the Thais will amble quite far into the future with their stable, relatively adaptable, essentially traditional bureaucracy.

NOTES

CHAPTER 1

1. James N. Mosel, "Thai Administrative Behavior," in W. J. Siffin, ed., *Toward the Comparative Study of Public Administration* (Bloomington: Indiana University, 1959).
2. Walter F. Vella, *The Impact of the West on Government in Thailand* (University of California Publications in Political Science, IV, No. 3 [Berkeley: University of California Press, 1955]).
3. David A. Wilson, *Politics in Thailand* (Ithaca: Cornell University Press, 1962).

CHAPTER 2

1. For convenience and simplicity the contemporary name, Thailand, is used throughout, except in quotations referring to the former name, Siam.
2. James C. Ingram, *Economic Change in Thailand Since 1850* (Stanford: Stanford University Press, 1954).
3. *Ibid.*, p. 9.
4. H. G. Quaritch Wales, in his *Ancient Siamese Government and Administration* (London: Bernard Quaritch Ltd., 1934), pp. 40–59, discusses the traditional society. Wales distinguishes between royalty (including nobles) and commoners.
5. Walter Vella, *Siam Under Rama III, 1824–1851* (hereafter *Rama III*) (Locust Valley, N.Y.: Association for Asian Studies by J. J. Augustin, 1957), p. 27.
6. Cf. Reginald Le May, *The Culture of Southeast Asia* (London: George Allen and Unwin Ltd., 1954). Also, Theodore Bowie, ed., *The Arts of Thailand* (Bloomington, Indiana: Indiana University, *et al.*, 1960).
7. Bishop Pallegoix's estimate, cited in Wales, *Ancient Siamese Government*, p. 59, as one-fourth, and by Vella, in *Rama III*, p. 26, as one-third; in any case the original estimate was a guess.
8. Wales, *Ancient Siamese Government*, pp. 53–54.
9. Vella, *Rama III*, p. 21.
10. Phya Anuman Rajadhon, "Popular Buddhism in Thailand," in William J. Gedney, ed. and trans., *Life and Ritual in Old Siam* (New Haven: HRAF Press, 1961), p. 65. For useful discussion of Thai Buddhism see also: Kenneth E. Wells, *Thai Buddhism: Its Rites and Activities* (Bangkok: The Christian Bookstore, 1960); Luang Boribal Buribhand, *The History of Buddhism in Thailand* (Bangkok: Chatra Press, 1955);

and Kenneth P. Landon, *Southeast Asia: Crossroad of Religions* (Chicago: University of Chicago Press, 1949). Hindu facets of Thai Buddhism are also shown in H. G. Quaritch Wales, *Siamese State Ceremonies: Their History and Function* (hereafter *Siamese State Ceremonies*) (London: Bernard Quaritch Ltd., 1931).

11. George Orwell's *Burmese Days* (London: Secker and Warburg, 1949) contains a discerning characterization of the conduct of a Burmese official, based on a rational calculation of merit-demerit, which is suggestive of the ways in which this calculus of karma has also been sometimes applied in the Thai social system. Beyond the simple prescription of admirable virtues, practical Buddhism contains a variety of formalistic measures of merit. To build a new temple is to gain great merit; to repair a temple built by another, however, is to enhance the merit accruing to the original builder. To offer food to a Buddhist priest is also to make merit; the monk in seeking alms is showing mercy toward creatures by giving them the opportunity to do good works.

12. H. G. Quaritch Wales, *Ancient Southeast Asian Warfare* (London: Bernard Quaritch Ltd., 1952), p. 147.

13. Phya Anuman Rajadhon, "Popular Buddhism in Thailand," in Gedney, *op. cit.,* p. 98.

14. Vella, *Rama III,* p. 33.

15. See, for example, Prince Dhaninivat, "The Old Siamese Conception of the Monarchy," in *Fiftieth Anniversary Commemorative Publication,* Vol. II (Bangkok: The Siam Society, 1954), pp. 160–175. Prince Dhani observes that the king was morally obliged to comply with certain ethical imperatives, and that his lawgiving power was conceptually limited. But neither the imperatives nor the legislative limitations were enforceable by any outside source, as H. G. Quaritch Wales has noted. The Thai kingship has been discussed by a number of authors, including Robert Heine-Geldern, in his article on "Conceptions of State and Kingship in Southeast Asia," *Far Eastern Quarterly,* II (November, 1942), 15–30. Kasem Sirisumpundh, in "Emergence of the Modern National State in Burma and Thailand" (Ph.D. dissertation, International Law and Relations, Wisconsin University, 1962), makes much of the superior place of the *Dharmasastra* in relation to the king (pp. 31–32): "Thus, a Thai or a Burmese monarch had no power to enact law. He was born to maintain order and peace and to protect his subjects. . . . His first task was to punish people contravening custom and to settle disputes between his subjects" (p. 32). Dr. Kasem's argument is valid that in ancient Thailand there was no *conceptual* basis for king-made law in the Western sense of general and permanent rules, although edicts which, practically speaking, were statutory in effect were hardly unknown. Dr. Kasem's characterization of the kingship seems more ideal than real. There is some danger of scholastic tendencies in intellectual analyses of the ancient kingship. Granted,

the king and his legitimacy were sustained both by rationalization and by elaborate ritual, and that these were matters of moment to the monarch himself. But in the last analysis, the legitimacy and efficacy of the kingship were not just functions of ritual and explicit rationale. The king *was;* he could change things, including the rationalized foundations of his own existence, as the Khmerization of the kingship showed. His position was not constitutionalized nor constrained by a priestly caste possessed of sanctions, nor by any abiding conviction that the gods would punish variations from the *Dharmasastra,* the sacred law introduced into Thailand by the fourteenth century. Of course, Thai kings were human, and rule and ritual must have given them assurance and relief from anxiety. But one gets the impression— from W. A. R. Wood's *History of Siam* (Bangkok: Barnikitch Press, 1924)—that the kings were often rather free-wheeling individuals. They were not, however, the omnipotent, absolute rulers that Wales makes them out to be—they lacked the instrumentalities necessary to an effective absolutism.

16. Wales, *Ancient Siamese Government,* p. 170.
17. Vella, *Rama III,* p. 16.
18. *Edict on the Method of Provincial Administration of King Day Srah* (or T'aiSri, or Pumintaraja, who reigned from 1709 until 1733) (in Thai) (Bangkok: National Library, 1928), translated by Wales, *Ancient Siamese Government,* pp. 126–130.
19. Wales, *Ancient Siamese Government,* p. 227.
20. Vella, *Rama III,* p. 24.
21. The following discussion of the characteristics of the traditional bureaucracy is largely based on Wales. There is, however, another description of the traditional pattern of Thai administration in an extensive memorandum written by King Chulalongkorn about 1893, *Pharatchadamrat nai pharbat Somdet Phara Chulachomklao song tharang phra baromrahatibai kae kai karn pokorng pandin* (King Chulalongkorn's explanation of the recent changes in the government), published with an introduction by King Prajadhipok in 1927. There is no fundamental disagreement between these statements. W. A. R. Wood's *History of Siam,* pp. 83, 94, is the source of information on King Trailok. He dates the governmental reorganization as A.D. 1454, while Prince Damrong, in *Laksana Ranpokkrong prathet Sayam taeboran* (Traditional Government of Old Siam) (Bangkok, 1959), p. 6, gives it as 1458. For our purposes such discrepancies are inconsequential—and illustrative of the common absence of completely authoritative sources on many of the details of ancient Thai history. Our aim here, of course, is not definitive history, but the description and examination of the general characteristics of the old bureaucracy, because of their relevance to modern-day administration in Thailand.
22. The word *kram* now designates a departmental element of a ministry.

In the Ayudhyan system it did not possess a precise organizational connotation; there were *kram* subordinate to *kram*. But the major *kram* were under *senabodi;* lesser *kram* were headed by men of lower status.

23. The following is based on Wales, *Ancient Siamese Government,* pp. 86, 113, 114, 121–122, 138, 202–204, 218–222.
24. *Edict . . . of King Day Srah,* quoted in Wales, *Ancient Siamese Government,* pp. 126–127.
25. The subject is dealt with at length in Wales, *Siamese State Ceremonies.*
26. A translation of the oath is found in M. L. Cort, *Siam* (New York: Randolph & Company, 1886), pp. 123–125. In the same book, pp. 260–264, the administration of the oath in a province is described. A translation of a portion of the oath is also found in Ernest Young, *The Kingdom of the Yellow Robe* (3rd ed., London: A. Constable, 1870), pp. 136–138.
27. Wales, *Ancient Siamese Government,* p. 219.
28. Wales notes: "The ease with which informers might reach the ear of the king with the most ill-founded complaint against a minister was a source of continued unrest." *Ancient Siamese Government,* p. 73.
29. Wales, *Ancient Siamese Government,* p. 246.
30. *Ibid.,* pp. 39–43.
31. Wales, *Ancient Southeast Asian Warfare,* pp. 141–142.
32. Wales, *Ancient Southeast Asian Warfare.*
33. This is drawn from Wales, *Ancient Siamese Government,* pp. 180–189; and from W. A. Graham, *Siam,* Vol. I (London: De La More Press, 1924), p. 370.
34. Wales, *Ancient Siamese Government,* p. 189.
35. Graham, *op. cit.,* Vol. I, p. 370.
36. This, at any rate, is Virginia M. Thompson's explanation of the beginnings of the tax-farm system; *Thailand: The New Siam* (New York: Macmillan, 1941), p. 544. Others, including Vella (*Rama III,* p. 23), assume that the farming out of tax collection was Chinese-inspired. Thompson's version makes a better story, but Vella's is more likely correct.
37. Wales, *Ancient Siamese Government,* pp. 233–234.
38. *Ibid.,* pp. 219–220.
39. Vella, *Rama III,* p. 23.
40. B. O. Cartwright, "The Huey Lottery," *Journal of the Siam Society* (Bangkok), XVIII (1924); reprinted in *Fiftieth Anniversary Commemorative Publication* (Bangkok: The Siam Society, 1954), Vol. I, pp. 131–149.
41. Vella, *Rama III,* p. 23.
42. Cartwright, "The Huey Lottery," in *op. cit.,* Vol. I, p. 149.
43. O. Frankfurter, "King Mongkut," *Fiftieth Anniversary Commemorative Publication,* Vol. I, p. 14.

CHAPTER 3

1. D. G. E. Hall, *A History of South-East Asia* (New York: St. Martin's Press, 1955), p. 199; cf. Chap. 18, "Siam and the European Powers in the Seventeenth Century."
2. *Ibid.,* p. 297.
3. Wood, *History of Siam,* pp. 203, 206.
4. Cf. Hall, *op. cit.,* Chap. 24, "Siam From 1688 to 1851."
5. Vella, *Rama III,* p. 115.
6. *Ibid.,* pp. 115–116.
7. H. S. H. Prince Vallabhakara, ed., *Siam: General and Medical Features* (Bangkok: Executive Committee, Eighth Congress, Far Eastern Association of Tropical Medicine, 1930), p. 34.
8. Kenneth E. Wells, *History of Protestant Work in Thailand* (Bangkok: Church of Christ in Thailand, 1958), p. 2. Dr. Wells notes that "the twenty-two Congregational or American Board Missionaries, in a period of eighteen years, 1831–1849, made not a single Thai convert. The Presbyterians worked from August, 1840, to August 5, 1859, before they baptized the first Thai Convert, Nai Chune. In thirty years, 1833–1863, the American Baptists made only forty-five converts, chiefly among the Chinese."
9. *Ibid.,* p. 9.
10. *Ibid.,* p. 11.
11. *Ibid.*
12. *Ibid.,* p. 14.
13. Cf. Bertha B. McFarland, *McFarland of Siam* (New York: Vantage Press, 1958). See also Vella, *Rama III,* pp. 35–43.
14. Vella, *Rama III,* p. 38.
15. For an extended discussion see Vella, *Rama III,* Chap. 9, "Relations With the West."
16. Vella, *Rama III,* pp. 3–5.
17. The following is drawn from Abbot Low Moffat, *Mongkut, The King of Siam* (Ithaca: Cornell University Press, 1961), particularly Chap. 2. Moffat's book, incidentally, is an extraordinarily eloquent and perceptive volume.
18. *Ibid.,* p. 20.
19. Translation of a letter to Phraya Suriyawongse Vayavadhana, ambassador to Paris, March 4, 1867, cited in Moffat, *op. cit.,* pp. 24–25.
20. For a more detailed discussion of the economic characteristics of the Bowring treaty and those which followed it see Ingram, *Economic Change in Thailand,* pp. 33–37. This entire volume is in a sense concerned with the broad economic consequences which flowed from the treaties.
21. Sir John Bowring, *The Kingdom and People of Siam* (London: Parker and Son, 1857), Vol. II, p. 227.

22. Ingram, *op. cit.,* p. 34.

23. Cf. Hall, *op. cit.,* Chap. 34, "Vietnam and the Beginnings of French Expansion."

24. Hall, *op. cit.,* p. 564.

25. Moffat, *op. cit.,* p. 25. See also Chap. 6.

26. Mosel, "Thai Administrative Behavior," in Siffin, *op. cit.,* p. 293.

27. An example of traditional Southeast Asian Oriental monarchical isolation: In 1880, long after Mongkut's death, a two-mile excursion by the neighboring King Tibaw of Burma was an epochal event: "If the Golden Foot goes by water, all bridges have to be destroyed, for never can descendant of Aloungpayah pass beneath where mortal has trode above." J. G. Scott, cited in Moffat, *op. cit.,* p. 27.

28. Moffat, *op. cit.,* pp. 26–27.

29. *Ibid.,* pp. 55–60.

30 Vella, *The Impact of the West on Government in Thailand,* p. 334.

31. Letter, King Mongkut to Wm. Adamson, manager, Borneo Company, Singapore Branch, 1862, quoted in Moffat, *op. cit.,* p. 167.

32. Malcolm Smith, *A Physician at the Court of Siam* (London: Country Life Press, 1947), pp. 85–86.

33. Cf. Hall, *op. cit.,* Chap. 37, "Britain, France and the Siamese Question."

34. Royal Memorandum 143/454, January 18, 1895, to Krammuen Damrong Rachanupap, Minister of Interior in *Qanuson nuangnainganchalong wan thilaluk sathapana Krasuang mahatthai kropop noksippiboribun* (*Sixtieth Anniversary Commemorative Volume*) (hereafter *Sixtieth Anniversary Volume*) (Bangkok: Ministry of Interior, 1952).

35. Damrong, "Conditions Existing During the Establishment of the Ministry of Interior," in *Sixtieth Anniversary Volume,* Part 2, pp. 37–42.

36. Vallabhakara, ed., *Siam: General and Medical Features;* cf. Ingram, *op. cit.,* p. 176.

37. Ingram, *op. cit.,* p. 176.

38 Damrong, "Conditions Existing . . ." in *Sixtieth Anniversary Volume.*

39. "Notification Concerning Presentation of *Biawat* Lists," and "Act Governing Revenue Office and Spending Agencies in Disbursement and Reimbursement Procedures," *Laws of the Fifth Reign* (in Thai), Vol. I (Bangkok: Wichakorn Press, n.d.).

40. The following discussion is from Chakra Hansakul, "A Study of Pay Policy and Administration in the Thai Civil Service" (Master's thesis, Institute of Public Administration, Thammasat University, October, 1959), Chap. 2, "Historical Development of Pay System in the Thai Civil Service."

41. Thus a young girl in the king's service initially received *biawat* at the rate of twelve to twenty-eight baht per year, depending upon the rank of her father. After puberty, the minimum rate increased to forty to sixty baht, although eighty to one hundred and twenty baht were more

common, and important actresses and concubines appear to have received more than two hundred baht. The information on this prototype of pay administration in an Oriental court crops up as a result of notifications issued by King Mongkut permitting the resignation of "inner-court officials," i.e., concubines, actresses, and young girls dedicated to the King's service by their fathers. As Chakra observes: "Girls in increasing numbers joined the king's service until it was 'overstaffed,' and the King could not recognize most of their faces or their names, but their number still multiplied. . . . King Mongkut found the way to remedy this problem was by retirement, but he chose the voluntary retirement instead of compulsory, declaring that he would like those girls to be free who had not had a child by him, who had not received insignia and *biawat* higher than two hundred baht, and who were not important characters of a play." Chakra Hansakul. *op. cit.*, pp. 45–46.

42. *Ibid.*, p. 47.
43. Arnold Wright, ed., *Twentieth Century Impressions of Siam* (London: Lloyds' Greater Britain Publishing Co., 1908), p. 68.
44. *Thailand Past and Present* (Bangkok: Publicity Committee, Ninth Pacific Science Congress, 1957), p. 58.
45. See, for example, James McCarthy, *Surveying and Exploring in Siam* (London: John Murray, 1900).
46. Wright, *op. cit.*, p. 206.
47. Wright, *ibid.*, p. 121.
48. McCarthy, *op. cit.*, p. 3.
49. *Ibid.*, p. 1.
50. Wright, *op. cit.*, p. 122.
51. Thompson, *Thailand*, p. 497.
52. Vella, *Impact of the West*, p. 340.
53. McFarland, *McFarland of Siam*, p. 75.
54. *Ibid.*, pp. 48–56. The following paragraphs are drawn from McFarland.
55. There were also three mission-operated schools in Bangkok: Samray Boys' School, the forerunner of Bangkok Christian College; the Wang Lang Girls' School founded in 1874; and Assumption College, a Catholic school established in 1885. The last of these schools appears to have been partly responsible for a trend toward English, as opposed to American, patterns of education which later became significant in the development of the public educational system.
56. A. Cecil Carter, ed., *The Kingdom of Siam* (New York & London: G. P. Putnams Sons, Inc., 1904), p. 208.
57. The following is drawn from Prince Damrong, *Laksana Ranpokkrong prathet Sayam taeboran* (Traditional Government of Old Siam), a lecture delivered in 1931, and printed in 1959.
58. The edict is published in the *Sixtieth Anniversary Volume*.

CHAPTER 4

1. As noted, related developments occurred in justice, finance, transportation and communications, education, military administration, and public health during the remaining years of the absolute monarchy; some of these were inseparably bound up with the development of the Ministry of Interior; all were to some extent influenced by that development; and none involved change of the scope entailed in the reconstruction of this ministry.

2. Damrong, "Conditions Existing During the Establishment of the Ministry of Interior" (*Sixtieth Anniversary Volume,* Part 2), is the source of this description.

3. As described by Damrong, "The old procedures of accomplishing the work were this": paper flowed from the provinces or from other sources into the working office of the Ministry, to be opened by the supervisory clerk, *Nai Wen,* having the duty at the time. After screening, the appropriate papers were submitted to the deputy minister for "preliminary consideration." The next morning the deputy minister together with Nai Wen would take the letters, together with the necessary documents, to the home of the minister. After the supervisory clerk had read the documents to the minister, the latter issued his orders. If his decision involved a reply, the deputy minister received the appropriate instructions from the minister, and then ordered a commission-rank (*sanyabat*) official to prepare the answer. Once drafted, this was resubmitted by Nai Wen to the minister for amendment. Eventually, a response was made. In routine matters the supervisory clerk would then prepare a letter himself in final form and send it to the seal clerk at the minister's home for sealing. The incoming letters were filed by Nai Wen in the attic of the working office. (Damrong then refers to his discovery in 1892 of many "bunches" of such letters from the reign of Rama IV, which had ended in 1868.) If the minister felt that an incoming letter raised a question for submission to the King, he would order the deputy minister to prepare an abstract for His Majesty. King Chulalongkorn's reaction to the procedures of the ministry was to grumble that "the Ministry of Interior now becomes the Ministry of Postal Service and asks my discretion for everything. It never uses its brain."

   Long after the modernization of Thai government had begun, the daily reading to the King of the traditional report on the state of the provinces had been maintained "in a very plain manner, concerning such matters as robbers, rainfall, and the condition of the rice crop." Its share of this report was presented by the Ministry of Interior on the traditional black accordion-folding cardboard, contained in a box which the royal secretary referred to as the "biscuit box of the Ministry of Interior" because of its resemblance to the boxes of tinned biscuits available in the markets.

4. Phraya Maha-ammarathyatibordi (hereafter referred to as Phraya Ammat), "The Story of the Ministry of Interior," Part 12, "Problems in the Creation of the Ministry," in *Sixtieth Anniversary Volume.*

5. Damrong, "Conditions Existing . . . ," in *Sixtieth Anniversary Volume,* Part 3, pp. 43–45.

6. Damrong, *ibid.,* Part 5, p. 50.

7. Cf. McCarthy, *op. cit.,* pp. 174–175. Nai Seng, referred to frequently by McCarthy by one fashion of expressing a later title of Phraya Srisdi (Phraya SriSahatep), had developed into McCarthy's chief assistant, and McCarthy's chronicle contains numerous references to the man and his work, both invariably described as "excellent." Nai Seng undertook a variety of responsible survey assignments and performed them independently. In 1891 his own brother, Nai Tat, was killed by Shan dacoits while participating in the frontier delimitation work on which Nai Seng and McCarthy were also engaged.

8. Phraya Ammat, "The Story of the Ministry of Interior," section on "Beginnings of Rural Administration," in *Sixtieth Anniversary Volume.*

9. Damrong, "Conditions Existing . . . ," in *Sixtieth Anniversary Volume,* Part 5.

10. Phraya Ammat, "The Story of the Ministry of Interior," section on "The Obligation of the Ministry of Interior," in *Sixtieth Anniversary Volume.*

11. Cf. Damrong, "Conditions Existing . . . ," in *Sixtieth Anniversary Volume,* Part 4.

12. Damrong, *ibid.*

13. Damrong, *ibid.,* Part 6.

14. Here is Prince Damrong's recollection of the formation of the idea of a system of regional government: "Communication between Bangkok and the provinces took many days. For example it took ten days to go to Phitsanulok [about 250 miles north of Bangkok, an ancient capital located on the Menam Chao Phraya]. The towns were scattered in various directions. It was impossible for the Minister to go out to these towns to inspect and improve them. The only way of control was issuing numerous orders to the governors together with direction for applying them. How did they interpret such orders? How did they carry them out? These things were not known by the Minister. Issuing orders to each province would be ineffective. A new solution was thus devised in conformance with His Majesty's thought that all provinces, five or six, were to be grouped into a *monthon.* The arrangement would be governed by the aim that the provincial headquarters shall be 'within the arm's reach of the great commissioners. . . .' They were the representatives and the consultants to the Minister. In other words, the great commissioners were to be the operators of a certain plan designed

by the Minister. This was the pattern that would accomplish His Majesty's purpose and was the one I conceived when I made my provincial inspection" ("Conditions Existing . . . ," *Sixtieth Anniversary Volume,* Part 6, pp. 56–61).

15. Vella, *Impact of the West,* p. 344.

16. Damrong, "Conditions Existing . . . ," in *Sixtieth Anniversary Volume,* Part 6, pp. 56–61.

17. As noted by Damrong in "Conditions Existing . . . ," *ibid.,* Part 6, from which the following is drawn: Monthon Ayudhya, or *Krung Kao* (Ancient Capital) as it was first called, was to control seven provinces linked by the Chao Phraya river system. Monthon Prachin would integrate four—later seven—districts on or near the Bangpakong River and the northeast section of the Gulf of Thailand. Monthon Nakorn Sawan would encompass eight provincial areas linked by the Chao Phraya-Ping river system north of Monthon Ayudhya; and still further north a fourth *monthon,* Phitsanulok, would link five provincial areas in the basins of the Nan and Yom rivers. Thus the *monthon* jurisdictions would encompass the chief territories initially under the Ministry of Interior.

In this modern day of radio and telephone it is easy to overlook the magnitude of the communications problems faced by the new Ministry —problems which had to be solved if the aim of integrating the nation were to be fulfilled. According to Phraya Rachsena, in Prince Damrong Rajanupap and Phraya Rachsena, *Tesapiban* (The System of Local or Territorial Government) (Bangkok: Klang Vidhya Press, 1952), pp. 92–113, a contact between Bangkok and a provincial headquarters in northeastern Thailand might require 8 to 12 days. When Prince Damrong acceded to the Ministry, an *urgent* communication between the capital and Luang Pra Bang, about 800 kilometers distant, required 17 days, with the return journey taking 13. A round trip to the important provincial center of Phitsanulok, 350 kilometers, took about 10 days. Twenty-four days were required for an exchange of communications between Bangkok and Nongkai, or between Bangkok and Ubonrachatani. Non-urgent communications might take several times as long, and during certain seasons of the year when floods impeded transportation even the most urgent communications might not be delivered.

18. Prince Damrong and Phraya Rachsena, *Tesapiban.* This was a collection of some of Damrong's writings, supplemented by Phraya Rachsena, a long-time official of the Ministry of Interior. This number includes Monthon Bangkok, not originally under the Ministry's jurisdiction. A total of 21 *monthons,* exclusive of Bangkok, were established at one time or another, with fairly frequent changes in numbers as needed.

19. Rachsena, in *Tesapiban,* Part 6, "The Beginnings of the Administra-

tion," p. 237. During his northern tour Prince Damrong, however, anticipated the need for prohibiting provincial governors from engaging in private business, and in his financial planning the conversion of governors to salaried officials was of a priority second only to the staffing of *monthon* offices with paid workers. (Damrong, "Conditions Existing . . . ," in *Sixtieth Anniversary Volume,* Part 6, pp. 46–61.)

20. Topics included: rural local administration, the issuance of regulations, provincial financial administration, provincial public works, management and care of animals used for transport, provincial judicial administration, administration of the land act, problems to be presented by monthon commissioners. Cf. *Sixtieth Anniversary Volume,* "The Tesapiban Meeting," pp. 145–150.

21. Damrong, "Conditions Existing . . . ," in *Sixtieth Anniversary Volume,* Part 6, pp. 56–61.

22. Rachsena, in *Tesapiban,* Part 6, "The Beginnings of the Administration," p. 237. The following is based upon Rachsena, *Tesapiban,* pp. 237–248. Graham (*Siam,* Vol. I, p. 322) cites the regulations as having been issued in 1896, but according to H. Warrington Smyth (*Five Years in Siam from 1891–1896* [London: John Murray, 1898], Vol. II, p. 250), they were approved by the Legislative Council in May, 1897. The Provincial Administration Act (*Khaw Bangkab Pokkrong Huamuang Chua-krow Paw Saw*) was adopted in 1898. Cf. Arsa Meksawan, "The Role of the Provincial Governor in Thailand" (Ph.D. dissertation, Indiana University, 1961), p. 116.

23. Rachsena, in *Tesapiban,* p. 239.

24. The following is based upon Arsa Meksawan, *op. cit.,* pp. 116–120.

25. Arsa Meksawan, *op. cit.,* p. 118.

26. Rachsena, in *Tesapiban,* pp. 289–290.

27. The mottled record of these later bodies is described in Arsa Meksawan, *op. cit.,* especially Chap. 6, "The Governor and the Provincial Council."

28. Initially, the title was *pu warajakarn muang,* the ancient term *muang* later being replaced by *changwad,* a more precise designation.

29. Wright, *Twentieth Century Impressions,* pp. 70, 91.

30. Smyth, *Five Years in Siam,* Vol. II, p. 250.

31. Wright, *op. cit.,* p. 92.

32. Smyth, *op. cit.,* Vol. II, p. 250.

33. Wright, *op. cit.,* pp. 92–94; Smyth, *op. cit.,* Vol. II, pp. 250–252; Graham, *op. cit.,* Vol. I, pp. 376–377.

34. According to Graham, *op. cit.,* Vol. I, p. 376.

35. Smyth, *op. cit.,* Vol. II, p. 251.

36. Smyth, *op. cit.,* Vol. II, p. 252.

37. Graham, *Siam,* Vol. I, p. 372.

38. Graham, *Siam,* Vol. I, p. 339.
39. *Ibid.,* p. 339.
40. James N. Mosel, "A Poetic Translation from the Siamese," *Journal of the Siam Society,* XLVII, No. 1 (June, 1959), 104–111.
41. The French episode and M. Rolin-Jaequermyns' role in it have been covered in various places. See: J. G. D. Campbell, *Siam in the Twentieth Century* (London: E. Arnold, 1902), pp. 177–180; and Graham, *op. cit.,* Vol. II, pp. 309–310.
42. These developments are described in Graham, *op. cit.,* Vol. II, Part 1; in Wright, *op. cit.,* pp. 70–204, and in Smyth, *op. cit.,* at various places, to mention just a few sources.
43. Graham, *op. cit.,* Vol. I, pp. 324–325.
44. Phraya Ammat, "The Story of the Ministry of Interior," in *Sixtieth Anniversary Volume,* Part 18.
45. The following is based upon Phraya Ammat's summary of the First Annual Report of the Ministry of Interior to King Rama VI, in "The Story of the Ministry of Interior," in *Sixtieth Anniversary Volume,* Part 19.
46. William W. Fegen, *Siam Directory, 1910* (Bangkok: Siam Observer Press, 1910), pp. 58–59.
47. A. J. C. Dickson, "The Teak Industry," in Wright, *op. cit.,* p. 171.
48. Prince Damrong, "Conditions Existing . . . ," in *Sixtieth Anniversary Volume,* Part 5, pp. 50–55.
49. Graham, *op. cit.,* Vol. I, p. 359.
50. Graham, *op. cit.,* Vol. I.
51. John H. Heal, "Mines and Mining Administration," in Wright, *op. cit.,* p. 185.
52. Graham, *op. cit.,* Vol. I, pp. 325–326.
53. "The Provincial Gendarmerie," in Wright, *op. cit.,* pp. 110–111.
54. Graham, *op. cit.,* Vol. I, pp. 326–327.
55. The following is based upon Phraya Ammat, "The Story of the Ministry of Interior," in *Sixtieth Anniversary Volume,* Part 19.
56. Graham, *op. cit.,* Vol. I, p. 328.
57. W. J. F. Williamson, "Finance," in Wright, *op. cit.,* p. 113.
58. J. Homan Van Der Heide, "Means of Communication, Rivers, Roads, and Canals," in Wright, *op. cit.,* pp. 200–202; and Ingram, *Economic Change in Thailand Since 1850,* pp. 79–84, 196–202.
59. Graham, *op. cit.,* Vol. I, pp. 353–356; Vallabhakara, ed., *Siam: General and Medical Features,* p. 22.
60. The following is derived from Phraya Rachsena, *Tesapiban,* pp. 299–309.
61. Soon after Prince Damrong's retirement, fiscal officials were transferred to the Ministry of Finance.
62. Prayat Smanmit's study, "District Administration in Thailand" (Master's thesis, Institute of Public Administration, University of the Philippines, 1959) contains valuable insights into the modern role of the

district officer in Thai government and a description of the development of the role of the district officer.

CHAPTER 5

1. Problems of semantics are involved here. If an organization is regarded as a system of action, then the bureaucratic processes with which we are concerned are appropriately regarded as aspects of the organization. If an organization is regarded as a static structure, then the bureaucratic processes which are the objects of concern in this chapter are patterns of action occurring within the organizational framework. In any case, the aim here is to isolate a critical aspect of the Reformation effort and to examine it, without getting bogged down in an avoidable conceptual morass. The following discussion should show that the bureaucratic processes can be described and analyzed, and that the analysis is thoroughly relevant to the case.

2. Ingram, *Economic Change in Thailand Since 1850*, Appendix B, p. 236.

3. Moffat, *Mongkut, King of Siam*, pp. 134–137.

4. The above is from the *Siam Directory, 1910*.

5. Ingram, *Economic Change in Thailand Since 1850*, describes in considerable detail the role of foreign financial advisers. Other discussions of the contribution of foreigners will be found in Vella, *Impact of the West*, pp. 342–344, covering the general use of foreign advisers during the reign of King Chulalongkorn; and in W. D. Reeve, *Public Administration in Siam* (London: Royal Institute of International Affairs, 1951), pp. 33–35.

6. Mosel, "Thai Administrative Behavior," in Siffin, ed., *Toward the Comparative Study of Public Administration*, p. 295. The whole matter of "The Use of Foreign Advisors and Officials in the Thai Civil Service During Rama V's Through Rama VII's Reigns" has been surveyed by Miss Rapee Kaocharern, in her Master's thesis (University of New Hampshire, 1963). (Rama V was King Chulalongkorn.)

7. Wright, in *Twentieth Century Impressions* (various pages), lists about a hundred of them. *The Siam Directory* for 1910 lists a total of 319 foreign officials as of 1909.

8. See Graham, *Siam*, Vol. I, p. 316. Colonel Gerini contributed to the work of the Siam Society and wrote the chapter, "Siamese Archaeology —A Synoptical Sketch," in A. Cecil Carter, ed., *The Kingdom of Siam*, pp. 213–226.

9. Francis B. Sayre, "Siam's Fight for Sovereignty," *Atlantic Monthly*, CXL, November, 1927, pp. 674–689.

10. Prince Damrong wrote extensively upon the subject. The following is based generally upon Damrong's piece entitled "Chulalongkorn University," in his *Compiled Writings* (Bangkok: Klang Vidhya Press, Department of Fine Arts, 1951), Vol. I, pp. 342–357.

11. There is some obscurity in the record. Prince Damrong refers to the

creation of the school, established "in front of the Pimanjai [Bhiman Chaisri] Gate" in 1899, in his above-cited history of Chulalongkorn University. Phra Pratum Dhevapibal, in a lecture delivered in March, 1941, based upon official documents of the Ministry of Interior, refers to the establishment of a Ministry of Interior training school at this time, which in 1902 became the Royal Pages School; and Phraya Rachsena, "The Training of Officials for Promotion," in *Tesapiban,* pp. 440–441, also makes reference to Prince Damrong's establishment of the civil service school in the Ministry of Interior, which in turn was the origin of the Royal Pages School. In any case, a school was established in 1899. In 1902 or early in 1903, Phraya Visutsuriyasak, the first head of it, became Undersecretary of the Ministry of Education and was replaced by Phraya Sivoravongsa, the chief of the Royal Pages Department, and it is probable that the school was then officially designated the Royal Pages School. Whatever the label, the institution was established in 1899.

12. This is based upon Phraya Rachsena, "The Beginnings of the Faculty of Public Administration at Chulalongkorn University," in *Tesapiban,* pp. 366–395.

13. One of them was Phraya Rachsena, whose writings on the development of the Ministry of Interior have been a most useful source.

14. Johnson, "Education," in Wright, ed., *Twentieth Century Impressions,* p. 233.

15. In 1906 the temple schools were recognized as the chief instrument of education in the provinces. It was agreed in principle that "all boys of school age ought to be required to receive instruction, and that this instruction, wherever possible, should be given by priests in the temples . . . ," and that the government should prepare and provide elementary textual materials free of charge (Johnson, in Wright, ed., *op. cit.,* pp. 233–234). At this time commissioners of education were appointed in each *monthon,* and the Ministry of Interior assumed responsibility for implementing these stated objectives.

16. Phraya Rachsena, in "The Selection of Officials to Fill the Positions" (*Sixtieth Anniversary Volume,* pp. 325–350), attributes this statement by Prince Damrong to the 1904 *tesapiban* conference.

17. The quotation and the discussion generally are from *ibid.*

18. The following is from Phraya Rachsena, "The Training of Officials for Promotion," in *op. cit.,* pp. 428–438.

19. Vallabhakara, ed., *Siam: General and Medical Features,* pp. 175, 176; Thompson, *Thailand: The New Siam,* p. 773; Graham, *Siam,* Vol. I, p. 254.

20. Graham, *Siam,* Vol. I, p. 355.

21. Wright, ed., *op. cit.,* p. 230.

22. Graham, *Siam,* Vol. I, p. 225.

23. *Ibid.*

24. Rachsena, "The Training of Officials for Promotion," in *op. cit.*

25. *Ibid.*, pp. 428–438.
26. Thompson, *op. cit.*, p. 244.
27. Chakra Hansakul outlines the status system in his "Study of Pay Policy and Administration in the Thai Civil Service," pp. 62–79. The case of Nai Seng aptly illustrates Mosel's observation that the bureaucracy was "a social system as well as an administrative system. An official was referred to at all times by the title attached to his office; it operated in lieu of his personal name. . . . (Family names in Thailand were not introduced until 1916.) If an official changed positions, was promoted, or demoted, or retired, he lost or changed his rank and title and name. Thus a man might have a series of completely different identities in the course of his lifetime. The result was an almost complete anonymitization and depersonalization of the officialdom" (p. 289).
28. Phraya Rachsena, "The Tradition of Decoration," in *Tesapiban*.
29. Chakra Hansakul, *op. cit.*, p. 71.
30. *Ibid.*, p. 91.
31. Mosel, "Thai Administrative Behavior," in Siffin, *op. cit.*, p. 290.
32. See *ibid.*, p. 291.
33. The quotation is from Mosel, p. 290.
34. The following is based upon Chakra Hansakul, *op. cit.*, pp. 47–92.
35. Adapted from Chakra Hansakul, *op. cit.*, pp. 54–55.
36. *Ibid.*, pp. 55–56.
37. Chinnawoot Soonthornsima, "The Relation of College Education to Pay Levels in the Thai Civil Service" (Master's thesis, Institute of Public Administration, Thammasat University, Bangkok, 1959), p. 28.
38. "Regulation of Ministry of Finance Governing Salary Rates of Provincial Officials, Ratanakosin Era 121," in *Laws of the Fifth Reign Ratanakosin Era 121* (Bangkok: Bamrungnukunkit Press, n.d.), pp. 142–144, cited by Chakra Hansakul, in *op. cit.*, pp. 56–59.
39. Chakra Hansakul, *op. cit.*, pp. 58–59, 83–84, is the basis of this paragraph.
40. Pension Act, R. E. 120, in *Laws of the Fifth Reign, R. E. 120*, pp. 179–190.
41. Quoted by Phraya Rachsena, "The Tradition of Decoration," in *Tesapiban*.
42. Prince Damrong, "Advice for Provincial Officials."
43. The role of King Chulalongkorn in nurturing the administrative values of the Chakkri Reformation is illustrated in the following incident, related by the late Phya Sridharamaraj in "Topics & Comments and Other Articles by 'Hermit,' " originally published as columns in the *Standard*, a Bangkok newspaper, and republished upon the occasion of his cremation, March 24, 1954: "I was appointed a judge one year before the age which is generally recognized by astrologers as the first critical year of every man's life. [He was appointed in 1908, at the age of 24.] But with me it was the year in which my career commenced. . . . The thing that impressed me most was the audience with King Chula-

longkorn, whose strength and wisdom stand highest in our annals. One evening in 1908 seven of us . . . were led into the Audience Hall by the then Undersecretary of Justice. His Majesty's impressive bearing and voice awed me to the dust. If I had not been so young and so ignorant of the world, I would then have felt very proud of our Great King. I did not feel then that I was too young to be on the Bench. . . . The country owes a great deal to Prince Rabi for having successfully organized our administration of Justice in less than ten years. Thanks to his training and discipline, our young judges, with very much lower salaries than that of our imported young legal advisers, could favourably compare with them. The audience lasted a few minutes. The seven of us stood in a row with flowers, candles, and joss-sticks for paying homage to our Sovereign before leaving the Capital to take our posts in the provinces. We were going to take over the administration of the courts in the provinces of Udorn and Ubol from the Ministry of Interior." In 1947, four decades later, an old man was yet impressed by his brief ceremonial contact with the king. And the king himself was willing to use his charisma to influence the attitudes of young officials, at best of the middling rank, who were going forth to do of the work of the new bureaucracy under the leadership of an exceptionally able Minister of Justice.

44. Wright, ed., *Twentieth Century Impressions*, pp. 204–205.
45. *Ibid.*, p. 204.
46. Phraya Rachsena, "Rewards to Officials of Other Ministries Attached to the Ministry of Interior," *Tesapiban*, pp. 425–427.
47. For a date on convictions, *Statistical Yearbook, Thailand, 1923* (Bangkok: Central Statistical Office), pp. 246–247; and for data on numbers of officials, *Statistical Yearbook, Thailand, 1935–1937* (same publisher), p. 340.

CHAPTER 6

1. Alfred Diamant, "The Bureaucratic Model: Max Weber Rejected, Rediscovered, Reformed," in Ferrel Heady and Sybil L. Stokes, eds., *Papers in Comparative Public Administration* (Ann Arbor: University of Michigan, I.P.A., 1962), p. 68.
2. *Ibid.*
3. John F. Embree, "Thailand—A Loosely Structured Social System," *American Anthropologist*, LII, No. 2 (1950), 181–193, has perceptively sketched the permissivity which seems to be a basic characteristic of the society.
4. Mosel, "Thai Administrative Behavior," in Siffin, ed., *Toward the Comparative Study of Public Administration*, pp. 301–302.
5. For materials relevant to impressions of the functions of Buddhism in Thai society, see—in addition to the sources cited in Chapter 2— John E. de Young, *Village Life in Modern Thailand* (Berkeley and

Los Angeles: University of California Press, 1955), Chap. 5, "Religious Beliefs and Practices"; also Wendell Blanchard *et al., Thailand, Its People, Its Society, Its Culture* (New Haven: HRAF Press, 1958), Chap. 5, "Religion."

6. For a suggestive insight into the apparent essence of the Oriental *Weltanschauung* in which Thai Buddhism shares, see F. S. C. Northrop, *The Meeting of East and West* (New York: The Macmillan Co., 1947).

Northrop's treatment is sweeping and idealized, but his abstractions are perceptive and suggestive characterizations of a "world view"—more precisely an aesthetic and an eschatology—in which "reality" and "meaning" have different connotations than in the West. At pp. 346–360 he presents a provocative analysis of Buddhism as a carrier of this world view. For example:

"Buddhism permits one to admit in addition to the undifferentiated all-embracing Nirvana the existence of whatever else similarly empirical scientific inspection or postulational technique operating in conjunction with experimental confirmation may validate. The only essential contention of the Buddhist is that one of the ultimate factors in terms of which the scientist and the philosopher must conceive the world to be constituted is the indeterminate, undifferentiated aesthetic continuum. . . . For the Buddhist and the Oriental generally the Christian notion of a determinate personality, soul, or mental substance which is both differentiated in its nature and immortal, refers to nothing which exists. . . . All differentiated, determinate things are transitory. . . . Thus the Oriental sage is continuously insisting that one must become self-less. . . . The way to secure peace of mind and religious contentment is, according to the Buddhist, not to go on, as the Western Christian does, optimistically assuming and cherishing the immortality of the complete, differentiated, determinate, unique personality. Such a procedure is false to the immediately apprehended fact that all differentiations, all determinate things in the complex, differentiated aesthetic continuum, are transitory" (pp. 352–353).

The *self* in this cosmology his two facets—"one a determinate, differentiated, unique element, distinguishing one person from any other person; the other the all-embracing, aesthetically immediate, and emotionally moving, compassionate indeterminate, and hence indescribable field component" (p. 353).

"Salvation" hence lies in the sublimation of *self,* in escape from temporality with its suffering and conscious selfishness into the world of the senses and individuals, a realm only suggested by the words "unconscious deathlessness," which is the ultimate quest of all mortals.

I would not wish to assert that such pristine conviction can be readily apprehended in the asserted and applied values of Thai laymen; I do infer that much Thai behavior is tinged with derivations of this outlook or something approximating it, and with other offshoots of institutionalized Buddhism. One of the most significant of these is the concept of *karma,* the ubiquitous idea that the state of a man's existence is a direct product of the totality of his thoughts and actions in a previous existence, i.e., a previous phase of his passage through temporality toward the ultimate, which is the transcending of temporality and the attainment of nirvana.

7. Such a posture would make the bureaucracy more attractive than business organizations, with their insistent emphasis upon output and efficiency. As economic enterprises developed in Thailand, the bureaucratic preference of most educated Thais has been pronounced. The relationship between preferences and presumptions about the impact of Buddhism is at least suggestive.

8. Similarly the questing scholarship characteristic of the West gained but a small foothold in Thailand in the course of the Reformation and after it. Thai Buddhism has as yet had no Aquinas, nor would he find anything analogous to an Aristotelian wellspring to tap if he were to exist.

9. See Ingram, *Economic Change,* pp. 170–174, 195–202.

CHAPTER 7

1. Ingram, *Economic Change in Thailand Since 1850,* p. 327.

2. The treatment of the 1932 revolution here, and in following sections, is based upon Thawatt Mokarapong, "The June Revolution of 1932 in Thailand" (Ph.D. dissertation, Indiana University, 1962). The interpretations, however, are not necessarily those of Dr. Thawatt.

3. Raymond B. Stevens, "Government and Administration," in Vallabhakara, ed., *Siam: General and Medical Features,* p. 1.

4. Vella, *Impact of the West,* p. 349.

5. For a perceptive discussion of this transformation, see Vella, *Impact of the West,* pp. 336–338.

6. *Ibid.,* pp. 349–352. See also Hall, *A History of South-East Asia,* p. 673.

7. Vella, *Impact of the West,* pp. 351–352.

8. *Ibid.,* p. 355; Hall, *op. cit.,* p. 673. It is possible that in 1688 King Narai was also killed in the strike against Constance Phaulkon. Quaritch Wales says so, in his *Years of Blindness* (New York: Thomas Y. Crowell Co., 1943), p. 7. Even so, the action was taken—if in fact Narai was killed—by nobles with a personal interest in the throne, and not by bureaucrats opposing policy per se.

9. Phraya Rachsena, "Establishment of Monthon Regions," *Tesapiban,* pp. 148–160.

10. Graham, *Siam,* Vol. I, pp. 328–329.

11. Ingram, *op. cit.,* p. 190.

12. One of Prajadhipok's early actions was to create a Supreme Council of State, a body of five senior princes to advise regularly on policy. He also established a five-man Financial Council to study economic

problems. Prince Damrong served on both bodies. (*Royal Government Gazette*, March 31, 1925, p. 438.)

13. Wilson, in his *Politics in Thailand*, pp. 167–172, outlines this development.
14. Wilson, *op. cit.*, pp. 172–173.
15. Thawatt, *op. cit.*, p. 108.
16. Thawatt, *op. cit.*, p. 48.
17. Fred W. Riggs, in *The Ecology of Public Administration* (Bombay: Asia Publishing House, 1961), first brought this most useful concept to my attention. In sociology, a distinction is customarily made between achievement and ascription as sources or criteria of status. *Attainment* is in a sense an intermediate concept. Status may be attained rather than either imputed or earned by actual or potential contributions to organization goals. Attained status is "earned," but it is earned by acquiring attributes which may or may not be indicative of achievement, if achievement is regarded as an acknowledgement of contribution or potential for contribution to the system.
18. Graham, *op. cit.*, Vol. I, p. 253.
19. Wilson, *op. cit.*, Chap. 4, "National Leadership" succinctly describes the nature of the political clique in Thailand. Fred Riggs, in a paper, "Cabinet Politicians in Thailand," traces the shifting structure of the cliques and analyzes the working of the clique system.

CHAPTER 8

1. The actual number of officials and other public employees is difficult to determine. In 1960 the Secretary General of the Civil Service Commission indicated that information on totals was not available. Payroll information from the Ministry of Finance, plus data on local teachers, showed the total number of civil servants rising from 164,725 in 1952 to 203,498 in 1957—a rise of 23.5 per cent. In the last years of the 1950s the civil service appeared to be growing at a rate of from 3 to 5 per cent a year. These data are from Chap Tharamathaj, "The Composition of the Civil Service of Thailand" (thesis, Institute of Public Administration, Thammasat University, Bangkok, 1959). Later data from the *Statistical Yearbook* indicated that total civil official employment in 1962 was about 240,000. Perhaps 100,000 might be added to this figure, if one were to include "temporary" nonstatus employees of the civilian ministries. And other public employees are to be found in 21 public enterprises (perhaps 10,000 in the Tobacco Monopoly alone).
2. See, for example, *Budget in Brief, FY 2505* (Bangkok: Budget Office, Office of the Prime Minister, 1961). The table, "Budget Expenditures Classification on Agency Basis," shows more or less equal expenditure allotments for defense and education in 1960, 1961, and 1962.
3. The organization structure of the civil ministries is described in the

Thailand Government Organization Manual Series (Bangkok, Institute of Public Administration, Thammasat University), a series of pamphlets, each describing a particular ministry, issued *seriatim* since 1959. The latest (March, 1964) describes the Ministry of Interior. A few earlier pamphlets are now out of date.

4. During 1957–1958 Fred W. Riggs identified 54 special companies and organizations established by the government itself. Many of these enjoyed special monopoly rights, tariff or quota protection, and so forth. High officials—even cabinet ministers—sat on their boards. Another 27 public corporations or agencies also operated on a revolving-fund basis. Fred W. Riggs, "Census and Notes on Clientele Groups in Thai Politics and Administration" (Indiana University, Department of Government, Institute of Training for Public Service, February, 1963; offset), p. 5.

5. Sahas Kanchanabanga, "Selected Fringe Benefits as Practiced in Thai Government Enterprises" (Master's thesis, Thammasat University, Bangkok, 1958), p. 9.

6. Winyoo Angkanaraksa, *Local Government in Thailand* (Bangkok: Department of Interior, 1958), p. 9.

7. *Thailand Population Census, 1960, Whole Kingdom* (Bangkok: Central Statistical Office, National Economic Development Board, 1960).

8. The formal place of municipal government is discussed by Frederick James Horrigan, "Local Government and Administration in Thailand: A Study of Institutions and their Cultural Setting" (Ph.D. dissertation, Indiana University, 1959), pp. 244–260.

9. The Ministry of National Development was organized as a combination of the existing departments of Highways, Irrigation, Mineral Resources, Land Co-operatives, Co-operative Credit and Marketing, Co-operative Auditing, plus the Office of the National Energy Authority, and the Thai Technical and Economic Committee. A planning department was also created, but only to plan for ministry functions. Another organization, the National Economic Development Board, is the national planning agency.

10. Thus "some companies which are fully private and have no official support or sponsorship enjoy the privilege of having high politicians serve on their boards of directors. It is widely thought that this results in special advantages from the government for the companies concerned." Riggs, "Census and Notes on Clientele Groups in Thai Politics and Administration," p. 6.

11. Systematic information about the job expectations of Thai students is limited. A survey by Prof. Edgar A. Schuler and Prof. Vibul Thamavit, *Public Opinion Among Thai Students* (Bangkok: Thammasat University, Faculty of Social Administration, June, 1958, mimeo.), indicated that more than half of all secular students interviewed expected

public employment; for a few schools in Schuler's sample the figure was 75 per cent or more.

12. The data are from the *Organizational Directory of the Government of Thailand* (Bangkok: USOM/Thailand, 1960, 1963).

13. Chap Tharamathaj, *op. cit.*, pp. 67–70.

14. The bases for the occupancy of positions by the military are varied. Control of important resources undoubtedly explains why a military officer heads the National Lottery. Political control is the aim behind the fact that the Public Relations Department is headed by a military man. But competence is also a dominating factor in some military appointments, such as the appointment of a military official as deputy secretary-general and then later (in 1965) as secretary-general of the Civil Service Commission.

15. "Any civil servant may resign from the service by submitting his resignation to his immediate superior. If such superior is not empowered to give approval, the matter shall be referred to the next higher authority in charge and the resignation shall become effective upon the approval of the official empowered. . . . The official empowered may in the interest of the service suspend his approval of a resignation for a period not to exceed one year from the date of filing the resignation." *Civil Service Act, B.E. 2497* (A.D. 1954), Section 35.

16. A restrained but eloquent portrait of the problems of establishing and maintaining an achievement-centered program in the Thai bureaucracy is found in: Lee M. Howard, John W. McDowell, Richard F. Peters, and B. A. Rae, *Report of an Assessment of the National Malaria Eradication Project of Thailand* (Bangkok: Agency for International Development, USOM/Thailand, February, 1964).

17. The "entertainment allowance" of Thammasat University during the last year or two of the Phibul regime was reportedly larger than the funds allotted for the salaries of full-time faculty members. Merely judging from the parties of those days, the allowance was substantial. It should be noted, however, that Thammasat University depended upon part-time instructors to teach most of its courses. In his perceptive sketch of the Thai social system, Embree also commented on this Thai characteristic: "Work is not regarded as a good in itself. . . . Pleasure is often considered a good thing *per se*" (Embree, "Thailand—A Loosely Structured Social System," p. 190).

18. One might argue that "national survival" is actually more of a goal than a value. But it has also functioned as a standard or criterion for guiding choice in Thailand. As an end it is so broad and basic that there is no point in characterizing it as a "goal" but not a "value."

19. For a detailed description of this development, see W. J. Siffin, "The Development of the Office of the President of the Council of Ministers, B.E. 2502–3," *Journal of Public Administration* (Bangkok), II, No. 1 (1960), 80–107.

CHAPTER 9

1. This and the following data are drawn from *Project for Modernization of Government Fiscal Management, Government of Thailand, Final Report* (Chicago: Public Administration Service, 1963; offset).

2. Robert F. Meagher, *et al., Public International Development Financing in Thailand* (New York: Columbia University Law School, February, 1963, offset), p. 16.

3. *Ibid.,* p. 17.

4. *Ibid.,* pp. 46–47, 53.

5. Turnover statistics are simply unavailable, but there is some fragmentary information: during 1954–1958 inclusive, 2,000 persons became eligible to appointment to third-class positions through competitive examinations, and almost 8,000 qualified for fourth-class appointments (Ura Gaewchaiyo, "The Development of the Thai Civil Service Commission," Master's thesis, Institute of Public Administration, Thammasat University, Bangkok, 1959, pp. 73–74). Several hundred others were appointed through "selective" examinations controlling initial access to specialized fourth-, third-, and second-class positions, as in medical work (Sirivat Viseshsiri, "Personnel Administration in the Ministry of Public Health," Master's thesis, Institute of Public Administration, Thammasat University, Bangkok, 1959, pp. 67–69). Payroll data, plus statistics on local teachers, show the total number of civil servants rising from 164,725 in 1952 to 203,498 in 1957, an increase of 38,773 or 23.5 per cent (Chap Tharamathaj, "The Composition of the Civil Service of Thailand," pp. 55–56). In studying a sample of 1,960 civil service positions, Nai Chap found evidence suggesting that the civil service in 1957–1958 was growing at a rate of about 3 to 5 per cent (*ibid.,* p. 57). The major expansion appeared to be in education, which would not be represented in the competitive examination data above, as local teachers are selected through examinations similar to those for the rest of the civil service, but not under the jurisdiction of the Civil Service Commission.

   In the last several years the rate of growth in the civil service appears to have outrun the rate of population growth, but, during the long period 1920–1957, the actual percentage increase in the number of civil officials appears to have been only about half as large as the percentage increase in the total population of Thailand (*ibid.,* pp. 55–56). This suggests that the current rate of bureaucratic growth is considerably greater than was true for a long time—a circumstance which has a number of interesting implications.

6. This is based largely upon Title 3, *Civil Service Act, B.E. 2497* (A.D. 1954).

7. As one might expect, there is also a "reform clause" (*ibid.,* Section 45), under which individuals who have been deficient in good morals, or insolvent, or recipients of criminal or bureaucratic punishment in the

past may be adjudged qualified by a unanimous and secret decision of the Civil Service Commission. Not much recourse is made to this clause.

8. *Civil Service Regulation 63, B.E. 2498* (1955).
9. *Civil Service Regulation 64, B.E. 2498* (1955).
10. Ura Gaewchaiyo, *op. cit.,* p. 74.
11. *Civil Service Rules Governing Syllabus and Procedure, 4th and 3rd Class Competitive Examination,* May 31, 2498 (1955). The confusing term "syllabus" refers to the material to be covered by the examination, which is spelled out in considerable detail.
12. Praween Na Nakorn's *Collection of Practical Problems Concerning the Civil Service Act,* published by the Commission staff, contains more than 600 pages and has gone through several editions. It is an excellent reference manual on civil service law, forms, and formal procedures as well as a key source of examination material.
13. Ura Gaewchaiyo, *op. cit.,* p. 71.
14. Sirivat Viseshsiri, *op. cit.,* pp. 72–73.
15. *Civil Service Act, B.E. 2476* (A.D. 1933), Sections 13, 23.
16. Ura Gaewchaiyo, *op. cit.,* pp. 75–81.
17. Horrigan's comments in his "Local Government and Administration in Thailand," on advancement in the field service of the Department of Interior are not entirely irrelevant:

"An interesting mythology exists around the question of 'how to get ahead' in the provincial service. One such Machiavellian code of long standing is still recalled, even if seldom implemented fully today: There are four roads to success . . . , in the order stated: (1) Flattery of superiors (*lia teen,* literally 'lick the foot'); (2) Presents to superiors (*sin kaeng,* literally 'strong property'); (3) Procuring for superiors (*kai dang,* literally 'red eggs'); (4) Merit (*kaeng wicha,* literally, 'strong knowledge').

"Within the provincial service itself there is a strong sense that promotion depends for the most part on personal relationships. A fine sense of discrimination is evidenced in standardizing the art of favoritism. According to this standard there are three types of superiors: First, the governor who has a clique or inner circle (*len puak*) composed perhaps of former students or other close adherents; secondly, there is the governor, whom one can assiduously cultivate in personal, informal contacts (*kan eng*); and, finally, there is the governor who is fair, just, and mature in judgments (*pen phu yai*), literally 'is big man.' With the former types, the present-day subordinate ingratiates himself by small presents of local produce (*kong kamnan*) as a symbol of his fealty and submission, or by praise and flattery (*prachob*). The road to success in Thailand too often leads through the superior's household rather than his office, and personal relationships rather than official performance is the testing ground for advancement" (p. 203).

18. *Civil Service Act, B.E. 2497*, Sections 25, 26.
19. *Ibid.*, Section 26.
20. Ura Gaewchaiyo, *op. cit.*, traces the evolution of the civil service structure from 1928. Data for the following are drawn from his most helpful study.
21. There have been changes in the functional classification of civil officials. Under Section 23 of the 1954 act there are now eight groups of officials—political, ordinary, state enterprise, royal household, police, teaching, special foreign, and special. But, except as noted above, they all must fit into the hierarchy.
22. Chap Tharamathaj, *op. cit.*, Figure 2, page 26. The data are for 1957. An examination of a sample of 1,956 positions as of 1958 was not inconsistent in its findings. The proportion of fourth-class officials may have declined somewhat in the past few years, due to an upgrading in the level of a sizeable number of teachers who have been receiving advanced training.
23. Chap Tharamathaj, *op. cit.*, p. 13. There is some difference between Ministry of Finance and Ministry of Education statistics, but it is not enormous. For example, for 1957 Ministry of Finance payroll figures showed 81,892 local teachers; the Ministry of Education report, *Educational Statistics, B.E. 2500,* showed 78,860 (Table 62, p. 129).
24. However, a civil service regulation generally requires that a first-class official must have two or more subordinates in the absence of a special waiver, implying that the classification of a nonsupervisory specialist as first class is regarded as exceptional—i.e., a variation from the general norm.
25. Chap Tharamathaj, *op. cit.*, p. 33.
26. *Notice Comparing Positions and Ranks of Civil Service Officials Under Civil Service Act, B.E. 2471* (Bangkok: H. M. Financial Council, February 23, 1929).
27. Some variation may occur, however, in the top of the salary ranges for individual positions such as section chiefs on the basis of CSC judgments about the skill and knowledge requirements of a position. Normally, these skill and knowledge determinations are based, however, upon the particular educational qualifications which happen to be possessed by the individuals in the posts.
28. *Administration of the Kingdom Act, 1952*, Section 34, as amended; cited by Horrigan, *op. cit.*, p. 148.
29. So Horrigan has found in his extensive study, *op. cit.*, p. 154.
30. Wilson, *Politics in Thailand*, p. 163.
31. The report, "A Program for Strengthening Public Administration in the Kingdom of Thailand" (Chicago: Public Administration Service, 1952, mimeo.), noted that "the increase which has occurred in the number of ministries and smaller units of organization and the creation of new organizations possessing an important degree of autonomy, of course, reflects the expanding number and variety of governmental

activities in Thailand as well as circumstances which are beyond the control of the Government. . . . The same trend—a growing number of divisions—is also in evidence within the departments. . . . It is possible that in such situations the excessive growth in the number of divisions has been partly a result of the relatively low official salaries which have prevailed and the small number of salary grades available to accommodate posts in the civil service which is growing rapidly in size and in its occupational complexity" (p. 35).

32. *A Public Development Program for Thailand* (Baltimore: The Johns Hopkins Press, 1959), p. 51.
33. *Ibid.,* pp. 223–224.
34. Chap Tharamathaj, *op. cit.,* pp. 27–28.
35. Wilson, *op. cit.,* p. 160.
36. The following is drawn from Lee M. Howard *et al., Report of an Assessment of the National Malaria Eradication Project of Thailand.*
37. *Ibid.,* p. 6.
38. *Ibid.,* p. 38.
39. *Ibid.,* p. 13.
40. *Ibid.,* p. 24.
41. *Ibid.,* pp. 20–21.
42. *Ibid.,* p. 34.
43. *Ibid.,* p. 16.
44. *Ibid.,* p. 25.
45. Satien Layalaksana *et al., Prachum Kotmai Prachamsok (Annual Compilation of Laws) B.E. 2471* (Bangkok, Bangkok Daily Mail Press), Vol. 41, pp. 241–255.
46. The preparation of the 1928 act, incidentally involved one of Prince Damrong's last contributions to the character of the Thai bureaucracy. He and the American adviser to the Ministry of Foreign Affairs and the British adviser to the Ministry of Finance prepared recommendations upon which the law was largely based. The act was drafted under the direction of a five-man royal committee chaired by H.R.H. the Prince of Chantaburi, chairman of the Royal Financial Council on which Prince Damrong also served, plus H.R.H. the Prince of Nakornsawan, the Minister of Interior, and the members of the royal family in charge, respectively, of the ministries of Finance, Foreign Affairs, and Education. A young man, Luang Sukhum Nayapradit, personal secretary to the Prince of Chantaburi, who had recently completed his college studies in the United States, served as secretary to the drafting committee. When, upon promulgation of the act, the drafting committee became the civil service committee, he was made its secretary and thus the chief administrative official of the civil service organization which was attached to the Ministry of Finance. After the 1932 coup, Luang Sukhum became secretary-general of the post-revolutionary Civil Service Commission, a position he continued to occupy until 1964. Luang Sukhum's brother was in charge of the Commission's

examination work from 1934 until his retirement in October, 1958. The continuity in the management of the Civil Service Commission is not only impressive—it is symbolically significant.

47. Ura Gaewchaiyo, *op. cit.*, p. 27.
48. The total 1931 budget deficit was reportedly about 10 million baht, according to Thompson (*Thailand: The New Siam,* p. 554), more than half of it—about 6 million baht—represented by Thailand's obligations on its foreign indebtedness incurred for public capital investment. Ordinary governmental expenditures within the kingdom exceeded revenues by less than 4 million baht in 1931 (Ingram, *Economic Change,* p. 237).
49. *Civil Service Act, B. E. 2476,* Section 57.
50. Ura Gaewchaiyo, *op. cit.*, p. 92.
51. E. J. Barbour, "The Needs of the Thai Civil Service System" (Bangkok: Public Administration Division, USOM/Thailand, March, 1964, mimeo.). The quoted passages are found at pages 4 and 5.
52. Manoo Choosanay, "The Role of Discipline in Administration of the Department of Interior, Thailand (Master's thesis, Institute of Public Administration, Thammasat University, Bangkok, 1960), p. 37. Except as noted, the following discussion is based upon Manoo's data.
53. Edgar L. Shor, "The Thai Bureaucracy," *Administration Science Quarterly,* June, 1960, p. 79.
54. Ura Gaewchaiyo, *op. cit.*, p. 84.
55. Manoo Choosanay, *op. cit.*, p. 49.
56. *Civil Service Act, B.E. 2497,* Sections 84–105.
57. *Ibid.*, Section 83.
58. *Ibid.*, Section 45. Favorable consideration in such cases is most uncommon.
59. Praween Na Nakorn, "Discipline of Civil Servants," *Civil Officials' Magazine* (Bangkok: Staff of the Thai Civil Service Commission, issued monthly), February, March, April, 1956.
60. *Ibid.*
61. *Ibid.*
62. *Ibid.*
63. Manoo Choosanay, *op. cit.*, p. 64.
64. Chakra Hansakul, "A Study of Pay Policy and Administration," pp. 130–131. The 1952–1964 estimate is from an unpublished USOM/Thailand paper.
65. Bangkok living costs for blue-collar and office workers have been studied rather systematically by industrial concerns such as Shell Oil Company and Lever Brothers Company, Ltd., for pay policy guidance. In September, 1958, the expenditure of a typical low-income worker with a wife and two children (one in school) was estimated at 706.21 baht per month, or about $36.00. In this income there was no provision for recreation, for medicine, or for capital outlays of any sort (quoted by Chakra Hansakul, *op. cit.*, pp. 133–137). A recent survey, *Advance*

Report: Household Expenditures Survey, B.E. 2505 (Bangkok: National Statistical Office), indicated that in 1962 the average family income in the Bangkok area amounted to about 706 baht per wage-earner, which is well within the pay range of the fourth class.

66. Chakra Hansakul, *op. cit.*, pp. 137–138.
67. *Ibid.*, pp. 119–123.
68. *Ibid.*, pp. 123–135.
69. *Ibid.*, pp. 128–129.
70. Chinnawoot Soonthornsima, "The Relation of College Education to Pay Levels," pp. 53–54.
71. *Ibid.*, pp. 55–56.
72. *Ibid.*, Appendix C, pp. 128–135.
73. *Ibid.*, p. 72.
74. Data are from *ibid.*, Appendix E, pp. 146–149.
75. This is based upon an unpublished paper, "Leave Policies of the Thai Civil Service," by Mayoora and Orasri Swangwan.
76. James N. Mosel, "Communication Patterns and Political Socialization in Transitional Thailand," in Lucian W. Pye, ed., *Communications and Political Development* (Princeton: Princeton University Press, 1963), pp. 184–228.
77. *Ibid.*, p. 227.
78. *Ibid.*, p. 187.

CHAPTER 10

1. *Statistical Yearbook, 1923,* p. 232; *Statistical Yearbook, 1956–1958,* pp. 95–99. Also, *Educational Statistics, 1957* (Bangkok: Ministry of Education, 1959), p. 246.
2. Ura Gaewchaiyo, "The Development of the Thai Civil Service Commission," p. 73.
3. Graham, *Siam,* Vol. I, p. 253.
4. *Educational Statistics, 1957,* p. 39.
5. *Ibid.*
6. Edgar A. Schuler and Vibul Thamavit, *Public Opinion Among Thai Students.*
7. Alan E. Guskin, with Tussanee Sookthawee, *Changing Values of Thai College Students, A Research Report* (Bangkok: Faculty of Education, Chulalongkorn University, 1964). This systematic study of the attitudes and expectations of 2,878 students is a study of values in a time of change rather than a study of changes in values over time.
8. Gabriel A. Almond, in Gabriel A. Almond and James S. Coleman, *The Politics of the Developing Areas* (Princeton: Princeton University Press, 1960), p. 17.

BIBLIOGRAPHY

Advance Report: Household Expenditures Survey, B.E. 2505. Bangkok: Thailand Statistical Office, n.d.

Almond, Gabriel A., and James S. Coleman, eds. *The Politics of the Developing Areas*. Princeton: Princeton University Press, 1960.

Arsa Meksawan. "The Role of the Provincial Governor in Thailand." Unpublished Ph.D. dissertation, Indiana University, 1961.

Barbour, E. J. *The Needs of the Thai Civil Service System*. Bangkok: USOM/Thailand, Public Administration Division, 1964, mimeo.

Blanchard, Wendell, *et al. Thailand, Its People, Its Society, Its Culture*. New Haven: Human Relations Area Files Press, 1958.

Boribal Buribhand. *The History of Buddhism in Thailand*. Bangkok: Chatra Press, 1955.

Bowie, Theodore, ed. *The Arts of Thailand*. Bloomington: Indiana University *et al.*, 1960.

Bowring, Sir John. *The Kingdom and People of Siam*. London: Parker & Son, 1857.

Budget in Brief, FY 2505. Bangkok: Budget Office, Office of the Prime Minister, 1961.

Campbell, J. G. D. *Siam in the Twentieth Century*. London: E. Arnold, 1902.

Carter, A. Cecil, ed. *The Kingdom of Siam*. New York & London: G. P. Putnam's Sons, Inc., 1904.

Chakra Hansakul. "A Study of Pay Policy and Administration in the Thai Civil Service." Unpublished Master's thesis, Thammasat University, Institute of Public Administration, 1959.

Chap Tharamathaj. "The Composition of the Civil Service of Thailand." Unpublished Master's thesis, Thammasat University, Institute of Public Administration, 1959.

Chinnawoot Soonthornsima. "The Relation of College Education to Pay Levels in Thai Civil Service." Unpublished Master's thesis, Thammasat University, Institute of Public Administration, 1959.

Civil Service Act B.E. 2476.

Civil Service Regulation 63, B.E. 2498.

Civil Service Regulation 64, B.E. 2498.

Civil Services Rules Governing Syllabus and Procedures, 4th and 3rd class Competitive Examination, May 31, 2498. Bangkok, 1955.

Cort, M. L. *Siam*. New York: Randolph & Company, 1886.

Damrong, Prince Rajanupap. *Compiled Writings*. Bangkok: Klang Vidhya Press, 1952.

——— *Laksana Ranpokkrong prathet Sayam Taeboran* (Traditional Government of Old Siam), Bangkok, 1959.

——— and Phraya Rachsena. *Tesapiban* (The System of Local or Territorial Government). Bangkok: Klang Vidhya Press, 1952.

De Young, John E. *Village Life in Modern Thailand.* Berkeley and Los Angeles: University of California Press, 1955.

Educational Statistics, B.E. 2500. Bangkok: Ministry of Education, n.d.

Embree, John F. "Thailand—A Loosely Structured Social System," *American Anthropologist,* LII, No. 2 (1950).

Fegen, Wm. W., ed. *The Siam Directory.* Bangkok: Siam Observer Press, 1910.

Fiftieth Anniversary Commemorative Publication. Bangkok: The Siam Society, 1954.

Gedney, William J., ed. and trans. *Life and Ritual in Old Siam.* New Haven: Human Relations Area Files Press, 1961.

Graham, W. A. *Siam.* London: De La More Press, 1924.

Guskin, Alan E., with Tussanee Sookthawee. *Changing Values of Thai College Students: A Research Report.* Bangkok: Chulalongkorn University Faculty, 1964.

Hall, D. G. E. *A History of South-East Asia.* New York: St. Martin's Press, 1955.

Heady, Ferrel, and Sybil L. Stokes, eds. *Papers in Comparative Public Administration.* Ann Arbor: University of Michigan I.P.A., 1962.

Heine-Geldern, Robert. "Conceptions of State and Kingship in Southeast Asia," *Far Eastern Quarterly,* II, November, 1942.

Horrigan, Frederick J. "Local Government and Administration in Thailand: A Study of Institutions and Their Cultural Setting." Unpublished Ph.D. dissertation, Indiana University, 1959.

Howard, Lee M., *et al. Report of an Assessment of the National Malaria Eradication Project of Thailand.* Bangkok: Agency for International Development, USOM/Thailand, 1964.

Ingram, James C. *Economic Change in Thailand Since 1850.* Stanford: Stanford University Press, 1954.

International Bank for Reconstruction and Development. *A Public Development Program for Thailand.* Baltimore: The Johns Hopkins Press, 1959.

Kasem Sirisumpunah. "Emergence of the Modern National State in Burma and Thailand." Ph.D. dissertation, Wisconsin University, International Law and Relations, 1962.

Landon, Kenneth P. *Southeast Asia: Crossroad of Religions.* Chicago: University of Chicago Press, 1949.

Laws of the Fifth Reign, Ratanakosin Era 121. Bangkok: Bamrungnukunkit Press, n.d.

Laws of the Fifth Reign, Ratanakosin Era 120. Bangkok: Wichakorn Press, n.d.

Le May, Reginald. *The Culture of Southeast Asia.* London: George Allen and Unwin Ltd., 1954.

McCarthy, James. *Surveying and Exploring in Siam.* London: John Murray, 1900.

McFarland, Bertha B. *McFarland of Siam.* New York: Vantage Press, 1958.

Manoo Choosanay. "The Role of Discipline in Administration of the Department of Interior, Thailand." Unpublished Master's thesis, Thammasat University, Institute of Public Administration, 1960.

Meagher, Robert F., *et al. Public International Development Financing in Thailand.* New York: Columbia University School of Law, 1963.

Moffat, Abbot Low. *Mongkut, The King of Siam.* Ithaca: Cornell University Press, 1961.

Mosel, James N. "A Poetic Translation from the Siamese," *Journal of the Siam Society,* XLVII, No. 1 (June, 1959).

———— "Thai Administrative Behavior," in W. J. Siffin, ed., *Toward the Comparative Study of Public Administration.* Bloomington: Indiana University, 1959.

Northrop, F. S. C., *The Meeting of East and West.* New York: The Macmillan Co., 1947.

Notice Comparing Positions and Ranks of Civil Service Officials Under Civil Service Act, B.E. 2471. Bangkok: H. M. Financial Council, 1929.

Organizational Directory of the Government of Thailand, 1960, 1963. Bangkok: USOM/Thailand.

Orwell, George. *Burmese Days.* London: Secker and Warbury, 1949.

Praween Na Nakorn. *Collection of Practical Problems Concerning the Civil Service Act.*

———— "Discipline of Civil Servants," *Civil Officials' Magazine* (Bangkok), February, March, and April, 1956.

Prayat Smanmit. "District Administration in Thailand." Unpublished Master's thesis, University of the Philippines, Institute of Public Administration, 1959.

Project for Modernization of Government Fiscal Management, Government of Thailand, Final Report. Chicago: Public Administration Service, 1963.

Pye, Lucian W., ed. *Communications and Political Development.* Princeton: Princeton University Press, 1963.

Rapee Kaocherern. "The Use of Foreign Advisors and Officials in the Thai Civil Service During Rama V's through Rama VII's Reigns." Unpublished Master's thesis, University of New Hampshire, 1963.

Reeve, W. D. *Public Administration in Siam.* London: Royal Institute of International Affairs, 1951.

Riggs, Fred. W. *Census and Notes on Clientele Groups in Thai Politics and Administration.* Bloomington: Indiana University, Department of Government, 1963, mimeo.

—— *The Ecology of Public Administration.* Bombay: Asia Publishing House, 1961.

Royal Government Gazette, March 31, 1925.

Sahas Kanchanabanga. "Selected Fringe Benefits as Practiced in Thai Government Enterprises." Unpublished Master's thesis, Institute of Public Administration, Thammasat University, Bangkok, 1958.

Satien Layalaksana *et al. Prachum Kotmai Prachamsok* (Annual Compilation of Laws), *B.E. 2471.* Bangkok: Bangkok Daily Mail Press, n.d.

Sayre, Francis B. "Siam's Fight for Sovereignty," *Atlantic Monthly,* CXL, November, 1927.

Schuler, Edgar A., and Vibul Thamavit. *Public Opinion Among Thai Students.* Bangkok: Thammasat University, Faculty of Social Administration, 1958.

Shor, Edgar L. "The Thai Bureaucracy," *Administration Science Quarterly,* V (June, 1960). *Siam Directory, 1910.*

Siffin, W. J. "The Development of the Office of the President of the Council of Ministers, B.E. 2502–3," *Journal of Public Administration* (Bangkok), Vol. II, No. 1 (1960).

—— ed. *Toward the Comparative Study of Public Administration.* Bloomington: Indiana University, 1959.

Sirivat Viseshsiri. "Personnel Administration in the Ministry of Public Health." Unpublished Master's thesis, Thammasat University, Institute of Public Administration, 1959.

Sixtieth Anniversary Commemorative Volume. Bangkok: Ministry of Interior, 1952.

Smith, Malcolm. *A Physician at the Court of Siam.* London: Country Life Press, 1947.

Smyth, H. Warrington. *Five Years in Siam from 1891 to 1896.* London: John Murray, 1898.

Statistical Yearbook, Thailand. 1923 and 1935–37. Bangkok: Central Statistical Office.

Thailand Government Organization Manual Series. Bangkok: Thammasat University, Institute of Public Administration, seriatim, 1959—.

Thailand Past and Present. Bangkok: Publicity Committee, Ninth Pacific Science Congress, 1957.

Thailand Population Census, 1960, Whole Kingdom. Bangkok: Central Statistical Office, National Economic Development Board, 1960.

Thawatt Mokarapong. "The June Revolution of 1932 in Thailand: A Study in Political Behavior." Unpublished Ph.D. dissertation, Indiana University, 1962.

Ura Gaewchaiyo. "The Development of the Thai Civil Service Commission." Unpublished Master's thesis, Thammasat University, Institute of Public Administration, Bangkok, 1959.

Thompson, Virginia M. *Thailand: The New Siam.* New York: Macmillan, 1941.

Vallabhakara, H.S.H. Prince, ed. *Siam: General and Medical Features.* Bangkok: Far Eastern Association of Tropical Medicine, 1930.

Vella, Walter F. *The Impact of the West on Government in Thailand.* (University of California Publications in Political Science, IV, No. 3.) Berkeley and Los Angeles: University of California Press, 1955.

────── *Siam Under Rama III, 1824–1851.* Locust Valley, N.Y., Association for Asian Studies, by J. J. Augustin, 1957.

Wales, H. G. Quaritch. *Ancient Siamese Government and Administration.* London: Bernard Quaritch Ltd., 1934.

────── *Ancient Southeast Asian Warfare.* London: Bernard Quaritch Ltd., 1952.

────── *Siamese State Ceremonies: Their History and Function.* London: Bernard Quaritch Ltd., 1931.

────── *Years of Blindness.* New York: Thomas Y. Crowell, 1943.

Wells, Kenneth E. *History of Protestant Work in Thailand.* Bangkok: Church of Christ in Thailand, 1958.

────── *Thai Buddhism: Its Rites and Activities.* Bangkok: The Christian Bookstore, 1960.

Wilson, David A. *Politics in Thailand.* Ithaca: Cornell University Press, 1962.

Winyoo Angkanaraksa. *Local Government in Thailand.* Bangkok: Department of Interior, 1958.

Wood, W. A. R. *History of Siam.* Bangkok: Barnikitch Press, 1924.

Wright, Arnold, ed. *Twentieth Century Impressions of Siam.* London: Lloyds' Greater Britain Publishing Co., 1908.

Young, Ernest. *The Kingdom of the Yellow Robe.* 3rd ed. London: A. Constable, 1870.

INDEX

Achievement norms, 219
Administrative manuals, 208
Alabaster, Henry, 55
Almond, Gabriel A., 281*n*
Angkanaraksa, Winyoo, 274*n*
Anonymous letters, 225, 228
Anuman Rajadhon, Phya, 255*n*
Appeals, by civil servants, 174, 175
Ascriptive norms, 93
"Attainment norms," 147, 233, 273*n*
Attitudes, toward the bureaucracy, 245
Autarky, 34–35, 194–195, 201–205
Authority, 25–30, 71–72, 75, 126–127, 164–167, 217
Ayudhya, 11

Bangkok, 16
Barbour, E. J., 280*n*
Biawat, 32, 53
Blanchard, Wendell, 271*n*
Boribal Buribhand, Luang, 255*n*
Boromotrailokanat (Trailok), King, 17, 18, 19
Bowring Treaty of 1855, 47–48
Buddhism, 9, 12–14, 131–133, 242, 271–272*n*
Budget Bureau, 168, 176, 177
Bureaucracy: as social system, 160–164; boundaries of, 152–159; legal-rational model, 126–127; return to traditional values, 144–150; traditional, 17–41
Bureaucratic centralization, 167–168
Bureaucratic growth, 94, 151, 213, 247–250, 273*n*

Bureaucratic processes, 91–93, 169–170
Bureaucratic reconstruction, 52–62, 69–75, 93–106, 126, 147–148; aims of, 68, 89
Bureaucratic stability, 149, 244–254

Careerism, in traditional bureaucracy, 32–34
Chakkri Reformation, 4, 5, 52–62, 68, 79–80, 88–89, 92–93, 144
Charisma, 27
Choosanay, Manoo, 280*n*
Chulalongkorn, King (Rama V), 50–58, 95, 126, 136, 137, 139, 257*n*
Chulalongkorn University, 101, 106
Civil Officials' Magazine, 215, 227
Civil Service Act of 1928, 118, 141, 197, 211–213, 279*n*
Civil Service Act of 1933, 197, 213
Civil Service Commission, 200–201, 203, 211–216
Civil Service examinations, 172–173, 179–188
Civil Service School, 101, 106
Class structure of contemporary bureaucracy, 196, 197
Committees: as a device for obtaining responsibility, 83–84; as a communications device, 238
Commoners, in traditional Thailand, 10
Communications, 54, 69, 122, 235–241, 263*n*–264*n*
Compulsory Education Law of 1921, 110

287